The Hollywood Kid

The Hollywood Kid

The Violent Life and Violent Death of an MS-13 Hitman

Óscar Martínez
and
Juan José Martínez

Translated by
John B. Washington
and
Daniela Ugaz

VERSO
London • New York

First published in English by Verso Books 2019
First publised as *El Niño de Hollywood*
© Debate 2018
Translation © John B. Washington and Daniela Ugaz 2019

1 3 5 7 9 10 8 6 4 2

Verso
UK: 6 Meard Street, London W1F 0EG
US: 20 Jay Street, Suite 1010, Brooklyn, NY 11201
versobooks.com

Verso is the imprint of New Left Books

ISBN-13: 978-1-78663-493-1
ISBN-13: 978-1-78663-492-4 (US EBK)
ISBN-13: 978-1-78663-491-7 (UK EBK)

British Library Cataloguing in Publication Data
A catalogue record for this book is available from the British Library

Library of Congress Cataloging-in-Publicatiovn Data
A catalog record for this book is available from the Library of Congress

Typeset in Fournier by MJ & N Gavan, Truro, Cornwall
Printed and bound by CPI Group (UK) Ltd, Croydon CR0 4YY

To Edin, with love and gratitude.

You said we were extensions of you. So this book is, in part, written by you. You live on within us, Dad.

To Marisa, the best place, the best place in the world.

All our lyrics are yours, Mom.

Contents

Preface

This is a book about scraps. It's about those leftovers that the enormous machinery of the United States chucks across its borders. Scraps are tossed into El Salvador, a country that grinds up much of what it receives. These human leftovers, however, are still living when they're expelled. And, in time, they bear fruit that will clog up the gears of both the machine that threw them out and the machine that's grinding them up. This book is about how these two countries deal with the scraps.

Miguel Ángel Tobar's story is a microhistory, a perfect example of the human cost of these international processes. Miguel Ángel was a sicario, a ruthless assassin for the Mara Salvatrucha 13 gang, a.k.a. MS-13. With more than fifty murders to his name, he might have become an underground celebrity in the United States, part of that club of serial killers who occasionally become fodder for the History Channel. But his life and crimes were committed in another part of the world, in a remote, hot and humid corner of western El Salvador. He didn't speak English, never set foot in LA—where the gang he belonged to was founded—and never was even able to pronounce the name of his clique correctly: "Haleewoo," he would say, meaning Hollywood. And yet, what transpired in the United States would mark both his life and those whose lives he ended.

We met Miguel Ángel by chance while working for the online magazine *El Faro* on a story about gang leaders and organized crime. The police detective we were in contact with, Gil Pineda, speaking to a junior officer, uttered a phrase one day that inadvertently launched two years of research. "Bring in the Kid!" Pineda said. Shortly thereafter, a thin slant-eyed young man wearing a large t-shirt and a Rastafarian hat appeared in the doorway. He wasn't much like the gangsters the media outlets might have led us to expect: a shaven-headed man with face tattoos. After shaking hands with him, we walked across the street and sat on plastic chairs outside his little shack. We talked for hours. He told us about his life, told us about the times he'd been a scared little kid trying to kill grown men. We met Lorena, his wife, and Marbelly, his undernourished daughter. From that day on, we kept visiting him. We went through his stories and compared them to details we gleaned from other sources: police reports, archives, other gang members, and ex-gang members, as well as from cops, judges, prosecutors, family members, victims, and forensic scientists. Even after he abandoned the little shack the state had given him—as part of a witness protection deal—we kept in contact, watching him try to forge a life in the sugarcane fields, fighting, hunting, and generally scrabbling away in order to survive. We got to know him as he grew unhealthily thin and, still the state's protected witness, he became so desperate he considered going back to robbing and killing in order to feed his family.

Over time we came to understand that Miguel Ángel's life revealed so much more than the difficulties of a single former gang member. To tell the story of an assassin, it's not enough to say when he pulled the trigger or where he was born. Over months and years, we came to realize that this man's life had been shaped by global politics. We came to understand that his choices, his personal agency, had always been limited, always tied to distant decisions made by US and Salvadoran politicians.

The life of Miguel Ángel was always constrained, always more a matter of compulsion than choice—though he didn't understand the forces working on him. He was the product of a long series of violent acts. Which is why some chapters of this book begin with events decades before his birth or thousands of miles north of where he came into the world. His ignorance of these forces left him both naïve and superstitious. Miguel Ángel was also the victim of malicious plotting. He was a scrap picked up by a criminal organization made up of other scraps.

A portrait of anyone, if done well, is a complex matter, comprising many shades and subtle nuances. Sometimes, Miguel Ángel acted reflexively. Sometimes, he seemed to have lived more than one life. All the while, he had original ideas and opinions about his condition and what had affected various aspects of his life. Amid the violence, in the center of his various survival strategies, he was always sincere. Although he easily could have, Miguel Ángel never lied to us. Or at least we never found out that he was lying. We corroborated one after another of his stories. Even when what he was telling us seemed impossible, we kept finding some document or testimony that backed up the assassin's word. We're still asking why he was so honest. Miguel Ángel never requested money or help. He never asked us for a single favor. He just talked. For three years he answered every question we put to him. On one occasion, he walked two hours through enemy territory, armed with a machete and a homemade shotgun, just to speak with us. He told us of his childhood and his past with both passion and detail. He talked to us of his hopes, his nightmares, his strategies, his failures, and of his worldview as a rural gang member. It took years—and a lot of patience—for us to understand his story, which is why we are now driven to retell it.

It would have been illuminating to see this man's life from afar, as if through binoculars. That viewpoint would have been compelling: bloody murders, shady rituals, machetes, pistols, bullets, and mortal wounds. It's what our country, El Salvador—the most murderous country in the world—is known for. But we decided to see it through a magnifying glass: To walk in his tracks, to follow his lead, and to probe into his violent realm. Because explanations—not justifications—are in short supply in this part of the world.

The idea that we—two brothers—should join forces as coauthors came about not only as a way to consolidate our knowledge of certain phenomena and sociocultural processes that we've been focusing on for the last ten years. It was also a means to unite methods of work—ethnography and reportage—in order to better understand our reality. We have both been, from separate intellectual trenches, committed to understanding the roots of the violence in our country. We have both carefully studied MS-13. We have spoken with dozens of its members, followers, enemies, and victims; we have lived with them for more than a year; we have spent long hours with them in the inhumane prisons of Guatemala, El Salvador, Honduras, Mexico, and the United States; and we have accompanied them as they sought to escape the violence by fleeing through Mexico and into the United States. We worked separately until, one day, we were together and met Miguel Ángel in a village called El Refugio. Since then, we have returned dozens of times to that village, as well as to the places where he killed and where, eventually, he was himself killed.

This isn't a book solely about the life of an assassin from the largest gang in the world, the only gang to be sanctioned by the US Treasury Department, a gang that is constantly included in Trump's incendiary rants and that has a presence in every department of El Salvador. This book is our way of understanding and explaining the backyard of the United States. "Shithole" is how Trump once referred to our country, speaking as if removed from what US politicians helped create, or helped destroy.

This is the story of something big. Something monstrous, transnational. This book is about a history of violence that endures—that is living, breathing, growing, and migrating. This is a story that is poorly understood, and it is told through the life of a nobody, of somebody forgotten, of somebody who was like so many others.

We focused on a scrap of the scraps and tried to convert it into a key to understanding this history. Throughout, we have tried to honor a painful idea we relayed one day to Miguel Ángel.

"Why do you want to tell my story?" he asked us in the dusty town where he was born, years after we had first met him.

"Because," we answered, ashamed, "we believe that your story, unfortunately, is more important than your life."

We hope to have justified that conviction.

Óscar Martínez and Juan José Martínez
El Salvador, May 2019

Part I

A Violent History

1

The End: The Death and Burial of Miguel Ángel Tobar

The Burial

Miguel Ángel Tobar knows no peace, not even in death.

It's noon on Sunday, November 23, 2014. Seven men struggle to get the body into the ground in the cemetery of Atiquizaya, in western El Salvador. The sun beats down on their backs.

Miguel Ángel Tobar's mother, a small woman with gray hair, seemed calm when the boy's father-in-law and brothers were digging the grave. Now that her son is being lowered inside his teak coffin, she kneels down on the ground beside him and cries out: "Why so young? Why again? Why another son? Why another murder?"

The coffin, a donation from the local government, has no glass window. Windowless coffins are often used out of respect for a family that prefers not to be left with the memory of a disfigured body. With Miguel Ángel Tobar, that's not the issue. His murderers didn't have the skillful aim he had, and they had to empty both their magazines to hit him six times in the back as he ran away.

Three bullets pierced his head discreetly, as it were, behind his ear. The bullets were kind to him.

Miguel Ángel Tobar's burial lasts only five minutes.

But hours were spent digging, judging the size of the hole in the ground, and digging some more. The preparations weren't very solemn. You might have mistaken the scene for a group of family members coming together to dig a well. The men, dripping with sweat, like laborers erecting a house, bickering about the depth and width. The women shushing their children's cries and watching the men work.

But once the men had roped the coffin and started to lower it, this everyday scene suddenly became the burial of someone they'd loved.

The mother screams for five whole minutes. She sways as if she's about to faint. Miguel Ángel Tobar's wife, Lorena, a shy eighteen-year-old hardened by life, allows herself to cry. Over the squeals and whimpers of their children, women sing evangelical songs as loudly as they can. They belt out words that describe celestial enclosures, an infernal lake.

The men, dry-eyed, lower their gazes to the ground.

Five graves away, four gangsters are playing dice.

Everybody knows that this cemetery is controlled by the Mara Salvatrucha 13. The gravedigger—who looked on as others did the grunt work of burying Miguel Ángel Tobar—knows it. The cemetery's security officer knows it, too. When someone asks, "Who are they?" he nonchalantly responds, "They're the guys in charge."

The burial of a gang member, no matter which gang, is governed by rules that can't be found in any manual. Whoever it is, he's allowed to be dead in peace. But today, that shaky rule has been left in the dust.

Two more gang members come out of the row of shacks flanking the cemetery and approach the four dice players. The players halt their game. Another youngster emerges and approaches the mourners. He's a thin, pale kid who's put on gangster attire fit for a gala: a round black Charlie Chaplin hat, a loose white t-shirt tucked into baggy black pants cinched by a belt, white knock-off Domba sneakers. The kid spits at the feet of the mourners and looks to catch someone's eye, ready for a challenge. No one meets his gaze.

Another gang member—materializing from a nearby ravine, and at first hovering at the edge of the scene—begins to inch closer, towards the other side of Miguel Ángel Tobar's grave. The site is surrounded, the mourners about to be trapped between the circling gang members and the ravine.

The father-in-law mumbles: "This is getting ugly." The last shovelfuls of dirt fill the tomb. One of the mourners, machete in hand, whacks off a head of izote, El Salvador's national flower,

Mourners sing evangelical hymns under candlelight in the Kid's mother's house. The songs have to be shouted to compete the reggaeton music from a nearby party. On the left is Doña Rosa, Miguel's mother.

and sticks it into the mound of dirt covering Miguel Ángel Tobar's coffin.

There's no time to pack the dirt, which is left with no tombstone, no cross, no epitaph.

The small, sorry-looking procession then quickly exits the cemetery. As they pass, other gang members come out of the shacks and tell the mourners to stay put. Instead, everyone just scrams.

Miguel Ángel Tobar, the sicario who betrayed the Hollywood Locos Salvatrucha, a "clique" (*clicas* in Spanish) of the Mara Salvatrucha, had departed the gang in the only way possible for someone who had lived his life.

In this country there can be no peace for someone like Miguel Ángel Tobar, El Niño de Hollywood.

Miguel Ángel Tobar was a member of the Mara Salvatrucha 13.

He belonged to one of the largest and most feared street gangs in the world, the only one whose leaders made the US Treasury's blacklist of transnational criminal organizations, on a par with the Mexican Zetas and the Japanese Yakuza. It's a gang that, for two straight years—2015 and 2016—made El Salvador the most murderous country in the world. To put this in perspective: In 2015, in cartel-occupied Mexico, Joaquín "El Chapo" Guzmán and the Zetas helped drive the homicide rate up to eighteen for every 100,000 inhabitants; El Salvador, meanwhile, had a rate of 103. In the United States, the rate is around five. More than eight murders for every 100,000 inhabitants is, according to the United Nations, an epidemic.

But before becoming the Kid of the Hollywood Locos Salvatrucha, Miguel Ángel Tobar was a semi-orphaned youth crushed under the heel of a war that had just finishing razing everything around him. In the mid 1990s, when Miguel Ángel Tobar first picked up a gun to join a gang-led war, the remains of the 75,000 victims of the other conflict were still smoldering. This twelve-year hell had begun in the 1970s, when El Salvador was a pressure cooker

An all-out civil war was raging then. The clandestine leftist groups had matured and begun to seriously organize themselves.

This wasn't a unified movement, but a collection of factions with diverse political ideologies. The middle-class youth, with mostly Catholic backgrounds and influenced by Asian communist movements, fell in behind the idea of a popular armed struggle. They formed the Revolutionary Army of the People, or ERP. Another group, which broke off from the Salvadoran Communist Party, linked up with a mass of industrial and agricultural workers to create one of the largest guerrilla organizations in Latin America: the Popular Liberation Forces (FPL). Insurgent groups sprouted from all sides, and the idea of armed struggle became more and more entrenched among the people.

At the other extreme, the pseudo-democratic government was composed of ultra-rightist military officers who'd led the previous coup d'état in 1979 and then defended their grip on power with all the notorious sadism of a Latin American army. Its right arm was the National Guard, whose name still sends chills down many Salvadoran spines. Manned by thugs, it functioned as a hit squad for the state and the small coffee-cultivating elite. In the 70s, the National Guard's information-gathering methods consisted of hanging buckets of water from a suspect's testicles or paddling a prisoner until he confessed where he'd hidden a stolen cow or a purloined necklace. Such methods were effective for terrorizing bandits or unarmed union organizers, but not so much for standing off guerrilla fighters galvanized by the spirit of revolution. The latter were much more agile in their combat strategies than the old and blundering state forces.

By 1975, bullets were flying in all directions. Guerrilla fighters bolstered their arsenals by kidnapping wealthy business owners and buying arms with the ransom fees. Contrary to the standard Marxist manual, they also developed a rear guard in remote agricultural communities, where the first camps and bases were established, and where the guerrillas filled out their ranks with campesinos tired of military oppression.

In 1979, everything changed in Central America. The three guerrilla groups in Nicaragua banded together and took down the Anastasio Somoza Debayle administration, the third generation of the Somoza dynasty still clinging to power. This was a ray of light for the Salvadoran guerrillas: the realistic possibility of installing a socialist government by way of the bullet. Fighting intensified. The campesino rear guard consolidated. And the US government, fearing it would lose control of its backyard, amped up its support of the Salvadoran army with both money and expertise. By the end of the year, an intelligence unit was formed, as well as an infiltration unit known as ORDEN. And, ultimately, the United States funneled something like $4.5 billion in aid to the Salvadoran government and military over a dozen years, coordinating with its leaders via the US Embassy in San Salvador and helping to cover up its crimes. It's been estimated that the United States sent military weaponry worth $1 billion to the country in that decade. On the other side, Cuba and the newly installed Nicaraguan socialist government were quick to support the Salvadoran insurgency with resources and training.

All these guns, however, needed arms to carry them. In a country whose population was 60 percent children, the result was inevitable. Thousands of kids younger than fifteen were recruited to both sides of the conflict.

El Salvador, a tiny country that would fit inside of California twenty times, threw itself and its armies of children into an abyss from which it would not emerge until 1992, with 75,000 people dead and countless more displaced.

Even before the war, Salvadorans had been coming to Southern California. But it was no longer a gradual migration—one by one, family by family. It was droves after droves. And the Salvadorans were fleeing, not migrating. They were fleeing with little more than they could pack in a night, and without even really knowing where they were going. It wasn't so important to get *somewhere* as it was to stop *being where they were*.

Almost none of the thousands of Salvadorans who came to California in the second half of the 1970s spoke English. Few had family there. Most congregated in the Angelino neighborhood of Pico Union, where they could find cheap apartments: up to four families squeezing into a matchbox.

Many were young kids who'd already known war. The recruiting process in El Salvador didn't entail getting a letter on your eighteenth birthday, as American kids experienced during Vietnam. No. In El Salvador it was military trucks pulling into poor barrios where packs of soldiers with lassos trapped kids and teenagers. The soldiers then shaved the rookies' heads, gave them a little training, and sent them to kill and die in the mountains.

In the mountains were the guerrillas. Hard-bitten guerrilla fighters who were also in the business of training kids and teenagers. A good number of those fighters, young and old, after seeing death up close, escaped to California where a network of the recently arrived was quickly forming. The more there were, the more they attracted other refugees. They thought California was the promised land.

"We fled the war. We didn't want more war. But over there we found another bunch of problems," said a veteran member of Barrio 18 who'd come to California in the '80s, after more than a year of battling guerrilla fighters in the Salvadoran mountains.

Los Angeles, where most migrated, was anything but a peaceful place where one could calmly put down roots. Another battle was being waged there, one also fought by youth.

The Salvadoran kids, who didn't speak English, were almost all put into special education classes. But language wasn't their only problem. These kids could probably assemble an M-16, no sweat, or distinguish the distant sound of a rescue helicopter from that of a combat copter echoing through the mountains. But they had no idea who Abraham Lincoln was, or what had happened at the Alamo in 1836. They knew which roots you could eat and which to avoid if your ration had run out, but they didn't know anything about square roots.

If classes were a torment for the confused Salvadorans, recess was a nightmare. The locals played baseball, American football, or four square—games they didn't understand. Others—some, like the Mexican kids, who had migrated earlier—organized themselves into groups that continuously fought and had a complicated system of hand symbols. They were members of something previously unknown to the Salvadorans: gangs. There were gangs of every type. Most were made up of Mexicans, and even so they attacked each other all the time—a trivial yet serious game, where

kids occasionally ended up dead. The school bathrooms and hall-
ways were tagged with esoteric symbols that marked the presence
of this or that gang. Leaving school at the end of the day was a
gamble. The new arrivals had to know where they could walk,
or risk crossing a forbidden line that would provoke a beatdown.
These gangsters saw the Salvadoran kids as prey. They weren't
organized, they were very poor, and they represented, above all,
unwelcome rivals. As the Mexican kids saw it, they already had
enough to deal with the black gangs. Now they had to worry about
these new savages. The Salvadorans were disrupting the understood meaning of the term "Hispanic."

"The Mexicans would assault us on our way to school, they'd
take our things. They wanted to squash all the *bichas* (little girls).
I mean they saw us as inferior, you know. They wanted to force us
into their gangs," said a veteran gangster sitting in a bar in downtown San Salvador, almost twenty years after the United States
retched him out like bad food. He doesn't say this in the tone of a
victim, knowing full well he doesn't fit that bill anymore.

It was this social rejection and violence that made the new arrivals band together. They didn't understand LA, and the city didn't
understand them. And yet, the city enclosed a secret that would
soon dazzle them.

AC/DC, Slayer, Black Sabbath ... heavy metal. Heavy, hard
music that couldn't be more different from the *rancheras* and ballads
crooning out in Salvadoran towns. Those irreverent and frenzied
compositions blared through the South Side barrios of LA and,
though the Salvadorans couldn't always understand the lyrics, they
understood the euphoria smoking off the well-tuned basses. At last
they recognized something within the great chaos around them,
something that meant they'd actually reached the United States.

They had suddenly come to understand one of the many languages spoken in the city.

Everything else melts away when you're standing in front of a stage, or even in front of an old radio in an alleyway in Pico Union, and you yield to an inner passion, bursting into a whirlwind of kicks and slaps. The metalhead movement, with its dark, satanic lyrics, was a magnet for Salvadoran kids. Long hair, heavy chains, and black boots became their identifying symbols. And it was one, small, almost imperceptible detail in the history of rock music that became the refugees' most cherished symbol.

As everyone knows, Black Sabbath and its lead singer, Ozzy Osbourne, were icons of heavy metal. Ozzy's emblematic symbol, a relic of the hippie era, was a peace sign, the two-fingered V. When, after years of alcohol and drug abuse, Osbourne was forced out of the band, a new star took his place: Italian-born Ronnie James Dio. This vocalist did away with many of the band's previous quirks, among them Osbourne's notorious peace and love sign. In its place Dio used an old-country gesture borrowed from his grandmother. The sign of the horns was part of a ritual to cure the "evil eye" or simply to spook away bad luck. You make it by sticking your pointer and pinkie fingers into the air. This sign would soon become the icon of heavy metal.

Among the Salvadoran kids in LA, the sign became known as the "Salvatrucha claw." Even today, Salvatrucha homies use it around the world.

By 1979, large groups of Salvadorans were being drawn together by heavy metal and satanism. They called themselves stoners.

In order to set themselves apart from other groups once and for all, the Salvadorans landed on a new name: La Mara Salvatrucha Stoner, or MSS.

The name harks back to a mostly forgotten film, *The Naked Jungle,* starring Charlton Heston. Made in 1954, it only premiered in Central America in the 1970s. It was an adaptation of a 1938 story by the German author Carl Stephenson, about a rich landowner in the Amazon whose property is devoured by millions of ants. The movie was popular across rural El Salvador, where these small windows into the Western experience marked the passage of time. It was so affecting that it inspired a new lexicon. The Salvadoran term *majada,* which colloquially referred to any group of people, was traded for *marabunta,* a type of army ant, or simply "mara." Initially the word had no criminal connotation. The second part, "salvatrucha," possibly coined by construction workers on the Panama Canal, is simply a reference to Salvadoran people.

The Mara Salvatrucha Stoner, a small cluster of autonomous cells that rarely interacted, wasn't at all organized. And its members were not as innocent as those of other young stoner groups. They became obsessed with the satanic lyrics of the heavy and black metal bands, and they took their adolescent games seriously. They'd congregate in cemeteries to invoke "the Beast." By the end of the 1970s, it wasn't uncommon to find stoner *mareros* cutting up cats, making blood pacts, and praying to Satan over the slabs in Pico Union's public cemeteries.

That's how the idea of the Beast was born. At first it was lifted from heavy metal titles, like Iron Maiden's *Number of the Beast,* but then it took on new meaning. It became synonymous with the gang itself, as well as with the imaginary dwelling space of gang members killed in battle, those who'd been murdered by other gangs. Like the Valhalla of the ancient Vikings, the Beast was a kind of home for warrior souls. And like Huitzilopoxtli, a sun god of the Mexicas, it thirsted for blood.

It's hard to get veteran gang members to talk about those transitional years, when they shed the guise of victims and metamorphosed into killers. Their memories are blurry. It happened without anyone paying much attention, a seemingly natural shift. Like growing up.

Even gang historians, like Professor Tom Ward from the University of California or the Mexican academic Carlos García, haven't come to fully understand this period. The fledgling gangsters were probably never entirely passive. Maybe it took them only a couple of years to realize that they already knew a violence cruder than that of their aggressors.

One thing is abundantly clear: sometime in the late 1970s, members of the Mara Salvatrucha Stoner cast off their victim role forever. The years when the Salvadoran schoolkid refugees suffered at the hands of Mexican or Chicano gangs began to recede. Members of the MSS became killers, waiting anxiously for the next provocation. Their union made them stronger.

"Over there in California they thought they knew what violence was. Fuck no! We taught them the meaning of violence," an old member of the MSS recalls, sitting with us in a café in downtown San Salvador. Two decades after having been deported from the United States, he still vividly remembers how the homie Salvatruchos swaggered, with large strides, down the Angelino streets. The Salvadorans knew all about war. They'd fled from one, and had come to feel no qualms about joining another.

The Vigil

In the village of Las Pozas, they're having a wake and a party. It's Saturday, November 22, 2014, and yesterday Miguel Ángel Tobar was killed. His body lies inside his mother's home. Many of the neighbors, meanwhile, are celebrating the founding of the village, and the mayor's office of San Lorenzo has organized a dance. Reggaeton blasts out of a pair of weathered speakers that seem to warp the music. The lights and racket are just blips in the absolute darkness of the surrounding fields and forests. A hard wind blows. By Salvadoran standards, it's a cold night.

Yesterday they killed Miguel Ángel Tobar. Today, to the sound of evangelical hymns, his family performs a vigil in the house where he was born. The truth is, given the difference in volume, the vigil thrums to the rhythm of reggaeton.

It's ten at night, and the men at the party are already drunk. They're eyeing each other, looking to pick fights. They stumble around, one hand on their hats, the other hand on a liter bottle of Cuatro Ases, a brand of Central American cane liquor or *guaro*.

Four soldiers keep to the shadows on the edges of the plaza. They won't get involved unless someone pulls out a machete, a pistol, or a shotgun. If the drunks just stick to shouting at each other, they'll leave them alone.

This is a dirt village. The streets are dirt, the houses are made with dirt, and, when the dirt dries, it turns to dust. And the dust never settles. Instead, it finds the corners of your mouth, the creases of your neck, your hair. It settles onto your sweat. But on this relatively cool and pleasant night, nobody's sweating.

In a house down one of the alleyways, almost in front of the village school, lies Miguel Ángel Tobar in his teakwood box. Old women surround him, whispering incantations—the standard prayers for this kind of funeral. At the head of the casket, seated in a plastic chair, the mother of the deceased stares at the dirt floor. She's a small woman, and the burden of a second murdered son seems to shrink her even more. A few months later she will die of cancer.

The house consists of one big room with three beds. Between each bed hangs a blanket for privacy. One of the beds is for the mother. The father isn't around. He hanged himself less than a year ago. He couldn't recover from the massacre of four members of his family by MS-13. There are some things you have to repeat, like commenting on the rain. The son's gang killed four of his dad's relatives. Four of his own relatives.

In another bed sleeps Miguel Ángel Tobar's older sister. Her husband is currently in prison for trafficking marijuana from Guatemala. In the third bed slept Miguel Ángel Tobar, his teenage wife, and his two daughters: three years old and three months old.

A group of men huddle in the backyard, drinking coffee and nibbling on sweet bread that the women hand out. The bread isn't from a bakery, it's just bread with sugar sprinkled on top. More than a dozen women sing and clap: "Here is the power of God, here is the power of God."

It's a miserable vigil. It lacks the drama of the usual gangster burial, where dozens of kids make offerings to the family and line up to say goodbye to their homeboy amid tears and vows of vengeance. None of that here. Miguel Ángel Tobar's funeral is a leper's funeral. None of his old gangster *compañeros* are here to pay their respects. They're either murdered or, thanks to him, in prison.

A man pokes his head in the door and asks a dumb question.

"Is this the dearly departed?"

It's the evangelical pastor. He's dark-skinned, very short. His funeral clothes are cheap-looking, and his shoes are dusty. He just walked two hours from his village. He's accompanied by two women in dresses, wearing veils over their faces. The pastor starts to speak about the beyond. He doesn't provide details of the beyond, he doesn't know what it's like, but he claims—with conviction—that it's better than this life. He takes his Bible and leads a prayer that the women follow, chattering incomprehensibly. Miguel Ángel Tobar's teenage widow, standing apart from the others, looks nervous. She's received threatening phone calls. She's scared the bullets that found her husband will find her next. The pastor finishes his sermon. He collects a few dollars from the relatives. It's common practice for these kinds of pastors—they don't receive a salary like a priest would. And yet this pastor doesn't follow the standard protocol. He finds the teenage widow and gives her everything he's collected. "Something to help you with, Mother," he says, and disappears into the darkness of the fields with his two companions.

Outside it's all reggaeton. Miguel Ángel Tobar's family had asked the organizers to push back the day of the event, as their house was only about a hundred yards from the dance floor and stage. It was a foolish request. Nobody was going to delay a party for the death of Miguel Ángel Tobar.

Miguel Ángel Tobar, half-naked, lies inside a white plastic bag on a metal tray.

A bead of viscous blood trickles from the bullet hole in the middle of his neck. The body is so fresh, the blood hasn't dried. After completing the autopsy, the Santa Ana forensic officers left him in his boxers—faded blue, the word *elegant* written on the elastic waistband. Of his four tattoos, only the deformed yin-yang on his right thigh is spared blood-spatter. The incomprehensible letters on his chest fall between the two bullet holes in his neck and the other bullet hole below his right nipple. On his left forearm, between speckles of fresh blood, you can make out the words: *mi vida loca.*

On the right side of his face, from his cheek and crawling up his forehead to his hairline are four furrows of dried blood. If you didn't know he'd died from gunshots, you might think a monster had clawed at his face.

Miguel Ángel Tobar, making a pretty dumb decision for someone who lived his life mere inches away from death, had returned to his family's house just two months before he was killed. Tired of living as a nomad, he came down from the mountains where he'd been hiding. He missed his teenage wife. He needed to provide for his two daughters. He knew that the imprisoned Mara Salvatrucha bosses he had betrayed had demanded his head. A band of killers was looking to avenge his betrayal. Some of them had founded the gang in the 1980s, in savage Southern California. They wanted to see him die. To suffer. They told him they were going to leave him smelling like pine, referring to the casket that would hold his corpse. They didn't guess that Miguel Ángel Tobar's funeral would be cheaper still: teak instead of pine.

Despite knowing all this, Miguel Ángel Tobar came home to the village of Las Pozas.

Las Pozas. Dirt, a school, an enormous ceiba tree, a cantina, a dirt soccer field, hills, heat.

Las Pozas was the retirement plan after his long stint as informant.

He didn't let any of the young toughs of the village join MS-13, even though he'd been one of the gang's sicarios. Miguel Ángel

Tobar called his crew of young neighbors *los ganyeros* (from ganja
—marijuana). They were eight or so young men stoked about the
marijuana Miguel Ángel Tobar brought over from Guatemala. For
them, selling pot on the village roadsides seemed like sophisticated
criminal activity.

Every month, Miguel Ángel Tobar crossed the border, which
was only a few miles from his house. He walked across hills and
fields, crossed a river, and would buy two, three, or five ounces of
marijuana. He smoked a bit with his ganyeros and then let them sell
the rest to divide the meager profits among themselves.

Miguel Ángel Tobar, a faithful soldier of MS-13, understood that
you shouldn't destroy your own home. But he prompted MS-13 to
destroy it all the same.

The ganyeros stood guard for him. They watched out for him
at night. They took turns as lookouts on the corner of the dirt
alleyway that led to his home. They called him if something came
up. Once, after a ganyero yelled for him, Miguel Ángel Tobar
had to come out of his house with a shotgun to scare away some
strangers.

Miguel Ángel Tobar knew that to get to him, his killers would
need to get past his faithful ganyeros. And then they would have
to confront him directly, confront the man who had earned his
name as a killer among killers. Which is why he only ventured out
when he needed to: one day he'd do work in the fields and earn five
bucks; another day he'd haul some pot over the border; another
day he'd hold up a shipping truck.

Friday, November 21, 2014, Miguel Ángel Tobar decided to
leave Las Pozas for a very particular reason. Born three months
earlier, his second daughter needed a name. Up until that point,
he'd simply called her *niñita*—little girl.

At noon that day Miguel Ángel Tobar rode his bike out of the village, following a series of dirt paths until, a half hour later, he reached San Lorenzo. He came into town from the back way, by Portillo Road—a dusty two-lane road that ends at the Chalchuapa River, the dividing line between El Salvador and Guatemala.

San Lorenzo was the exception in El Salvador. *Was*. No longer is. In 2013, there was not a single murder in the town. Not one. Up until November 21, 2014, when Miguel Ángel Tobar decided to slip away from Las Pozas to give a name to his daughter, there still hadn't been a homicide in San Lorenzo. Two years without a violent death.

Miguel Ángel Tobar walked into city hall, right in the central square. An old street sweeper saw him enter. So did an old woman who collects city bus fare at the station. So did a mototaxi driver lounging in his tuk tuk. All three witnesses remember thinking he looked nervous, that he walked quickly, that his eyes darted every whichaway. That's how they remember the Hollywood Kid walking into city hall.

He left an hour later. It was almost two in the afternoon.

He had given his daughter a name. Jéssica. The same day her father legally recognized her, he would also leave her fatherless.

Miguel Ángel Tobar didn't stop to talk to anybody. He got on his bike and started heading home. Rode three blocks. Got back on Portillo Road. And saw a mototaxi approach.

Night. Miguel Ángel Tobar was murdered seven hours ago. The blood that spilled out of his head lies thirty steps from his bicycle.

The police report: A mototaxi drove up with two male passengers, both fat, heads shaven, about forty years old. They attacked the victim. He abandoned his bicycle and ran. The first of six shots pierced his back. (The first red drops on the pavement appear one yard from the bicycle.) As the victim continued forward he was hit by two more bullets, one in the back of the head, behind his ear, the other in the ribs. He took another fifteen steps. (The blood drops are more abundant at this point.) He fell face down. He turned over to try to fight. The killers approached to fire three more shots. In the head and the chest. (The shells landed next to the puddle of blood, which was smeared, as if a wounded animal had tried to drag itself to safety.)

He fought.

The killers didn't take off for the hills but went straight back out through San Lorenzo in their noisy tuk tuk—sounding like a sheet of metal dragged across the road by the wind. The whole scene took place fifty yards from a police post. The police arrived twenty minutes later. They didn't pursue anyone.

At two in the afternoon, a hot November 21, 2014, in San Lorenzo, the state's protected witness, known by the authorities as

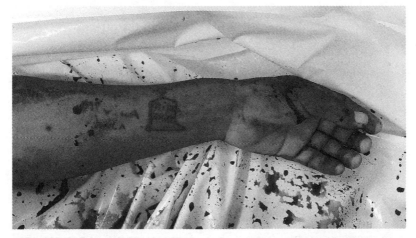

On the slab, a tattoo—*mi vida loca*—read between splashes of Miguel Ángel's blood.

the Hare or Yogui, a thirty-one-year-old gang member responsible for putting forty-six members of the Mara Salvatrucha 13 behind bars, was shot to death.

Miguel Ángel Tobar, the Kid of the Hollywood Locos Salvatrucha clique, had fulfilled his own prophecy by getting murdered.

2

The Beginning: A Child Tries to Kill a Man in the Coffee Plantation

An eleven-year-old boy was hiding in the coffee bushes, watching two men get drunk on cheap *guaro*.

It was December 24, 1994, and there was carousing all over the small Salvadoran town of Atiquizaya. The two men gulped down the liquor until a hot and muddled dream seemed to descend on them along with the torrid afternoon. One, a day worker from a coffee plantation, doubled over and fell to the ground. His companion, the foreman, yelled at him to stand up and keep drinking. The boy watched them from between dense branches. He waited, patiently, for the liquor to finish its job. After emptying the last of the bottles, with nothing left to drink and nobody to drink it with, the foreman staggered homeward.

The boy followed stealthily. He knew it was his moment. He walked down a dirt path that forked off the paved road heading toward the department's capital, Ahuachapán. He burst through the bushes and whacked the foreman, a hard blow to the head. The thick club knocked the man to the ground. The boy wanted to finish the job. He used a few big stones to smash his head and the back of his neck. The stones were as heavy as an eleven-year-old could lift.

The boy wanted to make sure he'd killed him. He went back to the dirt path that wound through the coffee bushes, watching over the foreman's body. A couple hours later it would be Christmas.

Under the first rays of light, a small delivery truck driving its route stopped in front of a heap of bloody clothing. That heap of rags, the drivers discovered, was breathing. They loaded the foreman into one of the hammocks that these kinds of drivers carry with them everywhere—so they can stop and take a nap wherever they find two trees. They drove him to the hospital in Ahuachapán.

The boy, still hiding in the bushes, was disappointed. He hadn't been strong enough to kill.

On that Christmas Eve, 1994, Miguel Ángel Tobar failed in his first attempt at murder. It was a skill he would later perfect.

The first coffee beans planted in El Salvador had arrived from India just after the drop in the price of indigo—the natural dye that had been the country's principal export—and the economic disaster that followed in 1850.

This economic debacle began with a singular event—an experiment conducted by a chemist's apprentice in a makeshift laboratory on the back patio of a London home. William Henry Perkin, an eighteen-year-old apprentice of Dr. August Wilhelm von Hoffman, the director of London's first chemistry school, had been running experiments with various materials. The mission was to discover a synthetic substitute for quinine, the antimalaria medication that colonial agents of imperial Britain so badly needed.

That April afternoon, young Perkin combined the contents of

one test tube with that of another and then applied heat. He mixed it around. Shook it. The resulting product would have no effect on malaria, but, inside the test tube, something marvelous was happening. Little by little, the liquid turned purple.

Young Perkin thought it was curious, nothing more, and wrote it up in his ledger. But when his mentor saw what he had done, he realized they'd made an important discovery: the first artificial dye.

At that time, almost all dyes were made of natural substances: ground-up insects or the resin of tropical trees. Indigo, extracted from the fruit of the anil plant, had been used for hundreds of years by indigenous peoples and, later, by Europeans. Now, it had suddenly become possible to dye cloth blue and purple without going through the laborious process of extracting and exporting natural indigo. Perkin became rich and famous, receiving four medals for chemistry and eight honorary doctorates. He built up an entire chemical industry and was knighted in 1906, a year before dying of pneumonia and appendicitis.

While the industry launched by Perkin enriched some, on the other side of the world, the smallest country of the Americas was blasted into crisis.

Little by little, the abundant anil plants began to wither. The plantations were abandoned, and hunger and poverty spread throughout the recently founded El Salvador. The country's elites and government officials had bet everything on the export of these leaves. When an economy is based on a single product, it's hard to adapt.

Gerardo Barrios, the president of El Salvador—who was eventually executed by firing squad—had a bright idea: repurpose the whole apparatus of agricultural exportation to serve another crop. Coffee. And that was the moment we all went crazy in El Salvador.

Coffee is capricious. It's a small tree or shrub that refuses to bear fruit at the wrong altitude. It needs abundant water and won't share its space with another harvestable plant. If it has too much shade, it dies. If it's exposed to too much sun, it dies. Above all, it needs attention. Unlike the anil, this tree and the processing of its fruits require constant labor.

The country's elites possessed the capital, the technical supplies, and all the necessary infrastructure to start producing coffee. They only lacked two things: land to plant the trees on, and field hands to harvest the berries.

And so their eyes fastened on the people who'd been ignored for more than 200 years: the indigenous population.

The colonial Spaniards had given to indigenous tribes, as a way of protecting them, communal land in the hills and mountains. High-altitude land, that wasn't worth much at the time. Indigenous peoples were relegated to the sidelines and backwoods when the country was founded. And then, suddenly, their lands became essential for the country's survival.

In the last decade of the nineteenth century, President Rafael Zaldívar signed a decree. The communal lands where the Indians worked, grew their crops, and protected themselves from the government, were taken away at the stroke of a pen. Most of these lands were taken directly by the state, which sold them to coffee cultivators.

The country had found its coffee fields. It only needed to find its laborers. The indigenous families who had just been stripped of their lands were now obliged to work them on others' behalf, for miserable wages. But coffee would demand even more of them.

Vagrancy laws were passed that let the state arrest people and force them to work for free, like slaves, so long as they were over twelve years old and couldn't prove they were already working on a plantation.

Both the land and the indigenous people were handed over to private interests.

In the first decades of the twentieth century, most of the country's coffee cultivation flourished in the west, and many Salvadorans desperate for work followed the coffee trail. Hungry, ragged multitudes, beggared by Zaldívar's decree, flocked to the western hills.

These masses were not, in reality, how they were portrayed in official culture: happy and carefree brown folk, dressed in traditional costume and singing as they shucked coffee berries. No. It was a despoiled army simmering with hate. Hatred of the Ladinos (the foremen, administrators, plantation owners) and even other mestizo campesinos slightly less deprived than themselves—all those whom the indigenous considered guilty for the theft of their land.

Decades passed, while poverty and hatred rose to a boiling point.

Some communist leaders tried to channel the discontent into a political movement. But by 1932, forty years of indigenous rancor at being forced to tend an alien shrub where their *milpas* and *ayotales* used to be—while also being raped, mistreated, and enslaved—could no longer be contained.

US missionary Roy McNaught woke with a start around midnight on January 23, 1932, in a village in western El Salvador. As he recounted later, he heard hundreds of indigenous workers attacking a nearby National Guard post, the telegraph and the mayor's office. Dozens more workers used sticks and stones to break down the massive wooden doors of the home of a wealthy coffee baron, Emilio Redaelli. The rebels had a few firearms—pistols and old hunting rifles—which they used to execute Radaelli. And then they did the same with his wife and kids. Next, they went for the liquor cabinet. They drank it dry before taking their fury to the neighboring village.

At least six communities were captured by the rebels. The same plan of attack was used in all of them. Take down the guard post, take down the telegraph, and ambush the homes of the rich coffee growers who'd taunted them for years. And yet, overall, little blood was shed. According to the American historian Erick Chin, the foremost expert on this period, the indigenous uprising barely saw a hundred people dead.

But it took the state by surprise. What happened in the weeks following the uprising has gone down as the bloodiest era in El Salvador's history. Speaking of El Salvador, that's saying something.

President General Maximiliano Hernández Martínez called his war minister, General Calderón, and his orders were clear: crush the rebellion, and make sure it stays crushed.

In an old, yellowing photograph, a group of men wearing hunting clothes pose next to a cart full of bodies. In another, a horrified young man peers at a pile of dead bodies—all of them, again, indigenous. In another, a priest reads from a black book to Francisco Sánchez, one of the leaders of the rebellion. In another, Sánchez hangs from a noose tied to a tree in downtown Izalco. They left his body exposed until it rotted—an example of what happens to indigenous people when they refuse to obey. When they don't harvest coffee.

At least 30,000 people, mostly young men, were murdered in western El Salvador in under a month. Many more were executed by the end of the year. None of those deaths were logged in the city's formal homicide registry.

The celebrated Salvadoran poet, Roque Dalton—a member of the People's Revolutionary Army (ERP), executed by the same ERP in 1975 after being wrongly suspected of being a CIA informer —wrote the following poem, *Todos* (All of Us), about the slaughter:

> We were born half dead in 1932
> we survived but only half alive
> each with a bill of thirty thousand dead
> that started accruing interest
> paying dividends
> and today suffices to spread death on those
> still being born
> half dead and
> half alive.
>
> We were born half dead in 1932
> to be Salvadoran is to be half dead
> the part that still kicks
> is the half-life they left us.

The haciendas continued to grow and harvest the wretched plant. Exporting and adding more shrubs, always more. Villages became small feudal enclaves. They had their own currency, their own corner shops, their own laws. And, fitting for El Salvador in those years, their own dictators. The foremen had become demigods. They took whatever they wanted, even if what they wanted lay between the legs of one of their female coffee harvesters. And if anyone talked back, they'd end up beheaded and left in a ditch.

The rich became very rich in the decades following 1932. The poor could hardly have been any poorer.

There's an indigenous saying that coffee, a cursed plant, thrives on blood. That's why coffee berries are red.

The boy—who would later become the Hollywood Kid—fled, running along the rows of coffee, disappointed in himself. But he took something with him that would be invaluable to his future. From the belt of the man he'd failed to stone to death, he took a .38 revolver.

The gun was of little consolation at first. Miguel Ángel hadn't been able to avenge his sister's honor or punish the foreman for his cruelty. Miguel Ángel could never undo what his father had allowed to happen, again and again.

Miguel Ángel's family was, during those coffee-growing years, a patchwork of other families.

His mother, Doña Rosa, had abandoned another family. Of that first family, one daughter and two sons remained. Two of her other children had died before their fifth birthdays. When I asked people who knew the family what those children had died of, they gave vague answers that meekly attempted to justify, in few words, the human life that had ended. They died of measles. They died because they caught something in the air. They died of a stomach bug. They died because of a soft spot on their heads. No one knows what they died of, but child death was normal in their world.

In the late 1970s, as the plantation owners saw their kingdom shaken by international competition, Doña Rosa got to know Don Jorge, the *miquero* of a hacienda.

Being a *miquero* means doing the work of an animal. A monkey, to be precise. The *miqueros* are in charge of stripping the high branches of shade trees. A good shade tree is tall but must be pruned, to compete as little as possible with the coffee shrubs below. The *miquero,* with a machete and a rope (but without harness or gloves) climbs up to the crowns of Japanese cashews, laurels, and other trees specific to the region. He lops the trees so that they cast shade, but not too much, and let through some sun, but not too much. If the *miquero* falls, it's his problem.

Doña Rosa got to know a *miquero* who fell. It sounded like a clap of thunder when Jorge hit the ground. They took him to his hut in the hacienda and prescribed rest and herbal tea, and he healed as best he could. It turned out he couldn't heal very well at all. His left arm remained bent and limp. The pieces of his broken bones barely knitted. His spine was left crooked, and he was in constant pain.

The *miquero* became a laborer. A laborer with one good arm, harvesting the beans that grew thanks to that perfect blend of shade and sun he'd made possible until he fell.

Years went by, the couple trudging from hacienda to hacienda, asking for whatever work they could find.

Doña Rosa and Don Jorge had four children. Sandra, the eldest, was born around 1979. Jorge in 1981. Miguel Ángel in 1983. And a little girl, whose name no one remembers, who died of measles when she was a year and a half old.

Doña Rosa, Miguel Ángel's mother, was a mother to three dead children.

Don Jorge, Miguel Ángel's father, was heir to the murdered indigenous people.

Don Jorge inherited his miserable job from those murdered people. He was born into plantation life, under the iron fists of the foremen.

They went from hacienda to hacienda until, in the 1990s, they finally settled on one. The hacienda was in Atiquizaya, in an area known—a cruel joke—as Paradise.

Don Jorge turned to alcohol and Doña Rosa's mind gradually grew feebler until she turned into a deranged old woman. The children basically raised themselves.

The foreman gave work to a crippled campesino with a large family. He even let him live in the hacienda. But he wanted a favor in return, for which he asked Don Jorge during one of his *guaro* benders: the eldest daughter. He didn't want her as his wife, he already had one of those. He just wanted her as an after-work treat.

Don Jorge accepted. He gave the foreman permission to rape his daughter Sandra as often as he pleased.

Over many months, the man would come around in the evenings to blow off steam with a fifteen-year-old girl. Afterward, he'd take out his *guaro* and get drunk with her father.

The foreman would order Sandra's brothers out of the house before he raped her. But, a few times, Miguel Ángel didn't leave altogether. Instead, he hid outside and, through gaps in the planks, watched his father's boss hump his older sister.

Miguel Ángel grew sick with hate. On December 24, 1994, while all Atiquizaya was celebrating, Miguel Ángel decided to kill for the first time.

He was a child—eleven years old—when he hid in the coffee bushes as two men nearby got drunk on *guaro*.

3

The Origin: The Civil War and the Refugees in California

March 24, 1980, 6 p.m.: a young man, tall and bearded, drove a red Volkswagen coupe to the chapel of a cancer hospital in the middle-class neighborhood of Miramonte, in the capital of El Salvador. Beside him was a sniper rifle loaded with an explosive .22-caliber bullet that would change Salvadoran history.

There were combatants in the country before 1980. The guerrilla forces had grown and were training both inside and outside of the country by the late 1970s. But, apart from the Farabundo Martí National Liberation Front (FMLN) led by Commander Cayetano Carpio, which at the time was the most powerful guerrilla group on the continent, they weren't well organized. The other guerrilla groups were made up of university students, poets, intellectuals, and unaffiliated but enthusiastic and romantic revolutionary youth. They lacked both determination and maturity.

The government wasn't a homogeneous bloc, either. The large landowners and the industrial elite felt vulnerable before the masses and their revolutionary ideas, which halted production every other week with strikes and street blockades. They'd stopped trusting the military, and the international policing of the US president, Jimmy Carter, appeared to this privileged minority little better than a communist force.

Only one figure had gained the unanimous respect of the military, the plantation owners, the industrialists, and the politicians: General José Alberto "Chele" Medrano. He was an old-school military man, a coarse and violent bully. Everything that was expected of a Salvadoran man. As chief of the National Guard, Medrano had won great prestige commanding the 1969 invasion of Honduras, part of a series of border skirmishes between the two countries that lasted barely 100 hours, which was later dubbed the Soccer War by journalist Ryszard Kapuscinski. The incident that set off the war between neighbors whose relations had long been tense, with the mass expulsion of Salvadorans from Honduras, was the series of qualifying matches for the 1970 World Cup in Mexico. El Salvador won two out of three against Honduras and entered the World Cup for the first time in history (failing to score a single goal).

The National Guard in those years was not unlike the gestapo in Nazi Germany. The institution was created in 1912 to pool the state forces and, from that moment on, they were feared throughout the country. They were a full-fledged military police force and, though the government soon formed the National Police, as well as the even more formidable Plantation Police, the National Guard continued to be a symbol of unchecked power across El Salvador. When the tensions between Honduras and El Salvador climaxed in 1969, it was General Chele Medrano who took charge. Financed by gold secretly collected by coffee growers, he traveled incognito to Europe to buy anti-aircraft batteries, modern rifles, and grenades for use against the Honduran army. The clashes, however, were inconclusive. The Salvadoran army killed more cows than people, and the troops devoted themselves to looting and destroying Honduran plantations throughout the operation. It was a war of the wretched. Like two malnourished boxers trying to hurt each other, but too weak to score a KO.

No one cared. The pyrrhic nature of the invasion didn't temper the pomp and circumstance with which General Chele Medrano and his national guardsmen were received in San Salvador after the Organization of American States, like a mother scolding her children, put an end to the offensive with the stroke of a pen. The general led the parade, armed, uniformed, and riding atop a black mule. In honor of him and his men, the street they marched on—one of the most important thoroughfares in the capital—was rechristened with the name it still bears: Boulevard of the Heroes.

From that day on, Medrano was known as the strong face of the military and the great protector of the coffee plantations. It was he who modernized the state's rule book of repression, becoming the primary shield against the counterinsurgency. The National Guard and police already knew how to torture. They'd employed torture for decades to subdue the masses who'd been pushed by poverty to commit petty crime. They were experts in squeezing outlaws, murderers, and thieves. Their methods of choice were hard kicks, hoods dipped in calcium oxide pressed against the face and, of course, the fearsome pail of water hung from the testicles.

But these methods would be inadequate against the insurgent groups of the 1970s. General Medrano knew it. He'd studied military tactics, and had learned a few tricks in the United States and Asia.

He can be credited with founding El Salvador's first serious military intelligence service, the National Security Agency of El Salvador (ANSESAL), as well as with building a network of informant campesinos, known as the ears of the military—the Democratic Nationalist Organization (ORDEN). To head ANSESAL he enlisted his right-hand man, a young officer who had traveled and fought with him in the inglorious war against the Hondurans, and whose intelligence and outsized capacity for violence set him apart from his peers. His name was Lieutenant Roberto d'Aubuisson.

Together they went to war on the incipient guerrilla fighters. Through the information gathered by ANSESAL, they located hundreds of organized campesinos, trade unionists, leftist thinkers, and community preachers—propagators of the liberation theology gaining ground all over Latin America. Leftists, union members, or church congregationists, as well as their leaders, would soon turn up dead, murdered in the street, beheaded, raped, sometimes with their throats clogged with the shit and piss they'd drowned in. Chele Medrano's mission was, in the words of one guerrilla fighter: "To kill the baby in his cradle." The baby symbolized the revolutionary process, and the killing was what it was. But that baby grew up, grabbed a rifle and headed for the mountains.

By March 1980, there was tenuous hope of a political truce. A group of young soldiers had carried out a coup the year before, bringing in a revolutionary junta made up of economists, doctors, politicians, and military officials. The archbishop of San Salvador, Monseñor Óscar Arnulfo Romero, told the masses to remain calm. The people had put their trust in this beloved archbishop, the man who accompanied them through their small villages and hamlets, and denounced state abuse from the pulpit of the Metropolitan Cathedral.

But El Salvador is a country of sharp turns. If it were a highway, it'd be full of switchbacks and rim-wrecking potholes. One of these unexpected swerves was made by General Medrano himself. He fell for a flower child—a rich and beautiful girl who, marijuana joint in hand, took leisurely drives around San Salvador in her convertible Mercedes. She was the daughter of a famous bandit of the 1930s, murdered by the regime of General Maximiliano Hernández Martínez, the same triggerman who'd killed many of the indigenous rebels of the west. Her name was Miriam Interiano. The general delivered himself up to Miriam and her bohemian lifestyle, until he was killed by a guerrilla ambush in front of his house in San Salvador. And so the winding path of the fearsome general came to an end, even as his legacy lived on.

The responsibility of organizing a counterinsurgency fell on General Medrano's gifted apprentice, Roberto d'Aubuisson. He gave up his military career when he was still a major, and, after the coup d'état and the establishment of the civic-military junta in 1979, became convinced that all this was part of a communist takeover plot. In fact, Major d'Aubuisson thought that almost everything, including some of the policies imposed by the United States, stank of communism. In his fevered mind, one figure in particular seemed to be nothing but a vile communist pawn: Archbishop Romero.

On March 24, 1980, the assassin's bullet foreclosed all hope for a negotiated end to the sociopolitical conflict. Romero was shot as he raised the communion wafer over his head and proclaimed: "May this spilled blood and sacrificed body be the seeds of liberty."

Afterwards, as a final seal to the declaration of war, in the middle of Romero's funeral, state soldiers, without an ounce of mercy, attacked the thousands of mourners who had congregated in front of the Metropolitan Cathedral. Tensions peaked, war had begun. Salvadorans found themselves on the battlefield.

Just as the 1914 assassination of the Austrian archduke Franz Ferdinand sparked the First World War, the assassination of Monseñor Romero, ordered by the arch-conservative Roberto d'Aubuisson, sparked disaster in El Salvador. The guerrilla fighters left their differences behind and formed a new coalition: the Farabundo Martí National Liberation Front (FMLN). Meanwhile, the state, with the backing of the Reagan administration, imported more weapons and created five new elite battalions trained by US military experts. These were killing machines. Men that would make Rambo look like a wind-up toy.

The National Guard and the two police units would remain in control of intelligence work and political repression, but actual combat decisions would be made, for the first time, by the Salvadoran army.

The northern tip of the tiny country became a rear guard for the guerrillas. The central zones were disputed. Only the west, the troubled and bloody west, would be able to keep to the margins of the conflict. The social trauma of the indigenous massacre of the 1930s had left its mark on following generations. By 1980, El Salvador, left without a Monseñor Romero to attenuate the conflict and stem the killing, launched itself into total war—a vortex of violence that would take twelve years to escape.

In the early 1980s, the Mara Salvatrucha 13 was relying on its godfathers. Two hard-as-nails godfathers. From the perspective of thirty years later, it all seems strange and unlikely. The godfathers didn't realize what they were creating, and they would be shocked to see the monster their child became. The first godfather was Ronald Reagan. The second, the 18th Street Gang, or Barrio 18.

In 1981, after a year of full-fledged war in El Salvador, Ronald Reagan became president of the United States. He was a hunk who had been famous in his youth for breaking hearts and manhandling cowboys in Warner Bros films of the 1930s and 40s. A Los Angeles native, he later became governor of rich and bountiful California. He brought the image of hard power back to the presidency. His predecessor, the Democrat Jimmy Carter, had been accused of being soft on the expansion of communism in Latin America. And so Reagan took the position of one of his characters, George Custer from *Santa Fe Trail*, and swept away the scum that was threatening the American lifestyle—both inside and outside of US borders. Central America was a special case. The US government lavished arms and military training on General Efraín Ríos Montt, the Guatemalan dictator accused of dozens of indigenous massacres. Despite Romero's magnicide, the United States supported the Salvadoran military regime by sending arms and financing the creation, as already mentioned, of five elite battalions to combat the guerrilla. It was like flicking a cigarette into a field of dry grass. The war reached such an intensity that it sent thousands fleeing for safety, the majority heading to Los Angeles, increasing the large population of Salvadorans that had already escaped to the city by the end of the 1970s. New blood to fill out the ranks of the Mara Salvatrucha, new blood to feed the Beast.

The mass of refugees and deserters ran slap into the second pillar of Reagan's domestic politics. "Drugs are enemy number one," he repeatedly declared in his speeches. And the Drug War would zero in on California.

By 1982, the small Latino gangs selling drugs had become a

government priority. To make matters worse, the 1984 Olympics held in Los Angeles were a means to, yet again, symbolically showcase the dispute between the world's two great Cold War superpowers and to cleanse the streets of riffraff.

Hundreds of gang leaders and members were jailed. Entire gangs were dismantled. The complex ecosystem of gangs was upturned by the new antidrug strategy, and the Mara Salvatrucha Stoner— the rockers turned gangsters—took advantage of the power vacuum. Reagan gave them everything they needed to grow. He ensured a constant flow of new members from Central America and at the same time weakened their biggest enemies in California. With such a giving godfather, it was only a matter of time before the Beast matured.

From the beginning the MS were a lawless army. They crossed into enemy territory and took what they wanted, trusting in their machetes and the hatchets they hid in their baggy pants. They challenged everybody they crossed paths with. And day after day, more young deserters—either from the army or the guerrillas—would come running north to be received with open arms. They taught the LA kids new ways of lying in wait for enemies and ambushing them. They had battle experience and, unlike the other Chicano gangsters of the time, were as tough as they come. The counterinsurgency training that Reagan provided to the military ended up training future MS members as well.

But they didn't understand the city. The complex war waged between Chicanos and Mexican Americans was a mystery to the newly arrived Salvadoran gangsters. The fight that *did* make sense was against the black gangs—the prodigious confederations of the Bloods and Crips. They understood that the Chicanos were fighting against the black gangs because they were different, and that was pretext enough for a festival of violence. And they understood why they, Central Americans arriving on already conquered territory, were attacked by the Chicanos. What they didn't understand was why the Chicanos had been fighting among themselves, and then decided on a truce, and then fought again, and then made up—a frenzy of alliances and enmities that seemed chaotic from the outside. Like baseball and four corners, the struggle on the street was a secret that the city refused to spill to them. The Salvadorans remained in a category all their own—something between an actual California gang and a haphazard group of violent friends.

Anthropologist Abner Cohen cites an Arab proverb that neatly explains the gangs' system of alliances and aggressions: "Me against my brother, my brother and me against our cousin, my cousin, my brother and me against the stranger."

That's how it was, and still is—the Chicano gangs violently fighting among themselves. And yet, when they were thrust into a penal system teeming with established black, white, and Asian gangs, they established a unified front that came to be known as Sur. But they needed guidance, and the guidance came from the Mexican Mafia. This group was formed by hand-picked gangsters from all the Chicano gangs of Southern California. It was a central committee, a gang of gangs inside the prisons. Hundreds of gangsters made up El Sur, but only a select crew of them became the Mexican Mafia, or La Eme (The M), as they're known in the street by those who dare utter the name.

La Eme is structured as a prison gang, and its laws are promulgated in the prisons. Codes of conduct and rules, such as: Do not kill from inside a vehicle; do not attack a gangster while he's with family; never turn down a fistfight; always wear blue, never red. Above all, obey La Eme. Do whatever it asks.

If a gangster doesn't comply, La Eme makes the whole gang pay. If the offense is serious, it can even set off a "green light"—the street's death penalty. From the moment a green light is given, all other gangs in the Sur system can go on the attack. Multiple gangs have been crushed by Sur's molars after committing cardinal infringements of the laws.

Richard, an ex-gang member of Barrio 18, thinks back on his experience during the 1980s as he drinks a fresh-squeezed juice in the Trashcan, a popular eating hall in Dina, one of San Salvador's most violent neighborhoods.

"When I got to Los Angeles, the first gang I ran into was MS, right around Lafayette Park," Richard, now in his fifties, recalls. "But I didn't like it. I don't know ... They were dirty drunks with shaved heads. They all had Black Sabbath and Metallica shirts on, and I just didn't like it. 'Hey, come with us, join up. We got your back here,' they were telling me, but I didn't like it. They were always high, smoking crack."

Richard arrived in LA in the early '80s, aged seventeen. He had been part of the Urban Commandos guerrilla unit, but the assassination of Romero, the intensification of the war, and the five battalions created by the Reagan administration scared him. He followed in the steps of his uncles and cousins and left for El Norte. Once in LA, he sought a new community, but was turned off by the MS gangsters. And then, soon, he found his new community. In the Shatto Park neighborhood, under a large oak tree that would cast a shadow over his life for more than twenty years, he found the homeboys of Barrio 18.

4
Welcome to the South: The Sureño Gang Rockers

The Death of Black Sabbath

Los Angeles in the 1980s was a complicated space. It contained both the whitewashed exuberance of Beverly Hills and the desperation of the poor Latino and African American neighborhoods. A cocktail mix of a swanky Sunday brunch with a spritz of blood from an alleyway machete fight.

The Salvadorans kept coming. Hundreds of them every day, carrying the dust of a civil war on their thin-soled shoes. As of 1981, the military-political conflict had come of age. The brutal repression of the organized masses had turned into full-fledged guerrilla warfare. Various insurgent groups unified to form the FMLN. By 1983, the guerrilla rank and file were men and women with grit and tactical experience in staging ambushes and attacking military garrisons. The war, in short, had been professionalized. The fight against the counterinsurgency was being run by high military officials, with the National Guard focusing solely on urban repression. The killing fields migrated from the streets to the mountains.

The Salvadorans arriving in Los Angeles, the mecca of US gangs, had been hardened by this violence. What Richard found in Los Angeles in the 1980s was not only the gang that would become his family for the next thirty years, but an entirely new world: all-consuming and violent, but also intriguing. The world of the Sureños.

Where he came from, what you did when you saw an enemy was simple. You aimed your weapon and fired. But it was different in the Sureño neighborhoods of LA. Each block and 'hood was dominated by a particular Latino gang, typically named after their barrio: Hawaiian Gardens 13, White Fence 13, Florencia 13, La Puente 13, Varrio Nuevo Estrada, Artensia 13, Pacoimas 13. All Hispanic, all at war. They fought with other gangs like Crazy Riders 13—the *locos* with the machetes and the hatchets—or the menacing, old-school Playboy 13, elegantly outfitted gangsters that defended Normandie Street wearing sport coats, short-brimmed hats, button-down shirts, ties, and shiny shoes. Pachucos that recognized fellow members by folding in their thumbs, index, and middle fingers and making bunny ears with their ring fingers and pinkies. But all of them, no matter what gang they belonged to, were playing the same game.

The "13" came from a simple substitution. All the nascent gangs were affiliated with the all-powerful Mexican Mafia. "M" is the thirteenth letter of the alphabet. That's why the Hispanic gangs used the number 13 in their names, signaling that they were part of the same Sur system and working under the shadow of the same Mexican Mafia—that gang of gangs that controlled the prisons and managed the system of punishment for all gang members who failed to conform to the code.

Richard found it all fascinating, and when he talks about those early years he shifts around in his seat and switches between Spanish and English, dredging up his old passions. One day, the gangs were his ultimate enemies. The next day, inside a Californian prison, they were his allies in a yard brawl against the black gangs.

Salvadorans took a few LA neighborhoods by storm—places where no one was thinking of brunch. The majority of those being jumped into the gang structure joined Barrio 18, which dated back to the 1950s, and whose lineage was also tied to the powerful Mexican Mafia. Despite some resistance from Mexican and Chicano gang members, the Salvadorans filled out the ranks of hundreds of different Hispanic gangs in the Sur system. The MS, however, still received most of the recent Central American recruits. And it became a gang built by them, run by them, and in defense of them.

The rookies quickly learned the basics of the game, but not all its subtleties. They came from a brutal place and didn't understand temperance. It was like trying to teach a Neanderthal the rules of boxing.

"The Crazy Riders 13, for example," Richard says, "became really dangerous when the Salvadorans showed up. They knew how to ride in a pick-up with giant machetes, along with files to sharpen them up. They were crazy, because most of them were Indians from San Miguel"—an eastern Salvadoran department.

Juan, a Salvadoran from Ilobasco (one of the areas most affected by the war) who was affiliated with a small gang in Orange County, the Shalimar 13, tells a dramatic story. Fellow gang members told him they were going to kill some enemies from the Alley Boy 13 gang. They gave him a pistol. But when Juan pulled the trigger, he discovered that there were no bullets in the gun. It was just a test—something all aspiring members needed to pass. The other gang members were laughing at him back in the car, ready to peel out before their enemies came to hunt them down.

But Juan, furious at having made himself so vulnerable, grabbed a gun his uncle had given him and shot a couple of them in the face. And then he jammed the barrel into another terrified gangster's mouth and told him never to pull shit like that with him again. They never did. In the ten years that Juan would lead the gang, they stopped using that initiation test. Juan was deported to El Salvador in 2010, and he told this story back in his native Ilobasco. The enormous tattoos he had all over his body, even on his face, wouldn't let him live in peace in El Salvador. The police hounded him. The gangs, both MS and Barrio 18, which had been in the country for decades at this point, threatened him. He went back to the United States to live without papers—not in California this time, but a state that was "less violent."

In the 1980s the Salvadorans put a lot on the line with the Sureños. Death in Los Angeles was a big deal, but where these guys were from, it was part of daily life.

To the Mara Salvatrucha Stoner gangsters, the squabbles with other party gangs and quasi-gangs seemed trivial. They were ready for a different league. In East LA, the La Raza Loca gang wanted to stand up to these long-haired goth kids flocking to their neighborhoods. But it wasn't a good idea. Only those who ran survived the showdown. Meanwhile, in the San Fernando Valley, an entire gang was caught off-guard in an abandoned factory. MS members utilized a technique they'd learned from Reagan's counterinsurgency battalions. The gangsters beat the rival gang members all night long, and then forced them to join their side. The Lafayette, Verendos, and Leeward cliques all took on some of these new members. And the Hollywood Boulevard clique wasn't going to be left out of the pickings, either. They were all looking to fill out their ranks and raise their status among the other Sureños. To win more battles they needed more soldiers.

In their own neighborhoods they started extorting drug dealers and beating up car thieves. While most Salvadorans entering the Sureño system were trying to understand the lay of the land, the gangsters of the Mara Salvatrucha Stoner didn't bother. They expected Southern California to adapt to them.

Barrio 18, enormous and well respected, was amused by the wildness of the inflowing gangsters. It was a natural association—at first. A lot of the new members of Barrio 18 were Salvadoran. Some of them were received with respect. They were invited to parties where they learned how to act like Sureños. They heard, in whispers, about the bosses of the M and how they ran Southern California from inside the prisons.

The MS grew up in the shadow of Barrio 18. It was a savage place to come of age.

El Burro, a Mara Salvatrucha 13 veteran, recalls his first confrontation, back in 1984, with the gangsters of Barrio 18, though he doesn't resort to the drama with which most gang tales are told. They had a couple of shootouts with a Barrio 18 clique called Tiny Winos. It went down close to a drug sale point, and it was a fight for the corner. Nobody was injured that day, but the Mara Salvatrucha and the Barrio 18 started distancing themselves from each other. Like brothers after a fight. Both sides knew that one way or another this rift was for life. The definitive break, however, didn't come for a few more years.

"We gained numbers, but lost quality," a woman in her fifties recalls, three decades later, in a coffee shop in one of the most exclusive neighborhoods of San Salvador. She was a protagonist in the early history of MS, one of the few women to hold power inside the gang structure. Now, though she maintains respect for the Mara and its trajectory, she keeps to the outer edges of gang life. Speaking to us for this book was about as close as she would go. And to ensure her safety, this is the only time we'll mention our interview with her.

"When we became Sureños we gained respect, but we sacrificed a lot. I was against it, along with a bunch of others in my generation. But we somehow needed to keep in step with what the majority wanted."

Little by little the new gangsters were being imprisoned in California. Once inside, they realized that no matter how tough they were on the street, all bets were off behind bars. They didn't have firm alliances with any of the Sureño gangs (apart from the friendship with Barrio 18) and they hadn't yet formally incorporated into the Sur system. Which means they weren't protected by the Mexican Mafia. The other Sureño gangs continuously subjected them to humiliation, and they were on their own in any brawls with black gangs in the halls and yards of the California prisons. Though it's still hard for them to admit this, they usually lost.

Without many other options, they began accepting the 13 at the end of their name, and, little by little, forgot their past as satanic hard rockers and dropped the "Stoner." By 1983, the gang had fully integrated into the Sur system, under the now notorious name of Mara Salvatrucha 13.

"The guys coming out of prison weren't like us anymore," a gang veteran recalls. "They didn't come out with long black hair. They came out as *cholos*, with shaved heads, baggy pants, big white t-shirts, earrings, and prison tattoos. They were different. They didn't listen to black or death metal. They'd turned into something more like Chicanos, *cholos*, like Sureños."

With the Mara Salvatrucha, pacts are signed with blood. The strange and romantic history of MSS, digging corpses out of cemeteries and robbing gravestones to the sound of heavy metal, needed its own burial. In late 1985, in an alleyway between 6th Street and Virgil Avenue, some homies, members of the Crazy Riders 13, beat an MS member to death. In honor of the recent stoner past that had spread like wildfire throughout Salvadoran culture, the kid had chosen a dark name for himself: Black Sabatt. He died in the hospital, under the tearful eyes of his homeboys. He was the first homie they'd had to mourn. This is how they paid their entrance fee, with blood. The stoners had died, and the Mara Salvatrucha 13 came bleeding into the Sureño system. Now they had a death to avenge, a token to play with.

These stories are told by the men and women who lived through them. Today, most of them are only tied to the gang through emotional links or old friendships. They recount these snapshots of bygone lives in busy cafés in downtown San Salvador, or dabbing their eyes over a beer at a bar in Dallas. They're no longer members of the Mara Salvatrucha 13, but they once were, and when they speak of the MS they do so as if they were talking about family, with respect. Some are teachers in elementary schools, others are plumbers, others again preach the virtues of God in Pentecostal churches in the slums of San Salvador or Guatemala City. They only ask, in exchange for revealing their secrets, that we don't use their names.

The Birth of the Fulton

In the San Fernando Valley, some forty minutes north of down-town Los Angeles, there's a street. It's not a very imposing street, nor very long. Lining it are apartment buildings, most of them low-cost, and framing these buildings are long alleyways that sometimes connect with other streets, or dead-end into a wall. In the mid 1980s, these alleys were the domain of the Salvadoran gangsters of the San Fernando Valley. What happened here to the Salvadoran youth was integral to the fate of Miguel Ángel Tobar many years later in his rural, coffee-dominated Atiquizaya.

In those years, the Valley was already an epicenter for Hispanic families. Attracted by the plummeting prices the further they got from the city center, hundreds of Salvadoran families started moving in. Some of the gang members who'd warred in the city were among them. Others, in that violent oblivion, decided to join the Mara only after they got to the Valley.

Living in San Fernando Valley meant climbing a couple steps up the social strata of undocumented migrants. Only Salvadorans who'd prospered in the city could migrate to the Valley and buy, at least the wealthiest among them, their own house with its own backyard. Some were able to set up stands in the bustling swap meets and flea markets. There they sold contraband, stolen goods, and t-shirts with small defects that were unfit to sell in the gift shops of Universal Studios.

The Salvadorans of the Valley were, for want of a better term, high-class. Of course, this should be seen in the relative context of the immigrant community. The kids had formed their own quasi-gangs. But unlike the wild stoners, these didn't attempt to dig up the dead or worship the Beast. Instead, they formed a lowriders club.

They called themselves Mini Toy, for mini Toyota, and were all about status symbols. They saw their cars as mobile murals. The lower your car was to the ground, and the more outlandish it looked, the greater your reputation.

Members recall cruising in a carnival parade of customized and remodeled cars—all driven by brown people. It felt like falling out of the Kid Frost music video, *La Raza*.

Most were Mexican or Chicano, but the Salvadorans had also secured a place in that scene. Maybe their cars weren't as eye-catching as the others, but they had other ways of winning the game. The Mini Toys and other Salvadoran car clubs started jockeying for position. With astounding speed, they went from wielding bats and chains to machetes and axes. Outfitted cars had nothing to do with violence, but those forgotten kids were always looking for trouble, trying to forge meaning in their lives. They found it in the hatred of the Other. In the conflict with the Other. It was the only way of life they knew.

The transition from car club to powerful MS-13 clique is not entirely clear. It's known that some gang members had come over from the Hollywood clique, or had some blood relation with members of both the Hollywoods and Barrio 18. But there isn't an exact date or a precise moment when MS-13 came to the Valley. It first emerged as a logo, an idea. Youths obsessed with Mini Toys started donning MS-13 t-shirts without really knowing much about the gang. They grabbed hold of a rumor, a war cry, a foreign flag that called to them, and they waved it up and down the Valley.

In the final days of 1985, the Salvadoran war had reached its climax. The guerrilla fighters of the FMLN knocked the army back every time they made a move. They attacked the largest military barracks, though without gaining any decisive advantage in the drawn-out war. The fighting had been going on for close to six years. Everybody was weary. That exhaustion further opened the faucet of Salvadoran migration to California. More and more deserters from both sides of the war came to the United States. Men and women whose lives bore the mark of violence, either because they'd inflicted it or had suffered it.

One of those deserters was a man about thirty years old, an ex-member of the National Guard and originally from the western Salvadoran city of Atiquizaya. With his down-turned nose and deep black eyes, he was almost certainly a descendant of the indigenous people slaughtered in 1932. His name was José Antonio Terán, but he was known in the Valley as El Veneno (the Poison).

When Terán arrived in the Valley, the Mara Salvatrucha 13 had officially joined the Sureño game. It hadn't yet ballooned to the size of gangs like Pacoima Flats, or the fearsome Pacoimas 13, Pacas for short. The first Angelino battle fought by this most recent iteration of the MS-13 was against a clique of the Barrio 18 known as North Side. Their battleground was a street. And the name of that street was Fulton.

The terrifying savagery the Salvadoran gangsters displayed in fighting for that piece of the Valley sounded the alarm bells of the area's criminal ecosystem. Those ex-combatants and refugees knew how to fight. And this daunting fact would be made ever clearer over the following years.

A former Salvadoran gangster, Fuentes, took notice of the new group. He saw that a strong *marero* muscle was being flexed in the Valley. Once involved in deadly fights to gain control of small segments of the city, Fuentes had recently adopted a new strategy. He'd started dealing both crack and cocaine. And he offered the

Salvadoran gangs a new type of relationship with drugs: selling them.

But there was one obstacle. For the Fulton Street clique to be able to sell Fuentes's wares they had to rid the area of another gang that had monopolized the trade. Along the way, the Tijuana Locos were wiped out.

The Tijuana Locos was a Sureño gang with a clear Mexican lineage. Its livelihood was also its ruin. The Locos smoked a large part of the crack and snorted a large part of the cocaine they peddled. And so they came up short to Fuentes, or, sometimes, they simply gave him nothing.

Fuentes offered the same business to the *mareros* of the Valley. He'd seen the beatings they meted out when any member was caught consuming drugs, and he liked their style.

In a matter of months, the Tijuana Locos had been extermi-nated. One on this corner, others in that alley. The new clique of the Mara Salvatrucha 13 became one of the most respected groups in the Valley, and other gangs soon learned their name: the Fulton Locos Salvatrucha.

A War between Equals

King Boulevard, 1989. In an alley behind a row of apartment build-ings, a party of Sureño gangsters is going full swing.

The Mara Salvatrucha had grown. In the land of Califas they'd watered their crops with blood, Sureño blood. The confrontations with other gangs had been brutal. The Drifters had bludgeoned the western clique's homeboys; the Crazy Riders 13 had bled out the Verendo clique; MS-13 was besieged on all sides.

The MS-13 was forced to bury many of their members. But then more joined them from Black Sabbath. Dozens more. The day of the party on King Boulevard, there'd been as many *mareros* present as there were members of the Barrio 18.

"The problem was this one kid who'd been MS, but came to the party as an Eighteen," El Zarco tells us, sounding a bit confused. He stares fixedly at a plastic table in a McDonald's in El Salvador, decades after the events. "He'd asked us for permission to get out and we'd given it to him. He said his mom was sick. But that was just a lie, he only said that to join the Eighteens. So at the party we told him that to get out of MS you have to go through the same ritual as you do to get in: thirteen seconds [of a beating]." He doesn't seem to totally trust his memory. His time in the California jails and his subsequent deportation to an unrecognizable El Salvador have done to his memory what a hurricane does to a roof.

He says his own clique, the Western Locos Salvatrucha, was present. He says that Boxer, of the Barrio 18, after witnessing the beating of his new homeboy Pony, asked for a "one-on-one"—a sacred request in the Sureño code. It's a fight between two gangsters, something akin to the duels of European nobility in the nineteenth century, something you can't refuse if you want to uphold your honor and maintain your good name. Zarco remembers Boxer as a tough guy. Representing MS was Popeye, one of the youngest members of the clique, a dark-skinned, long-haired kid, still rocking the stoner style. Boxer hit hard, Popeye did too. It was a tie. Then another Eighteen asked to fight, because someone had to save the honor of the gang that had claimed California for decades. The Soldier—representing the MS—accepted the challenge. He used to be in the Salvadoran army, and he won.

The Eighteens left, choking on their defeat. When they came back they brought an automatic rifle, but of the MS members, only Shaggy remained at the party. They shot him in the legs, and he bled to death. According to Zarco, at any rate. That's how he remembers it.

What's certain is that these gunshots, in the following decades, would mark the lives and deaths of thousands of men and boys across the United States and Mesoamerica.

One of those marked was only six years old in 1989, and living on a coffee plantation in western El Salvador. The future Hollywood Kid.

5
Assassin's Gaze: Getting to Know an MS-13 Traitor

January 2, 2012. As he taps away with two fingers on his old computer, Detective Gil Pineda tries not to melt inside his office in the small Salvadoran town of El Refugio.

In El Salvador, it's a pure formality to call winter winter and summer summer. The only two actual seasons are heat with rain and heat.

The detective has more than fifteen years' experience. He's around forty-five years old and has that mature firmness you acquire as the years tick by, before old age withers it all away again. A man like that throws a punch delicately, moving his fist lightly, without even clenching his fingers, though it's easy to imagine everything shattering to pieces with the force of that punch. A man like that laughs softly, never guffaws. "I don't understand what the hype is with getting a guarantee. I see other officers desperately searching for a judge that'll give them an arrest order. Every morning I tie my arrest orders to my feet," he once told us, lifting his right leg up to show a perfectly laced boot.

He's not tall. He's not short. He has a full mustache. He likes to carry a comb in his back pocket and his hair is always combed to one side. The first two buttons of his shirt are undone. He was chief of the homicide unit in one of the most conflicted departments—La Libertad—where there's a heavy MS-13 presence. He was also one of the police officers in charge of prison intelligence—the prisons that function as headquarters for gangsters. He wears a gold bracelet on his wrist and a gold chain around his neck. He smells of cologne. In a small holster he carries his 9mm Pietro Beretta.

The detective goes above and beyond in his work. He doesn't just carry out orders and make arrests. He enjoys his job. It excites him to get someone to snitch on their own gang and spill their secrets. He gives his own money to those snitches when the state forgets or simply refuses, and he does so even after he's literally beaten snitches into collaborating. One time the detective was talking about the Criminal, a face-tattooed member of the MS who he'd turned into an informant for the organized crime unit. How'd he get him to cooperate? "I only had to give it to him for a half hour," the detective responded easily, drinking a beer and eating fish cooked in lime and salt at El Camarón Cervecero, a restaurant on the pier of La Libertad.

He's a hardened man who, like almost everyone in his organization, skirts around the law from time to time in order to achieve his primary objective: destroying the gangs.

He's obsessed with how gangs are able to reconfigure a teenager's mind; that's why he takes pictures of their eyes when they start working together, and later when he suspects they've already killed. He's convinced that the expression in their eyes changes. "Look, look," he says when he shows off his photograph collection. "Look at that gaze, see how they eye each other up and down?

As if the other guy were an animal to be hunted down; see how each eyes the other, sizing him up."

"I've detained some hundred assassins in my life," the detective said later. This time we were in his dining room and he was eating fried chicken. "The majority were gangsters. I can tell whether a kid has killed or not. You can see it in him when he's making his extortion rounds. At first he has a look that's ... I don't know how to describe it, his eyebrows are in place, set straight across the face, and he has a normal look in his eyes, like a normal person, not like someone who's trying to achieve a goal. With time, they get that darkened look with their eyebrows constantly arched, and that expression stays there, locked into place. I took pictures of the *bichitos* collecting extortion fees, and I took pictures later, too, once they'd already killed. See?" He used the term *bichito*, derived from *bicho*, bug, a common term to refer to gang members, but also sometimes to civilians. "Their gaze changes," Pineda concluded. "The Kid never had a normal look. Ever since I met him, he had the eyes of a killer."

Now it's 2012, and Detective Pineda is overburdened, doing what he least enjoys: paperwork. Writing reports and drafting PowerPoint presentations so that his higher-ups or the prosecutors—mere office drudges, in his estimation—can understand the MS structure that he's been researching over the last two and a half years.

The office he works out of doesn't deserve to be called an office. It's a dilapidated shack with a tile roof and brick walls that are thinly whitewashed or bare. In that shack there are three desks that look as if they've been salvaged from the street. One of them supports a desktop computer, with a huge noisy monitor and a half-broken keyboard. In the back there are rickety toilets that only flush by filling a white plastic bucket with water and emptying it in a toilet bowl scabbed over with dark splotches.

There's one computer activity the detective enjoys: he likes to graph the gang structures. He collects pictures of the gang members and organizes them according to their rank within each clique. He shows off his results enthusiastically, the way a teenager might show off his World Cup or baseball cards.

"This is el Stranger," he says, pointing to a picture of a dark-skinned, obese man.

José Guillermo Solito Escobar, el Stranger. In his thirties, second-in-command of the Hollywood Locos Salvatrucha, recently got out of prison for aggravated assault.

"This is Liro Jocker," he says, pointing to a picture of a bald and burly white man, the stereotype of a gangster.

Jorge Alberto González Navarrete, Liro Jocker. The nickname comes from a phonetic play, from Little to Liro. He's a thirty-year-old man with skulls and crossbones tattooed all over his body, third-in-command of the Hollywood Locos Salvatrucha. He was deported from the United States after serving time for aggravated assault in June 2009 and, according to his deportation record, he used to be part of another MS clique in Maryland and was then known as Baby Yorker. The Kid would describe him as "a hard-ass bastard, a murderer."

"This is the Maniac," Pineda says, pointing to the picture of a skinny, hawk-nosed man wearing a button-up shirt. A man with a forgettable face; not someone you would cross the street to avoid.

Fredy Crespín Morán, the Maniac. Thirty-eight, an electrician by trade and treasurer of the Hollywood Locos Salvatrucha. He now works in public relations in the mayor's office of Atiquizaya, which is controlled by the Arena party.

"And the king of clubs. This is Chepe Furia," says the detective, pointing to the face of a dark-skinned man with prominent indigenous features, features he shares with those who were massacred in 1932.

José Antonio Terán, now nicknamed Chepe Furia. Forty-six years old, leader and founder of the Hollywood Locos Salvatrucha of the Mara Salvatrucha of Atiquizaya; ex-member of the Fulton Locos Salvatrucha of the San Fernando Valley, in California, where he was known as El Veneno, the Poison. And before that, a member of the fearsome National Police, the military police force, during the first years of the Salvadoran war. He migrated to escape the war he'd been fighting. Years later he returned to his homeland, branded with the letters he used to identify himself in the north: MS.

All of them were caught by Detective Pineda, and now face a jury trial for conspiracy and murder of a twenty-three-year-old informer named Samuel Menjívar Trejo—nickname Rambito—a vegetable vendor in the Atiquizaya market. Rambito was a lookout and aspiring member of the Hollywood Locos Salvatrucha, but since 2008 he'd been collaborating with Pineda and the police. He helped complete Pineda's deck of gangsters by telling him who was who in the lowest rungs of the gang.

One day at noon in 2009, two investigative officers of the sub-delegation of Atiquizaya asked emergency service agents to go down to the market, pick up Rambito, and bring him back to the station. The agents followed orders. They went to the market and, in plain view of all the other vendors, transported Rambito back to the station. The officers, José Wilfredo Tejada Castaneda, homicide detective, and Walter Misael Hernández Hernández, detective of extortions and head of the antidrugs unit of Ahuachapán, arrived at the station and took Rambito away with them. But they didn't sign the office log, not wanting to leave a sign of anything unusual.

The officers never returned Rambito, not to the market nor to the subdelegation office. But he was spotted that same afternoon, on his way back from buying two ropes, one blue and one green, and getting into the passenger side of a pickup truck. Chepe Furia was driving. In the back were Liro Jocker and el Stranger.

That night, in the western hamlet of Talpetate, some 120 miles from Atiquizaya, a passerby discovered Rambito's body in a ditch by the side of the road. It bore marks of torture and the head and torso were riddled with bullet wounds. The autopsy found traces of gunpowder on the left cheek. He'd been shot from less than two feet away. His feet and hands were bound with one blue and one green rope.

Rambito's death convinced Detective Pineda that to investigate the Hollywood Locos Salvatrucha it was necessary to leave Atiquizaya, the "city"—though it's more of a large town—where the subdelegation is located. The detective decided to relocate his entire team to a rural outpost in the municipality of El Refugio, a few miles away, a hamlet almost completely lost among coffee plantations.

The detective's PowerPoint, which he runs for us on his prehistoric computer, shows photographs of more than forty gangsters from the Hollywood Locos Salvatrucha. Rambito, a mere aspiring member of the clique, could never have given so many names. It's not possible for a mere pawn in the game to tell all the king's secrets. Rambito was an informant who divulged what little he knew, that's why the police never granted him protected witness status. On the totem pole of snitches, he ranked very, very low.

"We have a witness," the detective says, jerking his eyes and head toward the other side of the street. One of the clique's heavy lifters, he says. A former trusted hitman for Chepe Furia.

When we ask whether we can talk to this witness, the detective wavers for a couple of seconds and frowns. He loses himself in his ancient computer, saying that he needs to check something over. Then he yells over to the other sergeant, Pozo.

"Sergeant, go get the Kid."

In one of the shabbier neighborhoods on the outskirts of Atiquizaya, in the last months of 2009, a young man of twenty-seven was smoking his fifth crack rock of the day inside his house. The door to the house, really a shack, closes with a metal latch, but this time he's left it ajar. The Kid is stressed. It's not a good time in his life. Too many problems rolling around in his head. The Kid inhales a large mouthful of smoke. He hears the door clap open. He holds the smoke in his lungs, and then hears the clack of a gun. The Kid curls five fingers over the .40 he has strapped to one thigh and another five fingers around the .357 strapped to his other thigh.

"Hey, take it easy, I can see you're armed," the intruder says, holding his 9mm with both hands.

The Kid recognizes the calm voice. It's Sergeant Pozo, from the investigative office of El Refugio.

"I'm completely stoned," the Kid says.

"I just want to talk."

"I'm totally blazed off this rock."

"Fuck. So do you think we can talk?"

The sergeant holds his breath and decides to take his chances. He doesn't move a muscle as he watches the Kid get up from his seat and turn towards him with the two guns drawn. The Kid, his gaze locked on the sergeant, walks out of the house. Without letting go of the weapons he climbs into the bed of the pickup and says: "Let's roll." The sergeant puts his gun away and, with his heart in his throat, drives down the lonely streets toward the investigative office of El Refugio—an armed hitman of the Hollywood Locos Salvatrucha at his back.

Sergeant Pozo has finally succeeded in getting the Kid, a big shot in Chepe Furia's clique but besieged by some of the members of his own gang, to talk to the police about becoming a protected witness.

Like the majority of the officers and sergeants in the force, and especially the lower ranks, Sergeant Pozo lives in a neighborhood run by gangs. He may be a boss during the day, but at night he submits to the authority of the Mara Salvatrucha. This is one segment of the fine line between the state and the gangs in this minuscule country. In fact, the gangs *are* the state in some neighborhoods, counties, and villages.

Sergeant Pozo was assigned by Detective Pineda to flip the Kid. For a job like this, walking the dusty streets trying to convince an MS assassin into coming over to the other side, Sergeant Pozo earns $604.96 a month (the currency in El Salvador is the US dollar). The detective deployed other sergeants and officers to flip ranking gang members of the clique, but none of them were in the same kind of corner that the Kid found himself. This assassin had problems with other assassins. He'd seen a lot of blood spilled inside his own gang.

The Kid wasn't scared of a confrontation with a cop. He'd come through them before. If he hadn't found himself cornered, in a dead-end alleyway with his gang, the Kid would have spun around and Sergeant Pozo wouldn't be with us anymore.

As Pineda would later put it, digging into a surf-and-turf in La Ola Beto's in San Salvador: "The Kid's a good shot. When he fires he hits the victim in the head."

It's not the first time that detectives have tried to get the Kid to collaborate. Pineda is expert at sowing discord in the adversary's ranks and harvesting protected witnesses. More than once he's threatened to leave suspected gang members in enemy territory, to test their claim that they're not in a gang. He has video on his phone of a young kid denying that he was part of MS, and then later weeping during the interrogation. The detective threatened to send the video to other gang members. It's a trick to extract information, names, and ranks. Thanks to his unorthodox methods he's been able to piece together his puzzle. Since the end of 2009, he's tried to get members to flip one by one. It wasn't until he started suspecting that the Kid had been involved in the murder of a sixteen-year-old girl named Wendy, that he established a contact with someone close to the veteran Chepe Furia. He told Sergeant Pozo to do whatever he needed to get the Kid to talk. The sergeant's offer was simple: you're going to talk or we're pinning the murder on you. Pozo had been harassing the Kid for a while at that point—finding him on the streets of Atiquizaya and pretending to arrest him, so they could talk.

Once, Sergeant Pozo had a patrol of seven soldiers and two police officers detain the Kid.

"You going to book me or not? Because I'm not carrying today," the Kid said defiantly.

Sergeant Pozo kept his temper and explained to him that he wanted to help, but in order to do so he needed some help of his own. He told him he was going to charge him with crimes he hadn't even been involved with, starting with this one that he only witnessed: the murder of sixteen-year-old Wendy. The Kid was able to wriggle out of the threat, but only by showing some of his own cards: he had a lot of secrets.

"Okay, yeah, fine, if you want to help me, help me," the Kid said. "If not, you can book me now, or do what you want … 'Cause if you want to know all of Eliú's bullshit, the murder of that whore, the murder of that cop in the hall, who gave it to Wilman from the second floor of the house, the mototaxi drivers who had their brains oozing out, or the murder of Moncho Garrapata's wife …"

After that, the Kid disappeared for a few weeks. When the sergeant tracked him down again, he still had only this one card to play. Accuse him of Wendy's murder, and once he was up to his neck in court hearings, try to pin other murders on him. Threaten him with years in prison. And yet he knew that such a simple strategy wasn't going to work with an assassin who'd had the kind of experiences the Kid had.

Luckily, a better opportunity arose.

The Kid and the Beast

2005. Fifteen years after the end of the war, western El Salvador: two gang members are shooting the breeze. Boasting of past adventures and their "hits," as they call their kills.

Both belonged to Mara Salvatrucha 13, but were from separate cliques and families. One was known as El Chato, from the Park View Locos Salvatrucha, a clique formed in the 80s in LA's MacArthur Park, on Park View Street. The second man was a twenty-one-year-old member of the Hollywood Locos Salvatrucha, the brother clique established a few miles from Park View during the same turbulent decade. This was the Kid.

El Chato wanted to show off. He took out his phone and brought up a photo of a dead man. The Kid looked at it awhile, lifting the phone close to his face, and congratulated Chato.

"Shit, that dude got it fucking bad," the Kid said.

"See. That's how the Parvis leave their hits," Chato said, mangling the name of the Park View clique.

"Who was it?"

"Some *bicha*," Chato said, using the derogatory word for girl that they use to refer to their rivals. *Bicha* or *caca*, shit.

The two men said goodbye, and each went his own way. Afterward, the Kid knew that the Beast, the gang's goddess of violence, had turned its back on him. More blood would have to flow.

The dead man in the photograph was his older brother.

Months earlier, the Kid heard that his brother had gone missing. He figured the Barrio 18 had killed him. It wouldn't be unexpected for the kind of life his brother, a member of the Park View Locos Salvatrucha, had been leading. The Kid had started going almost daily to neighborhoods run by Barrio 18, taking on all the hits his clique was ordering. He killed some enemies, wounded some others—all with the conviction that he was avenging the murder of his brother. That's why what he saw on Chato's phone disturbed him so much. His fellow gang members had known. They'd been the ones to kill his brother. And still they let him risk his life confronting a deadly foe. They'd encouraged him, cheered him on, even gone with him. They loved the homicidal drive the death of a sibling had sparked in him. The Kid never imagined that his own gang, his brothers in arms, his homeboys—the Beast—could do this terrible thing.

His brother was known as El Cheje, an old word for woodpecker. He'd worked as a prison guard, ice cream vendor, and carpenter. Unlike the Kid, who was jumped into the Hollywood Locos Salvatrucha de Atiquizaya, he joined up with the Park View of Ahuachapán in the capital of the Ahuachapán Department.

But El Cheje made a very grave mistake. He killed another MS member. According to gang rules, his own death was thereby justified. The homeboy that El Cheje killed had robbed and threatened their mother, so El Cheje hunted him down and shot him dead. But he didn't just kill this homeboy. He also killed the homeboy's mother. The homeboy had bumped off his mom, so he did the same back, and worse. What the gang never knew was that El Cheje had carried out these killings along with his little brother, the Kid.

As time went by, the pair thought their revenge killing had become a thing of the past. That they had done it right, that nobody had found out, that their murder was lost among the coffee trees, lost in the dust of western El Salvador along with all the other anonymous corpses. But they were wrong.

The gang is like a gossip chain, deeds flying mouth to mouth. Somehow, a few members of the Park View Locos Salvatrucha had found out what El Cheje did.

When El Chato showed the Kid the photo of his dead brother, he didn't know they were related. He thought he was impressing a homeboy from another clique. Nothing more. Thanks to the same gossip chain, it didn't take El Chato long to realize that the photo he'd shown the Kid was his brother. El Chato saw what a blunder he'd made.

In the gangs' world, these kinds of mistakes have a simple solution —you fix them with death. This could have cost Park View a war with Hollywood. Better to preempt the war and kill the person who was wronged.

A few months after that day in 2005, Chato invited the Kid on a mission. He told him that he'd found an enemy from Barrio 18. He told the Kid not to bother bringing a gun, because they had everything prepared. The Kid accepted.

They were trying to "walk" the Kid. *To walk* in gang slang means to trick a victim into going somewhere he'll get murdered. "We're going up to the mountains." "We're gonna get high in a homeboy's house." "We're going to pick up some women."

The Kid accepted.

Rather than orchestrated by the whole clique, the Kid's murder was the idea of the same gang members who'd killed El Cheje and were now trying to clean up any evidence of their transgression. There were four of them: El Chato, El Zarco, and El Coco from Park View, plus Fly from Hollywood.

The Kid and El Chato walked toward territory controlled by Barrio 18. Supposedly they were looking for an enemy, supposedly the Kid wasn't armed. Both suppositions were wrong.

"This is where the *bicha* Cheje got it," El Chato said. "If you're indebted to the Beast you don't walk out of here." He was announcing the death of the Kid, maybe even confessing to the death of El Cheje. El Chato wanted to repeat his trick: leave an MS body in Barrio 18 territory. Problem solved.

The Kid responded with his typical enigmatic gang wisdom.

"Nah, if the Beast takes a liking to you, she keeps you tight. And if she doesn't love you, then nothing. Because when she taps you, it don't matter if you hide. And when she don't tap you, it don't matter what you try."

"Right on, homeboy," El Chato said—a form of amen. They kept walking. And then El Chato made a call.

The Kid has euphemisms for everything. If he kills someone

and dumps him in a well, he's sent him to get a drink. If he buries someone, dead or alive, in some field, he's sent him to count stars. If he shoots someone on a lightning mission, he's detonated him. While death may be simple for most of us, it has many shades for the Kid. It's like the Inuit with their many different words for snow. When the Kid tells stories of hits, he makes a shooting sound, plosive and strong, with his lips: *Pop. Pop.*

"Hey, get the pot ready," El Chato said into the phone. "I got a chicken for you."

Pop. Pop.

The Kid shot him twice in the face. One bullet entered right above his brow, at the end swirl of the Gothic "S" that El Chato had tattooed on his face. *Pop. Pop.* Two more shots to finish him off. And then he ran.

The Kid jumped on a bus.

"Listen, no more stops till I get off," the Kid told the driver. "And give me five bucks." He waved the 9mm around, terrifying the driver and the dozen or so passengers.

The Kid reported back that El Chato had been killed by Barrio 18 in an ambush. El Chato's ruse to trap the Kid actually gave credence to his story. He went back to his clique and, the next day, signed up for another hit on the Eighteens. This one was billed as avenging El Chato. You need to take a cover story all the way.

A couple of days later, it was Fly's turn. The only member of the Hollywood clique who participated in Cheje's murder.

Fly had tried to distance himself from the gang. He got a job as a private security guard, joining that army of men with 12-gauge shotguns who stand guard over almost every business in the country. It was five in the morning, and he was boarding a bus after his shift.

"Hey, homeboy," Fly heard someone call. He turned around.

Pop. Pop.

Just like for El Chato—two shots to the face. Just like they'd done to his brother. This time the Kid used a .45. High caliber for a pistol. Point-blank.

For El Zarco it was the same—waiting for a bus when two shots ripped through his skull.

And so began the Kid's troubles with the Mara Salvatrucha 13. Although he committed these murders in secret, people put the pieces together. They started whispering.

Things started to change. Suspicion, increased friction. The Beast the Kid had been running after started running after him.

This was the beginning of his battle to the death with his own gang, his fight with the letters that he once would have murdered for. After more than a decade of being its teeth, the Kid had become its prey. But this came at the end of his affiliation with various gangs. At the beginning there were other gangs that are now forgotten, having been overshadowed, finally, by the M and the S.

6
Tiny Wars

Gangs already existed in El Salvador in the 1980s. They occupied neighborhoods throughout Central America's northern triangle. But the gangs were eclipsed by the region's political-military conflicts. Adult problems overshadowing adolescent dramas. The passions of the present postponing thoughts of the future. Researchers who were in the region, major figures such as Jon Lee Anderson and Alma Guillermo Prieto, or the anthropologist Philippe Bourgois, didn't document the existence of these troubled youths taking refuge from the war by forging cryptic and obscure personas. They weren't the priority, which was understandable. Gangs weren't killing people in those days, or causing too much trouble. They didn't control large territories, barely holding a street corner, and their violence was negligible relative to the violence of war.

The first researchers who paid attention to these neighborhood groups—already technically gangs according to the 1920s sociologist Frederic Thrasher—were Wim Savenije, the former director of Flacso El Salvador, a Latin American social sciences institute; Miguel Cruz, a sociologist at the University of Florida; and Ellen Moodie, an anthropologist at the University of Illinois, Urbana-Champaign. They had woken up to the new type of identity being formed among youth in northern Central America.

These researchers noticed that the early gang members were young: adolescents averaging fifteen years old. They were forming small groups of very poor and troubled kids who were basically playing at war among themselves. These kids put meaning into their lives by forging rivalries. They lived to mess with each other and not get messed with back. They formed alliances. To define themselves they needed an Other, a hated competitor. There were hundreds of such disorganized, atomized mini-armies. Youths armed with bicycle chains, pipes, and machetes, whose names illustrated their rebel proclivities: La Mara AC/DC and their enemies La Mara No Se Dice (Can't Be Said); in central San Salvador there were the Mara Morazán and Mara Chancleta (Sandal); in the Mejicanos neighborhood, the Mara Gallo (Rooster); and in the La Rábida neighborhood there was Dark Justice. There was also a long list of minor gangs that petered out. Small-time thieves and pickpockets, but mostly kids with little meaning in their lives beyond the antagonisms whipped up against other kids like themselves. I hate, therefore I am. Since the 1980s, El Salvador has been full of small dissident groups whose voices were drowned out by the political cacophony. It was like playing the bongos in the middle of a heavy metal concert.

These small gangs, overlooked by the majority of academics and researchers, were the soil in which the mighty MS-13 and Barrio 18 gangs took root.

◄◄

In the late 1980s and early 1990s, the Salvadoran gang landscape was complex. To local tribes like Mara Gallo and Mara Morazán were added the student gangs that fought to control the center of San Salvador, lobbing rocks and staging knife fights in the name of the school emblems sewn onto their shirts. Students from the Technical Industrial Institute, for example, fought with students from the General Francisco Menéndez National Institute. Gaggles of teenagers dropped out of school to get revenge on other dropouts—spreading mayhem through the heart of the capital.

In the coffee-growing west, the end of the internal war left a lot of young people unemployed. Youth that grew up in the war were robbed of the chance to study or learn a trade. They had doctorates in violence, and they decided to keep on studying on their own. Many resisted laying down their weapons, and instead formed small collectives. The goal of these groups wasn't to bring socialism to the country or to defend the homeland. They didn't want to fight over ideas, but simply to fight for themselves. They robbed corner stores, held up trains, stole cattle, and kidnapped people. War had left them awash in weapons. Some of the guns came from Vietnam, passing through Cuba and Nicaragua. Others came directly from US manufacturers. Rifles, grenades, and machine guns originally streamed into the smallest country in Central America to defend political and economic ideas, and, failing to do so, fell into the hands of bandits who were fed up with fighting for others and hoping to win for themselves what the country had failed to give them: prosperity.

By 1992, Mara Salvatrucha 13 had become a feared gang in California. Though they were constantly under assault, they had seized a territory of their own. Almost two dozen cliques had organized themselves, in their own way, in Los Angeles—the mecca of

Hispanic gangs. The media and the authorities hadn't yet given MS-13 the notoriety they would in the twenty-first century, and if Twitter had been around, they wouldn't have elicited a single presidential tweet.

And yet, in the underworld, they'd already made a name for themselves. Researcher Carlos García, who's been studying the origins of MS-13 for close to a decade, explains that when the violence erupted in April of 1992, after the not-guilty verdict was announced for four of the five LAPD officers who beat up Rodney King, MS-13 members took advantage of the situation in an unexpected way. They waded into the chaos on the streets to join in with the attacks: MS-13 took up the fight against African Americans.

The Rodney King protests began close to MS territory, between Florence and Normandie. The latter of the two streets would give one of the most notorious cliques in all of the Americas its name. García explains that while the uprising began in the predominantly black, South Side neighborhoods, they quickly moved toward Koreatown, where MS-13 was based. The flame of indignation didn't randomly wander there, but was fanned by the tension between Korean and African Americans, especially as it would play out in corner-store conflicts and the competition for jobs and housing. Black residents complained of discriminatory treatment and price gouging, and the Koreans complained of stick-ups and thefts.

A year before the uprising, a clerk in a Korean American–run convenience store shot Latasha Harlins, a fifteen-year-old black girl, in the back, for allegedly attempting to steal a bottle of orange juice. All that can be seen in the surveillance video is the clerk and Harlins arguing. Harlins throws a few punches. And then the clerk shoots her in the back. Along with the Rodney King verdict, the Harlins killing fueled the fires of racial tension.

The easy explanation is that the disturbance was between the offended black communities and the California justice system. But that's too simple. It was an explosion, a pressure release, a carnival of ethnic violence. Various groups embittered with the state took to the streets. It was a free-for-all.

The fury of the black community was also directed toward Latinos. Some saw the Mexicans and Central Americans as invading their neighborhoods. MS-13 exploited the ethnic jockeying in an attempt to cozy up to Chicano gangs. As García explains: "MS took advantage of the situation by working against the blacks to gain points with the Mexican Mafia and definitively join the Sur system." It was an interesting move for a gang that, even if it had carried the 13 on the end of its name for years, was still considered countrified—a pariah. MS-13 mobilized an ancient logic: the enemy of my enemy is my friend. And the Mexican Mafia bought it. The transformation of MS-13—from a group of stoners to an embrace of *cholo* culture under the Sureño umbrella—was formalized during the uprising. A year later, in 1993, in a Los Angeles park, MS-13 made an offering of money and arms. Ernest Chuco Castro, a member of the Varrio Nuevo Estrada gang, accepted the offering in the name of the Mexican Mafia. It was official: MS-13 was part of the Sur system. They had formally entered the big league of the gang world.

By 1992, the concept of large gangs had made its way to El Salvador. Academics who claim that gang structures arrived in Central America with the deportees are correct, without a doubt, but within that truth lies a whole spectrum of subtlety. To understand the rise of the mega-gangs in Central America, you need to look hard at the microhistories trapped in villages, hamlets, and barrios throughout the country. In some places, the arrival of the deportees was a kidney shot to the social structure. So many people were being returned that they often attracted the interest of whole cohorts of Salvadoran youth in the capital.

El Burro

In a bar in downtown San Salvador, twenty-two years after the arrival of the MS, gang veteran El Burro (the Donkey) has already put back ten beers. The jukebox blares out bachatas, reggaeton, and old romantic ballads. The racket clashes with the mariachi bands trying to earn a few dollars nearby. El Burro is spewing stories; the scruples he expressed at the beginning of the night have vanished along with the froth washing down his throat. He tells us that when he came back to the country, having been deported in 1991, he didn't know that the United States was planning on deporting others just like him. Much less did he foresee that, sooner or later, he would run into old enemies from Barrio 18. One afternoon, as he walked alone and disoriented on the downtown streets, headed nowhere in particular, he saw a kid wearing Ben Davis overalls and a pair of Nike Cortez—both of which were unavailable in El Salvador at the time. They looked at each other for a few seconds. And then the other kid broke the silence.

"Hey, what's up, dog? Who you roll with?"

"The Mara Salvatrucha 13, homie. You got a problem?"

"I'm Eighteen. What's up?" And then the kid asked, in all sincerity: "So do we fight?"

Neither of them knew what to do—but they decided, at least for now, that what happened in California stayed in California. This is how a lot of the deportees came, unsure whether even their most intense hatreds should be relevant in the birth country that they hardly knew.

El Burro relates how, about a year later, he ran into another homie, an MS. They said hey to each other, hugged. El Burro asked if there were any more like him, and the other guy stared, surprised. He said there were a ton of them, and more were coming every day. El Burro stopped feeling so alone, and, little by little, his sense of belonging came back. Not of belonging to a country, but to a gang. Soon after hooking back up with other MS deportees, most of them old friends, he was inspired to start a little clique of his own. They baptized it with a name that he prefers not to make public, and soon started recruiting local youth. "It was the easiest thing in the world. In two months I worked up an entire clique in the hood," he remembers. After jumping them in for thirteen seconds, as he'd learned to do in California, El Burro tattooed them on their necks, chests, and arms with the two letters, followed by the number 13.

X

On the other side of the country, in the same years that El Burro had returned to El Salvador, a young man was trying to get through public high school in Sonsonate, a town close to Atiquizaya. That young man, now forty-six, is one of the oldest members of the Mara Salvatrucha. He was part of the first generation of recruits, those who were jumped in by the first wave of deportees, those who heard stories of Los Angeles straight from its protagonists. Now he is on the run from his own gang. After years of leadership, even standing as the national leader in El Salvador, he's now beleaguered by death threats after his fellow leaders started suspecting, without good reason, that he was about to squeal. All because he wanted to step away from criminal activity after fifteen years in a maximum-security prison. He wanted to be with his family, whom he was only able to see during prison visits for all those years. It's 2017, and the man is speaking from inside a detention facility in Texas, Men's Unit Three. This is where noncitizens go after serving their time and before getting deported. His only condition for talking with us was that we didn't use his name. We'll refer to him as X.

X saw the arrival of the deportees from a different perspective than El Burro. He didn't have to wander the streets aimlessly, looking to find his way. He just witnessed the arrival of a new style, something that had never been seen in his town.

"I studied in the Haití school. I had a friend, Francisco, we called him Minister, and one day he just split for California. Back then I wanted to be a doctor. The next year, when school would let out I would always see this guy with a shaved head and rumpled clothes, Ben Davis clothes, Cortez shoes, tattoos on one of his arms. He'd been deported. 'What's up?' he said to me one day. 'What's up, Minister?' I said back to him. 'That's not me anymore. Now I'm Shy Boy de Fulton.'"

And with that, Shy Boy shook the spray can he was holding and started tagging the school. It was the first graffito the city ever saw and took the shape of two square blocks. One with a Y shape in the middle to turn it into an M, and the other with two vertical lines, to turn it into an S. MS-13 Shy Boy FLS N (Fulton Locos Salvatrucha, and N for the north side of LA). Immediately afterward, as X remembers, Shy Boy hit play on a handheld recorder and "danced hip-hop." In reality, however, Shy Boy was playing a song from the group Tavares, a quintet of Cape Verdean-American brothers with a penchant for sequins. They played disco music, landed a couple hits in the '70s, and scored the *Charlie's Angels* film. Ralph, Pooch, Chubby, Butch, and Tiny performed slow, choreographed dance numbers. And yet, for some reason, Shy Boy found the music cool almost two decades after it had peaked and danced to it in the suffocating heat of Sonsonate. Shy Boy danced as well as he could. Watching him shake and slide in his bright white Nike Cortez, X and his classmates thought it was awesome.

From that moment on X divided his days into three parts. In the mornings, it was school; after classes it was dancing with Shy Boy and listening to stories about LA; and then it was off to work in the brick factory.

"In the afternoons, a bunch of us would be at Shy Boy's learning to dance. Girls came around. I liked one of them, La Bambi, they called her."

X thinks back to what drew him to those meetings at a time when there were no criminals or violence. It was just dancing, girls, and clothes. The biggest and most violent gang in the world didn't show up in El Salvador armed and menacing. It arrived in the form of young men dancing to what they thought was hip-hop on sidewalks hot enough to cook an egg.

The early gestation of the gang was the result of a bad decision by US authorities, who thought they could solve a problem by expelling it. They thought they were spitting out the window, but they were spitting straight up into the sky. Years later their policies would come back and splatter on them when the deported gang members returned and took over neighborhoods in New York, Virginia, Maryland, and Houston. But before this, when they had just arrived in El Salvador, the gangs swelled up with all the quickness and fury of a puffer fish, and for the same reason—so as not to be swallowed. Chewed up by poverty, by abandonment, by violence. They puffed themselves up to survive. Increased their numbers to fight back. It wasn't hard. The authorities didn't pay much attention. This war was just getting started as another twelve-year war was ending.

A year went by, and Shy Boy found company in deported young men like himself, who'd barely gotten to know the United States before they were sent back to their battered country. El Chino de Hollywood showed up, El Vago de Hollywood, El Horse de Fulton. The little group was expanding like a balloon.

In 1993, Shy Boy decided to start a clique. That was how things used to work. In between dances, a deportee just rolled up with an idea. Shy Boy, El Chino, El Vago, and El Horse started jumping in other kids. Today, there's a whole system of permission and loyalty checks you need to go through. Today, in order to join up, you need to kill someone and be jumped in for thirteen seconds. After initiation, you become part of the most murderous gang on the planet. Back then it was just the thirteen-second ritual of courage, and what you were joining seemed like a social club for disaffected youth.

"After you got jumped in, you could show up whenever you wanted to dance and hang out at Shy Boy's," X explains. "If you weren't jumped in, you could only come on Tuesdays. I even remember we won a contest dancing 'El Sapito' on Variedades del Seis. We won three hundred *bolas*," or about thirty-five dollars.

"El Baile del Sapito," the Toad Dance, was a popular song by the 1990s Salvadoran band, Bongo. The video, recorded at the site of various monuments throughout the country, shows four men and four women jumping and holding their hands up like someone who has a pistol pointed at them. The dance with its toddler-like simplicity was all the rage among working-class teenagers at the time. Variedades del Seis was a dance show that aired on Saturdays.

Hardly anyone these days remembers the relationship between "El Baile del Sapito" and one of the foundational cliques of the Mara Salvatrucha 13.

In 1994 the clique was rechristened the Hollywood Locos Salvatrucha, for a simple reason: little by little El Chino was taking over the leadership, and in California El Chino had belonged to the Hollywood Locos Salvatrucha. At the time, the clique had been operating out of the central park in Sonsonate. That was where they met up, and the shadow of anyone from Barrio 18 was already something to watch out for. X says that back then, people who'd never been to the United States didn't understand the rivalry. They only knew they needed to defend the park, not let the other side in, even if they looked almost identical. That was how it was. And it was fun.

One day, a few members of the original Hollywood clique, recently deported from California, showed up at the park. They took El Chino aside and told him the name would have to change, because most of the members hadn't been jumped in California, and it was disrespectful to the deportees. They could keep the clique, but they had to call it something else.

El Chino called a *mirin*—a phonetically derived word for meeting. *Mirin* has become part of standard gang vocabulary throughout El Salvador; it's a space where strategy is discussed, people are punished for mistakes, hits are assigned, and extortions planned. In 1994 Hollywood members in Sonsonate held a *mirin* to pick a new name for the clique. Brainstorming, someone mentioned that the bus fee collectors from the capital to Sonsonate call out, "San Cocos! Let's go! San Cocos, *vamos!*" San Cocos was a sort of nickname for the city. They voted, and the clique became San Cocos Locos Salvatrucha.

More than two decades after Shy Boy's first graffito, after "El Baile del Sapito" and the renaming of the clique, the San Cocos stand accused of murder, extortion, drug trafficking, and illicit association. They became famous in February of 2012 when they left five sacks in four locations of Sonsonate. Inside were the bodies of four men and one girl. The sacks were left in front of a courthouse, a police station, a military installation, and a jail. All the bodies bore signs of torture and asphyxiation. The unidentified girl was between thirteen and fifteen years old.

Some of the founders, like El Burro or Shy Boy, arrived already branded by gang life. And yet had they just been luckier, or been deported to another country, things would have turned out differently. Instead they found themselves in a country full of kids desperate for a less miserable life, kids like X, whose family story is classic. Two of X's brothers are in gangs, as well as two nephews and various cousins. Deportees and working-class youth seemed destined for each other. The United States was sending out a key to a door in El Salvador. The door opened onto a war that, twenty-five years later, is still raging.

El Smurf

Some youngsters didn't need to meet a deportee in person. It's a small country, and rumors run quick as a fuse.

In San Miguel, historically the most violent region of the country, there were hardly any deported gang members. El Smurf, an ex-MS gang member, remembers that when he was barely in his teens, around the end of the civil war, the kids in San Miguel were talking up these big gangs. But it was all hearsay. They didn't have a Shy Boy or a Burro. All they had was talk.

These kids hadn't seen the gangs yet. They hadn't seen the dances or the Ben Davis gear. And still, what they heard was enough to dazzle them.

A few deportees were returned to the region, but they kept their heads down. Eventually, El Smurf and his friends, students at one of the few private high schools in the region, decided to found their own clique. They wanted action and had no time to wait for deportees to come and set them up. About ten boys got together one day on an empty plot of land where, to the beat of early hip-hop and the scent of marijuana smoke, they decided that they were a cell of what would become the largest gang in the Americas.

It was that easy. El Smurf simply decided it was the right moment to found a clique. Spontaneity, of which little remains in today's gang structure, was an elemental ingredient in the early days.

Now that they'd decided on establishing a clique, they just needed a name, something modern, something cool. They held their own *mirin*. One of the kids had a rap magazine from LA, which somewhat increased his status. With the wisdom gleaned from flipping through the magazine, he proposed: "Let's call it Sailors. Imagine, we're *marineros*, the boat is MS and we're the *marineros*. 'Cause that's what Sailors means in English."

A few of them liked the idea. Others not so much, but the next line of argument was convincing.

"Think of it, the word *marineros* begins with an M and ends with an S, you know, it's like a code name."

And so one of the most powerful cliques of the Mara Salvatrucha 13 was born in eastern El Salvador, the Sailors Locos Salvatrucha, with a number of important cells on the US East Coast. The FBI has listed it as one of its top targets for the last five consecutive years. Thanks to a number of high-profile killings in New York and Virginia, its notoriety has grown since 2017.

El Smurf himself seems a friendly, happy man. His family was always middle class, and after a few years astray with his MS-13 homeboys, he went with his father to live in the United States. He's now a US citizen and teaches in a middle school.

Unlike most adolescents from the lowest rung of society who were taken in by the gangs, El Smurf always ate three times a day and always had shoes on his feet. But in those days the country offered very little, even to the middle class. If MS-13 was able to seduce kids with decent roofs over their heads, it's because it didn't seem like they were necessarily being drawn into criminality. It was a game at first, dangerous and childish, but just a game. Until, very quickly, it lost all its fun.

Twenty-three years after that day in the abandoned lot, as the bartenders of Bombshell—a swanky Houston bar—served beer and food to well-off Latinos, El Smurf admits that he misses the pace and chaos of those days. He says he came close to dying more than once, but, back then, giving your life for the gang and the clique made sense to him. It all seems very distant now.

"I never dreamed that the clique would become so huge and would spread so far. How could I? It started off with just a few of us. Just, well, to goof around, nothing more."

At the end of our conversation El Smurf offers a curious fact. The very day the Sailors were born, they ran into a problem: their initials, SLS, already corresponded to another clique, the San Juanes Locos Salvatrucha (SLS). To get around this, Melqui, another one of the kids from the private high school, decided to add an extra letter. A *W.* Why? Because it was cool. Plus, in the magazine, he'd seen some rappers making a *W* symbol with their fingers and it seemed cool to be able to do the same thing to represent their clique. "SLSW" would soon be appearing on walls throughout the city, asserting the clique's dominion.

Researchers and journalists insist that the *W* has to do with West Side, or the letter *M* flipped upside down, but they're wrong. It was the brainwave of a group of kids flipping through a rap magazine, wanting to belong to something cool.

And so MS-13 entered El Salvador, clearing pathways through a thicket of violence, recruiting disaffected youth by promising them they could become part of the historical war against Barrio 18. MS landed in the country through deportees like El Burro, but its subsequent rise was owed to an idea that spread like wildfire from mouth to mouth.

In western El Salvador, too, there were already small gangs, more rural than their eastern counterparts. In the early 1990s, Atiquizaya had the Mara Gauchos Locos, the Meli Meli 33, and the first transnational gang in the region: UVAS (*Unión de Vagos Asociados*, or the Union of Associated Loafers). The UVAS established a presence in the capitals of Guatemala and Honduras with small cells which, over the years, eventually disappeared. It's still possible, however, to find former UVAS members who tell their stories, digging up vague fragments, squeezing their memories.

In this part of the country, MS didn't breeze in like a rumor, like dust blown on the wind. It arrived with a man of indigenous descent who was well versed in violence, a former soldier in the National Guard and an ex-member of the Fulton Locos Salvatrucha of the San Fernando Valley. In Atiquizaya and its environs, MS arrived in the shape of José Antonio Terán, also known as Chepe Furia.

Women

When you talk about gangs, you talk about men. This book is no exception. Our history of the Mara Salvatrucha 13 is mainly protagonized by men because more of them tell the stories and explain how the gangs function. And yet, when the Stoner cells were digging skulls out of graves and invoking the Beast, there were girls and women digging right alongside them. Later, women as well as men arrived in El Salvador in handcuffs and chains, stepping off the deportation flights into the unknown ordeals that awaited them.

When MS-13 conquered the South Side, the women changed their style, too. Their rock-and-roll–inspired clothes were ditched for overalls and American football jerseys. Their voluminous hairdos concealed blades to attack their enemies, and their pockets were stuffed with bags of pot and wads of cash. Maybe the young women didn't jump into brawls as eagerly as the young men, but they played important roles in the development of the gang.

As the gangs took on elements of masculine Chicano and *cholo* culture, they also borrowed the idea of the *ruca* or *jaina* (terms for a Chicana girl or girlfriend). The sassy, aggressive woman who was comfortable in the clique and willing to stick a knife into an enemy was also seen as a protector and comforter, a mother, a self-sacrificing and neglected lover. In the gang's formative years, its female members assumed the double role of warrior and comforter.

In the 1980s, a few female members in LA stood out, more than their male counterparts, as capable gang administrators. Their success came from the fact that they were not only willing to resort to violence, but also understood restraint. They knew when a gentle threat was more effective than grabbing somebody by the balls. And, even if they never acquired the same status as men, they rose up in the ranks. Some more than others.

And then the gangs arrived in El Salvador. They melded with other groups, smaller gangs and crews, and returned to a mindset that relegated women to the status of a thing or an animal. The image of the beautiful *chola* with a teased hairdo and lips painted dark red, a .38 revolver hidden between her breasts, was a California image. For the Salvadoran gang member it was a legend, like the story of the Amazons.

Though there are more women than men in the wider gang structures of El Salvador, over at least the last ten years women have lost the ability to found new cliques. The only accepted roles for women are those without a voice and without a vote, without even the ability to participate in the *mirins*.

Apart from the idealized figure of the mother, male gang members see women as an adulteration of the purity of the gang. In their worldview, mothers alone merit the dignity of devotion. Otherwise, women only get in the way of a gangster's total devotion to the mara.

Medea (not her real name), one of the first women to join the MS-13 in El Salvador, benefitted from the Angelino ethic that still prevailed in the 1990s. She was one of many new gang members in Quezaltepeque, a rare metropolitan area in this mostly rural country. But Medea also saw that ethic change. As the gang's culture became more Salvadoran, female roles within the clique went up in smoke. Medea went from being someone to being someone's property.

A few years ago, Medea was violently raped by members of her own clique. Homies from another clique were also invited to rape her. Recently, while eating at a Pollo Campero (a popular

Salvadoran fried chicken joint) in a mall in San Salvador, we told her that one of the men who raped her had been gunned down by police in what the authorities had tried to pass off as a two-sided confrontation on a coffee farm. When she learned of the murder, Medea said, "Listen, I hate them. I'm not in it because I want to be. At first, sure, but now it's only because I have to. I hate them."

We reminded her that, at one point, they were her homies.

"Yep. But after all they did to me, not anymore. I like it when they get killed. I give thanks to God when they kill each other."

Within the gang, women are rejected as probable traitors who you're not only allowed, but encouraged, to avoid.

One young male explained why cliques kill so many of their own women: "Look, there's no gangster who hasn't been betrayed by a woman at least once."

He continued: "The thing is, women are treacherous, they're destructive." And he was talking from the perspective of a gang with members such as the Hollywood Kid—traitors working with the police to put fellow gang members behind bars.

Chepe Furia was a powerful man in both Atiquizaya and the surrounding areas. The gangster who would turn Miguel Ángel Tobar into the Hollywood Kid slowly gained control over many of the institutions of western El Salvador: the mayor's office, garbage collection, three MS-13 cliques, some policemen and judges and even, as we'll see, the power grid.

Two stories testify to the man's power. The first involves a cowardly congressman.

The congressman accepted to be interviewed in early 2012, but he laid down some ground rules first. Too many rules, perhaps, for a man who moves through life with two bodyguards, who is an elected representative of the Ahuachapán department, endowed with the awesome power to write new laws for the department's 350,000 inhabitants. These were his rules: don't reveal my name, don't reveal the exact location of the interview (not even the city), and don't reveal my political party. Only then did the congressman agree to talk about Chepe Furia.

On the agreed day, we marched behind the congressman into his party's office. Inside were seven other people, suffocating in the heat and pretending to be busy. One of them, on seeing the congressman, hunched with furrowed brow over a sheet of paper on the table in front of him. The paper was blank. The congressman told them to leave the room, that he didn't want any of them there. In little more than a minute, the room was empty. The congressman closed the large metal doors to the street, then locked them. He opened a small window-grate, and one of his bodyguards poked his head in, ready to heed his boss's order: "Stay at the door until further notice."

Finally, the congressman sat down and said:

"Alright, what do you want to know about Chepe Furia?"

Hesitantly, he outlined a rough sketch. He said the gang leader had friends in customs, the prosecutor's office, the mayor's office, the courtrooms, and the police force. He said things that even the courtroom janitors knew by then. In fact, the most revealing statement had come before the congressman said anything at all. The room vacated, the heavy doors locked, the bodyguard patrolling the street outside: a national representative who thought it necessary to hide his own name just to whisper the name of Chepe Furia.

"I mean, we're not talking about just any delinquent, this is a mobster with eyes and ears planted all over the state. And, you know, I won't always be a public servant," he said, trying to justify himself.

The second story that showcases Chepe Furia's power concerns his first battle with Detective Pineda. Once again, it's necessary to start by skipping ahead: Chepe Furia won that battle.

It had been seven months since the detective had reeled in his first star traitor, the Hollywood Kid. Over several long interviews, the Kid had told the detective and his investigators the secrets behind his clique and the man who'd created it.

This was a complicated exchange. The detective knew he couldn't leave the Kid locked away in the police outpost of Atiquizaya. It had only been a year since the two sergeants, from that same office, had detained Rambito shortly before he turned up tortured and dead in a ditch. The sergeants accused of delivering Rambito to his enemies had not yet been charged, but the detective, thanks to information given to him by the Kid, already knew who they were. Pineda didn't even want to think about how easy it would be for Chepe Furia to have the Kid assassinated. Who would stand guard at the outpost of Atiquizaya? Chepe Furia's little rats? And keeping the Kid in the dingy outpost of El Refugio wasn't an option, either. There was simply no space. The Kid would have had to sleep outside like a dog, next to the perpetually clogged toilets. Adding to the complication, the Kid had demanded two things in exchange for his cooperation. First, permission to smoke pot. If they wanted his secrets, they had to let him roll his joints. Obviously, this would have been hard to manage if he was living in the police outpost. The second demand was even more challenging. At twenty-seven years old, the Kid had hooked up with a girl of fourteen. He wanted her with him, no matter what the law said. The Kid's demands were impossible to fulfill in a state-run safe house typically shared by gang members, ex-gang members, petty delinquents, innocent witnesses, and victims. It's a microcosm of the country, where no one feels at ease. One can stay alive, sure; but feel comfortable or secure, no. The Salvadoran police say that many of their witnesses renege on the deal after going to one of these houses and realizing that the state's offer means living there for months on end, perhaps years, as long as the process lasts. One investigative police officer said that some gang members prefer to face a criminal trial over staying in these houses.

On one side, the detective faced the corrupt police force of Atiquizaya; on the other, the demands of an MS-13 hitman.

But the detective, who double-knots his boots every morning, could deal with the Kid's legally dubious demands. And he felt confident enough to outsmart corrupt officers. He did both things. He convinced the relevant authorities to give the Kid the title of plea-bargain witness, a delinquent whose crimes are pardoned on condition he testifies about the crimes of others. Pineda convinced his superiors that this wasn't merely another low-rung gang member who could make their case for one, or two, or even five homicides. The Kid was the key to dismantling a clique of more than forty-five members who had infiltrated the highest state institutions. The detective's maneuverings got results. Results that are to be expected in a country such as this: fifty dollars and a monthly basket of basic necessities. Four pounds of beans, two of rice, some packets of tomato sauce, salt, sugar, oil, packaged noodles, four rolls of toilet paper, two bars of soap, two toothbrushes, and one tube of toothpaste. That was it. One basket, once a month, for two people.

El Salvador's National Victim and Witness Assistance Program, responsible for evaluating the situation of plea-bargain witnesses, also delivers their monthly rations. The police put in fifty dollars to cover rent for a single room on a plot measuring five square meters. The little shack stood right in front of the police outpost of El Refugio. In fact, the detective, if he looks away from his ancient computer, can see the tiny box of gray cement.

The detective had found an answer to his riddle. The Kid would remain in his sight. So long as he was in his own little hut, it was easy to ignore the fact that a girl lived with him and that he spent his evenings smoking the marijuana he grew on the same plot.

In that little room, on that barren lot, the Kid would live less than seven months before the detective decided that his case was ready, his deck of gang members was complete, and it was time to trap the king and all his subjects.

More than 500 police officers from several units around the country assembled at the Cavalry Regiment headquarters of San Juan Opico, more than an hour away from Atiquizaya, one October evening in 2010. Their orders were to conduct raids on seventy homes of the members of Chepe Furia's clique. The task forces were bussed to the central park of Atiquizaya and dispersed. The city was under siege. The detective led over fifty agents to the San Antonio neighborhood. Among the operatives was Sergeant Tejada, one of the men who'd later stand accused of having handed over Rambito. They were after six separate targets, but the detective was focused on one, the capture of his king of spades, Chepe Furia.

Atiquizaya has little more than 30,000 inhabitants, many of its streets are paved with stones or left unpaved. Chepe Furia's web of foot soldiers ran from the police force to the garbage collectors and extended far beyond the city. It was an enormous operation and many details slipped past the detective. At this juncture, they were unlikely to find the mobster in his house, asleep and unaware.

Almost as soon as the officers entered San Antonio, the electricity went out across the whole neighborhood, turning it into what seemed an abandoned ghost town. Maybe as a sort of cruel joke, the only gang member left in the area was of the lowest level, El Cuto, son of a tortilla vendor and one of the lookouts posted close to where Chepe Furia lived. The chief prosecutor of western El Salvador, Mario Martínez Jacobo, remembers that one of the few locals who hadn't also fled told him that a car had come not ten minutes before and whisked away Chepe Furia.

A majority of the clique was soon captured in the surrounding neighborhoods—both low- and mid-level gang members. More than twenty-five were tried for eleven homicides, and more than thirty were accused of conspiracy, including, in absentia, Chepe Furia.

Having won this round, the boss disappeared from Atiquizaya for the next two months.

And yet he had such confidence in his network that at the end of that time, on December 24, 2010, a squad of soldiers doing a routine patrol in San Antonio spotted him along with his father, looking relaxed as ever. The two were greeting visitors outside Chepe Furia's corner store, in front of the soccer field he'd had built.

As soon as he heard of the sighting, the detective got the interim judge of the specialized trial court of Santa Ana, some thirty minutes from Atiquizaya, to sign an arrest warrant, and drove to San Antonio to deliver it to the soldiers himself.

It was fortunate for the detective that this particular interim judge was in session. The presiding judge, Tomás Salinas, was on vacation and had already rejected evidence against Chepe Furia presented by the prosecutor's office after the failed operation in

San Antonio. Salinas had refused to order Chepe Furia's arrest in his absence—even though, on November 24, his supervising organization, the Specialized Unit against Organized Crime, had urged him to do so, because there was sufficient proof to identify Chepe Furia as the leader of the gang.

Pineda recalls that Chepe Furia's attorney "was pulling out her hair in rage," and demanded to know why the order had been signed by the interim judge and not by Judge Tomás Salinas. Meanwhile, the wanted man himself peacefully watched the scene play out, casually perched on one of his store benches.

No doubt he knew that, though he had finally been caught by the man who'd been chasing him for years, he still had one more card to play.

But to play that card, he first had to go to prison. Chepe Furia, formerly known as El Veneno of the Fulton Locos Salvatrucha of the San Fernando Valley, asked to go to the Apanteos Prison. According to Salvadoran prison jargon—categorized by type of inmate—Apanteos prison is only for "civilians." That is, any criminal not associated with either of the two major gangs—MS-13 and Barrio 18—including petty delinquents, robbers, murderers, kidnappers, rapists, and fraudsters.

One of the greatest failures of the Salvadoran government was handing the prisons over to the gangs. They gave up a space in which, by its very nature, the state is supposed to ensure that aggressors are both punished and rehabilitated. But politicians feared that the homies would end up slaughtering each other if they were all mixed together. Since 1999, when members of the Barrio 18 launched a grenade at members of the MS in a juvenile detention center, various local Salvadoran governments started carving prisons into jigsaw puzzles. These puzzles had a handful of pieces. The MS, the Barrio 18, La Raza (the largest "civilian" prison gang), *los pesetas* (men who were traitors to their own gangs), and Los Trasladados (another civilian prison gang). And then, around 2005, the Barrio 18 split in two, the Revolutionaries and the Sureños. Each side demanding their own space inside the jails.

These turf wars were fueled by dead bodies and government ignorance. Before the split, it was thanks to a massacre that the Barrio 18 secured a home of its own within the prison system. On August 18, 2004, in the Mariona prison, more than 400 gang members and thousands of civilians drew blood however they could: with machetes, sharpened scrap metal, knives, and Molotov cocktails. By the end, eight members of the Barrio 18 and twenty-four civilians had died. Three days later, the Eighteens were moved to their own prison.

In contrast, the MS very gradually acquired more turf. At first, during the '90s, they were helpless against groups of civilians who ruled the jails like feudal lords. The MS were treated like lepers— beaten, humiliated, and raped. They were carted from one prison to another, from solitary confinement to high-security wings, all blocked off just for them. Their homeland never cared whether or not they returned from the United States, but the prisons had been waiting for them with open arms, and with the ugliest of intentions. Some of the national leaders of the MS got to know each other, frightened in their new, designated rooms, with their bones broken and their open wounds still fresh. Month after month, as more deportees became inmates, the MS prison population grew, gathered steam, and finally decided to rise up. During the '90s they were isolated for their own protection, but, as of 2002, they were isolated to protect the rest of the prison population.

In early 2001, adult MS members were able to secure two sectors in the Apanteos prison. There were 150 MS scattered throughout the eight areas of the facility. The ones who'd been there longest started to throw *wilas*—messages written in code—to the MS members housed in the other areas. These messages were written in lime juice, which the recipient would read by holding a lighter underneath to make the words appear. The coded writing was perfected over the years. A gang member learned to read the third letter of a word, and then the second letter of the following three words, and then again the third letter, until a complete word or sentence was formed. These were usually orders.

X, the MS member who kicked off his gang career by dancing to Tavares under the Sonsonate sun, lived through those years. He became a pariah, isolated from the civilians. Terrified, he used to beg the guards to open a door for him, to let him out, because the guys from La Raza were after him with their paring knives.

He remembers the celebrities who passed through the prison—gang heroes. Their gang names are famous, while their "surnames" pay tribute to the places they were deported from: Colocho and Cola de Western, Diablito and Crook de Hollywood, Morro de Normandie, Skiny de Stoner, Flaco de Francis, Chory de Fulton.

"We'd throw each other *wilas*. We were scattered throughout the prison. We were sick of being raped, robbed, beaten down. The prison exploded. We were like one hundred fifty against four hundred civilians. When three civilians turned up dead, that's when they brought us together into two sectors, sector three and sector six. For the first time we were all together. And so we started to organize," X said from his hideout in Texas in 2017.

A gang that infiltrated a country, an international mafia that President Trump tweets about, a terrorist organization as defined by Salvadoran law, developed largely behind bars and thanks to thoughtless officials who reckoned it was a good idea to lock gang members up with their own.

There was no going back. There's still no going back. Each gang has its prison, or at least its sector within a prison. In time Apanteos was left with only one sector for women linked to MS, while the rest of the sectors went on to house civilians.

In December 2010, when Chepe Furia refused to link up with his own in Apanteos Prison, it was ruled by Los Trasladados. These were a group of civilians who'd organized to defend against La Raza, and then went on to set their own fires.

Chepe Furia tried to be discreet, to go unnoticed, to pass for just another common prisoner in the civilian sector nine of Apanteos Prison. He failed.

The warden of Apanteos remembers how the day after the top boss arrived, three inmates asked to meet with him. They all had one question: "Do you know who you've just put in with the civilians?" One of the inmates answered: "Don Chepe, the greatest mobster in all the west." Another described him as "leader of the clique of Atiquizaya, the leader of all organized crime." The warden, realizing that someone would try to kill him, decided to move Chepe Furia to a sector known as La Isla, the Island, reserved for inmates whose lives are at risk.

Better to isolate him than have another lifeless body in a prison that had already rioted multiple times. In the common areas there weren't eight, or three, or even two gangster leaders. There was one. And he was Miguel Ángel Navarro, thirty-five, known as the Animal. He was a rural thief from the coastal department of Sonsonate in western El Salvador. He'd been locked up for more than a decade and had racked up many more crimes while in prison. He'd earned his gang name because of his body, buffed by field-work, and his skill in hand-to-hand combat. One inmate, a fink who got his information by shining the shoes of members of Los Trasladados, said he once saw him rough up five inmates at once. Single-handed. That was the Animal.

The Animal didn't like gangs. The warden knew this. That's why the few MS members in Apanteos, or the relatives and collab-orators of MS, were secluded in sector eight, shielded from death by walls and fences.

No one questioned the iron grip Los Trasladados had over Apanteos Prison. Not even the Mexican Zetas. In those days there was a Mexican inmate in his thirties, Enrique Jaramillo Aguilar, originally from Apatzingán, Michoacan. He was arrested after a brawl at a Salvadoran nightclub. The police found a surprise in his black, Guatemalan-plated SUV: a secret compartment opened by an electric switch. Inside the compartment was a Galil rifle, two M-16s, one 30.30 carbine, two shotguns, a revolver, a military flash grenade, and eleven cell phones. They originally convicted him of illegal weapons possession. Shortly after, a twenty-nine-year-old Salvadoran was watching the news and recognized the voice of the recently arrested Mexican. When his face flashed across the screen, her mind flooded with painful memories. She didn't know Jaramillo's real name, but she knew his alias: Omega, a member of the Zetas drug trafficking gang, which operated out of Reynosa in the northern Mexican border state of Tamaulipas.

That woman became a protected witness under the name "Grecia," and was forced to leave her country after testifying. She said she had been a migrant. That she'd left El Salvador on April 13, 2009, headed for the United States. She went with a coyote (people

smuggler) named Ovidio, who sold her to the Zetas in the state of
Tabasco for $500. Grecia was raped for several months in a brothel
in Reynosa called La Quebradita, run by a Zetas member named
Omega. Grecia managed to escape during a military raid on the
brothel and testified in Mexico, before returning to El Salvador.
Jaramillo had also managed to escape. When the forensic inves-
tigators examined Grecia, they found a tattoo on her right calf: a
butterfly perched on two branches. The branches formed the letter
Z. She also had a vaginal infection and pelvic inflammatory disease.
Grecia's testimony ultimately lengthened Jaramillo's sentence in
Apanteos prison by landing him an additional trafficking conviction.

Well, not even Jaramillo, a member of los Zetas who walked
around El Salvador armed to the teeth, could walk the walk in
Apanteos. The prison warden remembers how he smugly called
himself a Zeta, and even told some of Los Trasladados that he was
planning a "tactical operation." His insolence landed him in the
hospital. Jaramillo never again claimed to be a Zeta, and maintained a low profile from then on.

Chepe Furia, the famous MS leader, had no chance of surviving
in the Animal's kingdom. The Island seemed like his safest bet.

But the Island, that small cell between sector eight and sector
nine, was full of other shipwrecked men. Mostly leaders of La Raza
who'd been threatened by Los Trasladados, and some leaders of
La Mirada Locos 13, a gang that originated in La Mirada Avenue
in Los Angeles and later resettled in La Presita, a neighborhood of
the eastern town of San Miguel.

No one knows exactly what happened on the Island, but a few
days after Chepe Furia's transfer, he asked to see the warden. He
said he had "issues of ego" with the other inmates on the Island,
and admitted to being a member of the MS-13. The warden, a

suspicious man with a military past, forced any gangsters who wanted to be interned with their fellows in sector eight to sign a document, formally recognizing their *taca* (gang name) and clique.

In the handwriting of the Hollywood Kid's mentor, this document states: "Chepe Furia, Hollywood Locos Salvatrucha de Atiquizaya."

Chepe Furia was transferred to sector eight. There were no heavyweights there; those were all in the Ciudad Barrios and Gotera prisons. Here there were active members mixed in with collaborators, relatives, and various menials working lower gang roles, mostly stakeout and surveillance jobs such as *chequeos*, *paros*, *paros fijos*, and *postes*. The gang has a vocabulary all its own.

Chepe Furia was, as the warden put it, "out of place" in sector eight. He did his best to keep a low profile. Maybe he knew his stay wouldn't last long.

In December 2011, Judge Tomás Salinas returned from his vacation. Promptly, only thirty-eight days after the kingpin's arrest, Judge Salinas held a posthearing review for Chepe Furia to see if he could await trial outside of jail. To succeed, the defense would have to prove that their client posed no flight risk, evidenced by having a good job, a stable family, or some other strong tie to the area. In the saturated Salvadoran prison system, where overcrowding exceeds 400 percent, it's not a privilege to get bailed only a month into custody on remand, but rather a luxury reserved for select prisoners—presidents, congressional representatives, and millionaires.

Chepe Furia was granted this luxury.

According to the prosecutors and police detectives on the case, Judge Salinas vigorously defended Chepe Furia. After hearing the prosecution and defense, the judge argued that "just because the police and one plea-bargain witness" say so doesn't make Chepe

Furia the leader of a criminal organization. He also deployed a strange logic, one that seemed as improper for a judge as for a leader of a criminal organization. He expressed surprise that they would accuse him of conspiracy and not of homicide, because "to be a [gang] leader ... one has to commit several murders." At times, said a prosecutor, "the judge acted like another defense attorney for Chepe Furia." In fact, Judge Salinas wrote in his opinion, "We cannot judge a person based on what the media says or what the prosecutors say." Even Chepe Furia's garbage disposal exploits were used as a point in his favor: "This person has a contractual agreement with the mayor's office of Atiquizaya." The judge, a specialist in organized crime, concluded that there was no reason to think José Antonio Terán would jump bail. He set a $25,000 bond (which Chepe Furia paid that same day with two mortgages) and told him to hand over his passport and visit the Atiquizaya police post every Friday, to sign in and make his presence known.

Chepe Furia, the man who escaped a 500-officer operation, the one who'd signed a document claiming gang membership in Apanteos prison, who'd made the Hollywood Kid a hitman, walked out the front door of the Santa Ana Court. A free man.

The following Friday, February 4, Chepe Furia didn't check in at the Atiquizaya police post. He didn't do it the following Friday either, nor any Friday afterward in 2011.

Chepe Furia had slipped the state's grasp for the second time.

Chepe Furia's second escape made clear what many already knew. He wasn't a run-of-the-mill gangster. Hardened by war, educated on the streets of Los Angeles during the boom of the Sureño gangs, Chepe Furia returned to El Salvador as a new type of gang leader. A mobster, a master, a gangster with a brain.

That's why, when Detective Pineda received a court order in March 2011, instructing him to recapture Chepe Furia, his first, exasperated thought was "Oh, fuck it."

Judge Salinas didn't only issue an order that its oversight agency, the Supreme Court's Criminal Division, would later consider "completely wrong" because "the risk of escape was evident"; he also ignored dozens of people who claimed that Chepe Furia was a mobster mastermind and different from all other gang members. When Chepe Furia escaped for the second time, he'd already climbed to the top and established a small empire in western El Salvador. Before his arrest, he would breeze around the region in his gray car with polarized windows. The car wasn't his, it belonged to Alex Iván Retana, better known as El Diablo. We're not talking about a simple gangster here but an ex-prosecutor who is also a car thief who ran his own car repair business, which, according to the police investigation, he used as a front to sell cars stolen in Guatemala and El Salvador. The advantages of living on a border.

According to immigration officials, Chepe Furia also often traveled to Guatemala in 2010 in the car of the son of a former congressman named Mauricio Ascencio. The Ascencio family also had a used car business on the border. Ascensio was captured and indicted in 2013 as a member of the Texis Cartel, an organization heading the watch-list of the United Nations Office on Drugs and Crime. Chepe Furia was not only on the good side of judges like Salinas, but also rubbed elbows with ex-government and public officials. The mayor of Atiquizaya, of the right-wing Arena party, even sent a letter to the judge when Chepe Furia got out of prison. The letter said Chepe Furia worked in garbage collection and was known as a community leader in San Antonio (the place where the lights had gone out during the police operation to capture him).

Two lawyers familiar with his case aptly described him during that time. "He's a gang member who defies the gang member prototype," said a prosecutor named Rodolfo Delgado. "He's the intellectual of the clique. He's always been smart, and that's helped him gain the trust of many people," said another, René Martínez, the chief prosecutor for the entire department at the time of the operation. "He has complete control of the area," said the deputy director of police, Commissioner Ramírez Landaverde.

In the words of some who knew him, Chepe Furia was the affable benefactor of his neighborhood, a genial fellow who remembered people's names. In the words of one plea-bargain witness—the man who deceived him, the Hollywood Kid—he was a ruthless killer who handed out death sentences to rivals and foes, all while enjoying a cut of meat in a roadside restaurant.

But the enmity between the two started many years later. The passion initially sparked from the admiration of a lost kid for a man with big ideas.

The Hollywood Kid's Prelude

"Once you've made the jump and have murdered, you've made a pact with the devil, you're part of the devil, you've surrendered your soul, man. And, soon after, you'll have to give your whole self over, too, because that's how it is on the streets, when it's your turn, it's your turn," says the Kid in 2013, four years after first turning on his gang, sitting in the sheltered shade of a wall, in the empty lot he was living in.

It's midday and the furious heat suffocates the backyard plot. There's a sweet smell in the air, the smell of fallen fruit, and people outside are moving slowly, as they would by the side of a pool. The police officer that guards the Kid, his personal custodian, is a little more alert today. He glances nervously at those who pass by the gate made of sticks and wire.

The guard is jumpy because there was a bit of a problem yesterday with some of the drifters in the area who come around to smoke—yes, the Kid smokes in his little shack—or to buy weed—yes, the Kid grows and sells. The problem was resolved with a couple of swings of a machete, not lethal, but they were painful, and doled out by the Kid. He says he sells marijuana because the pension he receives from the state is so small and he has to support his daughter and young wife, Lorena. This might be a far cry from how one would imagine the life of a protected witness: another city, another identity, and other difficulties. But there's none of that here; the kid is in his same city, with his same identity, and only a gate made of sticks and wire to separate him from the world. With a simple "good afternoon," anyone could walk through that gate.

The Kid gets out of his chair and asks Lorena, who's still a minor, to make coffee. He asks her in gang slang, flipping the syllables in almost every word.

"*Rramo, otro torra nepo feca rapa trosono y tocipan.*"

She soon emerges with three cups of weak coffee and a plate of toasted sweet rolls. Some life-saving clouds sweep over, and the heat becomes bearable for just a couple of minutes. The Kid is young, twenty-nine years old, but today he seems like an old man—someone with endless yarns to tell. Like an old minstrel, sitting in a battered chair, he remembers his time as a hitman, when he first began to kill.

And so he will remember all the stories. This battered lot will become, for two years, before worse times arrive, a theater of the bloody tales of the Hollywood Kid.

━←

Some twenty years ago, in the early 1990s, on a riverbank on the outskirts of the city of Atiquizaya, a group of boys were huddled in a circle. They watched intently as one of them repeatedly sank a machete blade into the neck of another. The child executioner was Miguel Ángel. He was possessed, he wouldn't stop until the job was done. He'd been offended by the jokes the other kid kept making about his legs. Girly legs. The Kid decided that killing him was the best way to end the mockery once and for all. The others didn't get involved, they just waited patiently for it all to be over, distracting themselves by breaking off the branches of a nearby mulato tree, which they would use to cover the young body. The same tree that indigenous people used in their worship of Xipe Totec after the Spanish colonizers had prohibited it. Xipe Totec, "Our Lord the Flayed One."

The group of kids were members of a small gang—one of so many in western El Salvador—called the Gauchos Locos. Much as they tried, nothing they did could completely hide their rural roots. Their gang names always gave them away: the Goat, Fly, the Cat, the Chicken.

Many of these small, juvenile gangs, and this one in particular, were difficult to define and classify into a single category. One day they killed a boy, leaving his body under mulato branches, and the next they amused themselves by stoning the skinny cows of Don Chepito. They erratically swung from benign mischief to barbarism. The group was made up of mostly kids. Not yet teens, no longer children. They roamed the hills and roads of western El Salvador, stealing chickens and smoking pot. They were the living remnants of the war that had finally sputtered to a close. Their playthings were bullets and blood.

When the machete stopped falling over the boy, and he finally stopped breathing, they all decided to leave the remains where they were, barely hidden under a mound of reddish branches, so that he'd be taken by a current or a hungry mountain animal, as if he were an offering to the bloodthirsty and beneficent gods of their grandparents. Then they went about their tasks, hunting black crabs for lunch. They knew no one would miss the dead child.

They were just that, the children of no one, lost boys.

Miguel Ángel's life seems to confirm the idea that everything is a cycle, a vital cycle that ends as it began. The body of the child-murderer ended up under a spray of izote blossom, the national Salvadoran flower, laid there by a compassionate campesino. His life, at least his life as a hitman, began under a mulato tree, the tree of blood sacrifice.

Part II

Shacks

7

Chepe Furia's Boys

"If you were born on the streets you die on the streets. That's what life is like here. You're ready to die on the streets. We got a long history, man, going back to the war. We were born of the war. We lived the war, and it was the people of the war that made these gangs. We started over there in '90, '93, we started to band together in groups, but these groups weren't the gangs of today. I'm turning twenty-eight years old today. Back then we started out real young. Young people got into groups that stood as lookouts over the neighborhoods. I was MG: Mara Gauchos Locos 13. The guy who started the gauchos came from the United States. We occupied the toll booths, the highways, the edge of town, the downtown, and the park where all the busses parked, that's where we were in control. And any little new thing you had, we'd take it from you, we'd put a knife to your throat and we'd take whatever you had, we'd even take your shoes if you had shoes newer than ours. We were fifty kids, all out on the street. Those of us who had a record would hide from the cops. Keep out of town. We had farm tools and hand cannons [home-made firearms]. It was rare to see someone with a real gun, it was hard to get hold of that sort of thing."

Miguel Ángel, sitting outside his shack, is remembering the old days. It's January 4, 2012.

Miguel Ángel's shack is rugged: dry dirt ground, exposed brick, and a tile roof. And yet you can't say it's dirty. Inside the little room there's two old bed frames with thin mattresses on top. Three bundles of folded clothes lie on top of one of the cots: one is a man's clothes, another is a woman's, and the third is fit for a little girl. All the clothes are threadbare. Miguel Ángel's are way too big for him. Ill-fitting hand-me-downs.

The ground outside is drenched. It rained last night. The heat is relentless in this town. A constant force. But the smell of humidity and burnt coffee manage, at least, to wake up the mind a little bit.

Like always, the police officer that guards the lot is watching TV in the main house. Two buildings frame the lot. A big one, where the family who owns the property lives, and, about five yards away, the shack where Miguel Ángel lives. In between are two cement washbasins, where one can wash dishes, or clothes, or children. Miguel Ángel's *mujer*—that's what he calls sixteen-year-old Lorena, *mi mujer*, my wife—uses one of those basins to bathe Marbelly, who's now two years old.

Miguel Ángel looks emaciated. He's been confined to his little shack for almost two years, going to and coming from trials. Putting a mask over his face to confront his homies in court and feeling ridiculous every time. No matter how much they call him the Hare or Yogui in the case files, everyone knows he's really the Hollywood Kid. The court tries to protect his identity by distorting his voice to make him sound like a mouse or a zombie, by having him wear a mask, hide behind a screen, use an alias. None of it works.

"Other little groups sprang up: Los Meli 33, Los Valerios 13, and Los Uvas, then Los Chancletas in San Lorenzo, and that's how it went, man, a whole bunch of groups banded together. The deal was that in the dance halls you represented your barrio, man, and the others represented theirs, and all hell would break loose, and, shit, in those fights there were police and *maras* all mixed up in there. Then all of a sudden this dude shows up, Moncho Garrapata, who's Chepe Furia's first cousin. That son of a bitch shows up and brings this Eighteen from up north. He's come from Mexico and he starts calling out his people, the son of a bitch, all his people in the sectors that he controls, in the areas of Chalchuapita, La Periquera, La Línea. He starts grabbing hold of all these triggers, you know how these dudes will jump you for no reason, with no warning, and then he picks up the little girl, the Eighteen, the son of a bitch picks her up. And when he had them all up and ready, in walks Chepe Furia."

Miguel Ángel is skinny. Protruding ribs. A clavicle that's a showy necklace of bones. And yet he's also solid. Compact. The muscles he built working the coffee plantations, the cornfields and bean farms since he was a boy, still cling to his skeleton like a vine to a tree. Today, he tells stories while crouched down on the ground. There's something animal about him, about his essence. You feel that this underfed man could pounce on you, tear you apart like a wildcat. He could charge at you like a wild boar. And he could definitely, as if he were still a gang member, hack you to pieces with a machete.

"The first time Chepe Furia came around was in '94. Fuck, Chepe Furia rolling up, and all the *maras* just watching the trucks go by, and this guy with his tricked-out car. The fucker came rolling in, with his lowrider and his brand names. He was like twenty years old back then. The crazy fuck had been deported, but he already had his people here, and real quick he'd started getting things fucking organized," says Miguel Ángel, still on the damp dirt.

Over the course of January and February, we visited Miguel Ángel's shack on an almost weekly basis. Our access, which at first required persistent calls to try to convince the detective, became rote. We even started coming without notice.

Miguel Ángel never lost his animal, predatory essence. It only takes a few minutes of conversation for blood to appear in his stories—it always does—and then the look in his eyes, along with his whole demeanor, changes. When he remembers, he gesticulates as if he were back in in the scene he's describing.

He's seeming more and more like a caged and desperate animal. He's going nowhere, and he knows it. A man used to quick results —I fire, you die; I demand, you fork over—doesn't understand the concept of justice. What's justice? How do you shoot it? He understands himself as a prisoner of history, of his country, of his time. Pursued by his own gang, targeted by the other gang, harassed by the police, he'd had to turn himself in. There's nothing in his life but guns, with the Kid in the crosshairs. Giving him this little shack, this mound of earth, seemed a good idea in the beginning of 2010, but after spending almost two years locked up, going and coming from spilling the secrets of the Mara Salvatrucha in court, getting threatened, threatened, and threatened again, interviewed by prosecutors in suits who don't understand his language or his world, testifying before a judge under his new, plea-bargain witness name, Yogui—which he hates—with a stifling mask over his face and the voice-over of a mouse, the animal in him sometimes doesn't feel like a predator. It feels like prey. And he hates that feeling. It's not in his nature.

He, whom others hid from.

He, the stalker.

He, the hunter.

He, *pop*, *pop*.

He, the Hollywood Kid.

A predator, even if taken out of the jungle, won't forget his essence.

Chepe Furia and the Lost Children

They say the hamlet of Las Pozas is a good hideout. Through the hills, you can run all the way to Guatemala. The authorities can't make it here without being seen.

To get to Las Pozas by car you need to drive through Atiquizaya, an hour and a half beyond the capital, cross the center of that dusty town, skirt its central park dotted by small restaurants and food stands, drive another few blocks, pass tile-roofed houses, take a right past the church, take a street that's usually closed for the village's patron saint festivals where greasy fried food is gobbled down, keep driving down a two-lane asphalt street, leave behind fields and more fields, pass a bicycle repair shop, a one-lane bridge, Mara Salvatrucha graffiti tags, a white Barrio 18 tag on a tree trunk, several narrow roads that snake up toward the hillsides and, in the distance, the Chingo Volcano, then take the exit for San Lorenzo, a place where everyone stares at you as if you hadn't come from the capital but from Mars in a spaceship, drive down a few cobblestone blocks and cross the dirt road where rickety signposts read, "Las Pozas," and keep on driving, another twenty minutes and you see the enormous ceiba tree towering over a school at the entrance of town.

Yeah, the hamlet of Las Pozas is a good hideout.

And every stranger that takes the exit to San Lorenzo will get eyed with suspicion. And once they enter Las Pozas their presence will only stand out more. The town is on high alert whenever an unknown car enters. It's as if everyone—people and dogs alike— are put on pause, all of them frozen for just a second. The town is made up of a large tract of land with five roads fanning out from the school like a star, some leading to the mountains bordering Guatemala. Rows of makeshift houses line each street. They are tattered improvisations of shelter, a few bricks, sheets of laminate, tile, plastic, and stone. The roads are very narrow. Only one car can fit. And it's impossible to make a U-turn. You have to drive into the forest to find a little bit of room to make your turn. Three stores sell knick-knacks and Coca-Colas. There's a cantina and a soccer field. That's it.

People who live in the surrounding areas say that many of the men who hide here were once members of car-thieving gangs or are plea-bargain witnesses. Many make a living by trafficking marijuana to Guatemalan border towns. They trudge through the hillsides hefting large sacks of herb to sell to men waiting for them in pickups.

When people talk about the "authorities" of Las Pozas, they're not talking about the police. As if it were still at war, this corner of El Salvador is not patrolled by the organizations created after the peace accords; the government sent in soldiers instead.

Las Pozas is a place of nomads. People who lost their jobs, people on the run, people expelled from the coffee plantations by unjust landowners. Mostly dysfunctional families, made up of the pieces of other families. The children of these families understood only one verb: survive. Many of them dulled life's disappointments the same way their parents did, with the help of cane liquor.

The town cantina is owned by a forty-something campesino whom everyone knows as Cockroach. He's a friendly, good-natured old man, vulgar like nobody's business. Cockroach packs obscenities into every sentence.

"Those fucking little *bichos* were legless, the faggots. They were fucking flying through the last hour of work in the *milpas*, the fags, so they could come running with their dollars to piss it all away here, the sons of bitches."

Cockroach was talking about the lost children, the descendants of those nomads, of those stray bits and pieces of other families. The children of war.

One of those kids was Miguel Ángel Tobar, a regular at Cockroach's bar since the age of ten.

It took a while for Cockroach to understand how such a ragged brat could so often afford to buy a liter of Cuatro Ases. Las Pozas was full of poor folks and, though a bottle of rotgut only cost some ten colones (a little more than a dollar), that was big money in that forgotten corner of the world. A man wouldn't get paid much more for a full morning's work harvesting coffee.

Cockroach remembers Miguel Ángel as a kid who was "happy, who didn't seem like he would kill a fly, but with a shitty, weird family ... Who'd have imagined?"

Miguel Ángel would show up to the bar at all hours. Sometimes at noon. Sometimes early in the morning. Sometimes when Cockroach was trying to sleep. A village cantina is allergic to formalities. It sets its schedule according to the needs of the drinkers. Cockroach remembers Miguel Ángel running into the bar and asking for his bottle of *guaro* and, with hardly a word, bolting back out the door.

Used to seeing machete fights inside his cantina, Cockroach noticed the kid's hurry, but that was all that stuck out to him.

And then, other kids he didn't know started showing up. They would do the same: storm in all excited, ask for a liter or two of Cuatro Ases, and then dash off as if somebody were chasing them.

Cockroach started to get curious.

The cantina was on the far side of the village, about 300 yards beyond the school and the big ceiba tree.

One night, Miguel Ángel came in and asked for his usual. Then, like always, he dashed out with the bottle. Cockroach followed him with a flashlight. Miguel Ángel rushed over to the ceiba tree where Cockroach saw a black, double-cab pickup truck. He walked closer. Beyond the pickup, sitting on the roots of the ceiba, was a man in his thirties surrounded by about five kids with plastic cups into which the man was splashing some of the clear *guaro*. The man noticed Cockroach, who waved. The man waved back.

A couple of nights later the man himself stopped by the cantina. Cockroach remembers him as being friendly, and that he was with another, bald guy, with tattoos on his neck and peeking out from under his unbuttoned shirt. They ordered drinks and then the first man stood up and approached the black counters separating the barkeep and the bottles from the drunks. He thanked Cockroach, asking for his name. "Everybody calls me Cockroach."

"And me, Chepe Furia," the man said. "Nice to meet you."

Chepe Furia and his sidekick left the cantina. Cockroach had seen the face of a legend. But Chepe Furia wasn't like the white dog or the creaky cart of the tall tales told around these parts. He was a man of flesh and blood, a man who had a big nose and drank Cuatro Ases with the neighborhood kids.

In western El Salvador you occasionally hear the whispered names of famous bandits and stick-up men—men whose names you don't dare speak aloud in the cantinas. One of those names was

Chepe Furia's. These weren't the names of gangsters: gangs were hardly a concern when people started hearing about Chepe Furia. From that first day Chepe Furia and his companion walked into the cantina, they started hanging around. Sometimes, Cockroach recalls, they'd show up without any money.

"They liked to show up whenever they wanted, sometimes real late at night. 'Open up, Cockroach, you son-of-a-damn-bitch.' And they'd bang on the door until I got up to serve them. But they would always end up paying. They'd send Miguel Ángel to pay the next day, or a couple days later."

Chepe Furia always was a man with a plan. He wasn't getting drunk with the kids because he liked their company. He saw his future in them, his muscle. He was training them to fight in his name.

Miguel Ángel remembers that Chepe Furia would show up in Las Pozas, back in 1995 and 1996, with kids and teenagers from the nascent gangs in Atiquizaya, Ahuachapán, Turín, and El Refugio. To recruit more, Chepe Furia made an alliance with a sixteen-year-old everybody knew as El Farmacia. He was, like Miguel Ángel, a member of the Gauchos Locos 13. For years in El Salvador, you could find everything in pharmacies: medicine, soft drinks, knick-knacks, candy, magazines, newspapers, even cigarettes and beer. El Farmacia was the same—you could meet all your expectations with just one kid. "That motherfucker," Miguel Ángel remembers, "he'd get you anything you wanted. If you told him, get me that thing, by that afternoon, he'd bring it to you. Ten bucks, five bucks he'd charge you so he could buy his pot. The *bato* was in the know."

Chepe Furia understood that El Farmacia, thanks to his skill, was an important needle with which he could sew together various groups of local youth. If the rural gangs had their differences and resolved them with clubs and knives at parties, their hate still wasn't irremediable. It wasn't even close to the hate that MS-13 and Barrio 18 would develop for each other. They only hated each other for something to do, or to be able to distinguish themselves from each other. They hated to be a part of something, to feel a little less deprived. Chepe Furia understood that he could use this adolescent hate and turn it into another kind of hate. A transcendental hate. A hate that would last a lifetime.

In El Salvador, we know about hate.

The lost boys were encountering something new. Chepe Furia was able to bring them together because he was different. Bedraggled and hungry, the local kids all had something in common. But Chepe, with his pickup, a 9mm in his waistband, buying Cuatro Ases like a lord, was different. He was what they aspired to be.

In the next town over, Atiquizaya, Moncho Garrapata had the same agenda, but under the banner of Barrio 18. Chepe Furia knew that a confrontation over territory was on its way, and so he started preparing himself. Uniting the lost boys wasn't hard. But now he needed to steer their aggression, take all those miserable lives and give them a unifying purpose: to kill the Eighteens. Meanwhile, he would turn himself into their chief.

He explained to the kids what a meeting was, the kind the Californian gang members called in order to make decisions, but he Salvadoranized the word, spelling it like they pronounced it: *mirin*, with a hard-rolled R. Chepe Furia held his *mirins* at the soccer field in Atiquizaya's San Antonio neighborhood, close to where his parents lived, and where, years later, he'd humiliate 500 police officers by switching off the public grid as they chased after him.

Language is important in war. It unites. It differentiates. Chepe

Furia taught all the kids to despise the Eighteens even in common speech. He taught them to call them *las bichonas, los uno caca, los cagados, las chavalas* (roughly: bitches, shits, shitheads, little girls). Miguel Ángel remembers that Chepe Furia implemented two rules at one of the *mirins*. The first: "Respect for me, I got the latest word from the Mara Salvatrucha, and I'm the founder of the Hollywood Locos Salvatrucha." For these kids, MS-13, "the big one," as they called it, was this man who'd been deported from *el norte*. The second rule: "We're going to jump you all in again." A lot of the boys, like Miguel Ángel himself, had gone through thirteen seconds of blows and kicks, without being able to fight back, in order to officially join the neighborhood gang. The deportees that had founded those small, now extinct, gangs had brought some of the Sureño rituals with them.

Next, Chepe Furia gave them a creed.

In a country as tiny as El Salvador, there is a lot of copying and repetition. And violence seems to have a memory of its own. Chepe Furia (stealing a phrase from Roberto d'Aubuisson, the murderer of archbishop Óscar Romero) substituted *barrio* for *El Salvador*: "Barrio first, barrio second, and barrio third."

The gang grew. The lost boys shed their precarious identities and gained a new, collective identity. Soon they would even have new names, their nicknames taking over to the point that if somebody called out to them with their birth names, they might not even turn around.

"In those days," Miguel Ángel remembers, "we had some .22 pistols and a 9mm that belonged to that asshole. Sometimes he'd lend them out. He'd send us to go rob and ... sometimes things got hairy. If somebody took a stand, you'd have to waste them. We'd go robbing the *Formos* milk trucks ... Three hundred pesos [about thirty-five dollars] ... We're going to grind somebody, they'd say. This is for the clique, they'd say. Everything for the clique, they'd say. Clique first, clique second, clique third, they'd say. That is, for the barrio. Barrio first, second, and third, they'd say."

The lost boys started to integrate into the MS-13. And they expressed their loyalty to the man who founded their clique. They also started moving closer to where he lived in the San Antonio barrio. They squatted abandoned houses—they called them *destroyer* houses—and converted them according to their needs. Chepe Furia provided them with ample pot, and they stole electricity from nearby public utility wires to make them a little more habitable.

The life of gang soldiers didn't change much after they earned their letters. It was, and is, a mafia, but a mafia of the poor. The secret is that their dream was not to be somebody rich, but just to be somebody. A different person from who they were. Because some of them, like Miguel Ángel, had not only always been poor, but had always been humiliated. They were the brothers of raped sisters and the sons of alcoholic fathers. They were nomads. They were trash. They were lost children.

Nobody would want to be Miguel Ángel Tobar.

El Ozzy de Coronados. El Diablito de Hollywood. El Flaco de Francis. El Shy Boy de Hollywood. El Camerón de Normandie. El Gato de Fulton. El Smookey de Western. El Zombie de Adams. El Negro de Orphan. El Shorty de Fulton. El Crook de Hollywood. El Chiche de Fulton. El Tigre de Parvis. El Oso de Coronado. El Comando de Normandie. El Greñas de Coronados. El Laky de Parvis. El Risas de Fulton. El Tiny de Western. El Spider de Fulton. El Popeye de Western. El Indio de Hollywood. El Burro de Witmer. El Zarco de Western. El Extraño de Adams.

El Tortuga de Coronado. El Vampiro de Fulton. El Negro de Normandie. El Cola de Western. El Psycho de Adams. El Cachi de Leeward. El Cuchumbo de Novena. El Rebel de Normandie. El Flipper de Parvis. El Trigger de Fulton. El Snoopy de Western. El Garrobo de Normandie. El Viejo Pavas de Seven Eleven. El Rata de Leeward. El Triste de Coronados. El Maya de Western. El Crimen de Adams. El Chino de Western. El Chivo de Centrales. El Revuelo de Parvis. El Santos de Normandie. El Monkey de Novena. El Negro de Harvard. El Vago de Hollywood. El Morro de Normandie. El Skinny de Stoner, El Caimán de Hollywood ...

El Veneno de Fulton.
José Antonio Terán.

Rechristened as Chepe Furia de Hollywood.

It wasn't just one. Dozens poured in during the 1990s.

The United States rejecting them.

The United States deporting them.

The United States vomiting them.

The United States not knowing what it was doing.

Migration is a cycle.

They were being recruited from all over El Salvador.

The lost children of El Salvador.

The gang leaders of El Salvador.

A country under construction.

A country in ruins.

A country without a thought for its lost children.

War deported from the streets of California to the streets of El Salvador.

One war ending. Another beginning.

El Salvador's hardest lesson: the end of war is not necessarily the beginning of peace.

8

To Kill a Witch

Even from outside Miguel Ángel's shack, you can smell the penetrating scent of pot. The air is so still that the smoke lingers, hovering above our heads before slowly dissipating into the blue sky of western El Salvador. The police at the outpost across the street ignore the spectacle. They're used to it. Inside the shack, on this January day of 2012, Miguel Ángel is smoking a joint as fat as a finger. He offers us a brief, hoarse hello, wanting to hold in the precious fumes as long as he can. He speaks and inhales, lets out a little smoke and then sucks it back in, swallowing back the gulp that had started to pour out. He's enjoying himself so much that just seeing him makes you want to take a puff, to relish the dense smoke as much as he does.

Lorena, his teenage wife, is washing Marbelly in the cement sink and preparing a weak, translucent coffee. Something's cooking in a pot, smelling spicy and healthy. At first glance, this could be the home of any young campesino couple.

Miguel Ángel wasn't expecting visitors. When he knows people are coming, he puts on an old button-down shirt and shoes, and skips the marijuana. Today, he's barefoot and shirtless, wearing threadbare pants. His hair is mussed, his eyes are red, and his mind is full of smoke.

He wasn't expecting visitors or an interview, but stories are crowding on his tongue, and he's ready to tell them to anybody willing to sit and listen. When he begins to talk, however, a battle begins between the stories he wants to get out and, maybe more important, the smoke that he wants to keep in. It's like listening to someone trying to stifle a coughing fit.

When Chepe Furia first arrived, in 1994, Miguel Ángel had already tried to kill several people, but he'd only succeeded with two: a kid he left dumped under a pile of branches next to a river and an old man. The latter meant almost nothing to Miguel Ángel.

Precious smoke. Miguel Ángel enjoyed few things more than a pipe of marijuana and cultivating cannabis on the site where he lived as a protected witness.

He wasn't going to waste much breath talking about him in the shack. The old man wasn't a gang member, and his death didn't count for anything, didn't earn him any respect. It was like scoring a goal against a team without a goalie, when there's not even a game going on.

The victim was an elderly goatherd who'd crossed paths with Miguel Ángel when he was still a boy. The goatherd, who knew Miguel Ángel as a bum and a thief, offered him a drink of Cuatro Ases. Miguel Ángel took a swig. The old man then said that he'd give him money if he let him "treat him like his wife." Miguel Ángel said sure, and when the man celebrated by tilting back the bottle of Cuatro Ases, Miguel Ángel punched him hard, right in the middle of the chest. The old man fell backward to the ground, and landed flat. He struggled to get in another breath.

"He choked because I whacked him with everything I had. And you know, if you get hit when you're drinking, you drown," Miguel Ángel says while examining the roach of the joint between his fingers, deciding on the best way to inhale the last of it.

The young Miguel Ángel snatched the bottle of Cuatro Ases and stole a few coins from the old man's pocket, watching him as he choked, or at least that's what he thought was happening: that the old man, beaten up by years of drinking *guaro*, died right at his feet. That was the last Miguel Ángel saw of him: laid out, eyes closed, not seeming to breathe, and not having been able to treat the Kid like his wife.

Along with the poverty and violence he suffered, the criminal life first left its mark on Miguel Ángel when he was still just a boy. From that day on, after killing (or attempting to kill) the old herder, he was filled with terror every time he heard the tinkle of goats' bells. He thought the bells were the soul of the old man following him around, looking for what that young kid still owed him.

The goatherd—a regular figure in the village—was named Chepe Toño. Memories, especially memories more than two decades old, tend to dissipate like puffs of marijuana smoke, but Miguel Ángel has hung onto a crisp image of the scene: one hard punch and the old man was dead. Later, in El Refugio, the other kids would tease Miguel Ángel by chanting: here comes Chepe Toño!

In any case, that murder didn't count as a gang murder. It didn't add a point to his name, at least not as the homies counted them. It wasn't the kind of kill Chepe Furia wanted from his lost children.

Marbelly is fresh-faced and dripping wet from her bath. It won't take long, however, before she's rolling around in the dirt again. Miguel Ángel pinches what's left of his joint between his fingers. A small ember glows between his lips. He burns himself and then finally tosses the butt. He spits ash off his tongue. Spits again. And then he starts to tell us about his first murder as a member of the Mara Salvatrucha 13, as a soldier for the Beast, as part of the tradition of assassins that began thousands of miles away from this little shack, in a strange land called California.

The Witch

By mid-1996, Chepe Furia had successfully planted the seeds of his gang. It was nothing like an established and structured mafia, but just a group of kids and teenagers bewitched by an older and more intelligent leader. They were ready and willing to do whatever Chepe Furia told them. After all, they had no one to tell them much of anything else. Soon it was Miguel Ángel's turn to make a pact. To seal in blood his agreement with the Beast, he would have to kill in her honor.

Mara Salvatrucha 13 has a good memory. Its horrifying past has become part of its structure. The young gangsters learned to imitate what they saw, learned how to make it their own.

Years back in *Califas*, when they were still inspired by Black Sabbath, the gang started to play the Sureño's bloody game: requiring new members to make their first kill. The Mara Salvatrucha 13—the Beast—taught her children what she'd learned. Meting out death is the price of admission, the seal of total submission.

Miguel Ángel's first true hit was a baker. A youth from a small village, El Zapote, who, just like Miguel Ángel, was seduced by the irresistible ideas exported from the north along with the deportees. He was an Eighteen. Exactly what Miguel Ángel had been waiting for. After months of walking with the Beast, finally he had a chance to make a blood offering and become one of her legitimate children.

As leader of the mission they sent El Hollywood, a teenager with experience whose job was simply to make sure everything went smoothly, to be witness to Miguel Ángel's initiation. They carried a 9mm pistol—a luxury for the neighborhood gangs, who still wielded machetes for whenever they were forced to carry out makeshift, artisanal hits.

Pop.

El Hollywood took the first shot, hitting the baker in the chest, knocking him to the ground. But then the pistol jammed. The baker, back on his feet, took off into the coffee fields, hoping to hide in the undergrowth, but that was precisely where Miguel Ángel was waiting for his opportunity. He hacked him with a machete in the face, and then in the chest, and then again in the face. The baker had stopped moving, but Miguel Ángel didn't stop. He grabbed the baker by the hair, raised his machete again, and sank the blade into his neck. When El Hollywood arrived, with his pistol still jammed, he found Miguel Ángel staring into the eyes of a decapitated head. He was still holding it by the hair. Right in front of his face, the face of death. He dealt the head a couple of kicks, and a couple more kicks to the headless cadaver, and then he and El Hollywood lost themselves among the coffee trees.

At twelve years old, with a machete for a weapon, Miguel Ángel sealed his pact with the two letters.

"They said the guy was a witch, and it was true, because I tried with that pistol afterward and no problem, a fucking good shot. And then later again with the same gun ... thunder, man. So that's why I cut the dude's head off, because they say that witches can put their brains back together. When El Hollywood came over, he found me holding the head," Miguel Ángel would tell us in his shack, seventeen years after decapitating his victim.

The two boys ran through the coffee trees until they reached a field. They took a path to Miguel Ángel's house, where they rested a while. Covered in blood, they burned their clothes and scrubbed their shoes.

El Hollywood ran to tell Chepe Furia and the other gangsters that the mission had been a success. The Beast had birthed another son. Now all that was left was the formal act, the ceremony. The jumping-in. The thirteen-second beating.

But being a teenage assassin, Miguel Ángel was worried about two things: the first was that his dad would find out about the half-bottle of Cuatro Ases he'd stolen and drunk with El Hollywood to calm their nerves after the decapitation; the second was that if they jumped him in during the week, he'd get in trouble at school for being all bloody and dirty and in trouble at home for ruining his uniform and his best pair of shoes. These were his childish fears.

Chepe Furia, like a kind godfather, soothed his disciple's worries. He decreed that the jump-in would be the following weekend so that Miguel Ángel wouldn't have any issues at school. These are the decisions you need to make when you're the leader of a pack of teenage killers.

The clique at that time, Miguel Ángel recalls, consisted of twenty-two members.

Miguel Ángel's life is cyclical, and he returns to his origins again and again, tying his life to the lives of other men who have been just as deprived as him, who've also bled and suffered in this part of El Salvador. They decided to jump him in on May 3—a sacred day for the indigenous community, a day of celebration for the god Xipe Totec, the Flayed One. The Flayed One is the god of rain and harvests, the god who restores life after his own death, who skins himself in sacrifice in order to restore the life of others.

In his capacity as founder and leader of the Hollywood Locos Salvatrucha de Atiquizaya, Chepe Furia directed the jump-in. In this performance of power, everything has its place. Chepe handpicked three established members to give Miguel Ángel his initiation. He made sure to assume a role in which he'd be able to keep his hands clean. So Chepe stood on the sidelines and slowly counted to thirteen as the fists and kicks rained down on Miguel Ángel. Chepe was the conductor of an orchestra, and the symphony was a beat-down.

At the beginning of the twentieth century, the French anthropologist Arnold van Gennep termed certain symbolic actions "rites of passage." He described ritualized moments in which a person passed from one social category to another, abandoning all that pertained to his earlier life as he entered into a distinct social position.

One … two … three … Seconds lingering in the air, seconds as long as days. Chepe counted slowly. Thirteen seconds never last as long as they do for the Mara Salvatrucha 13. Marijuana smoke floating above the ritual, bottles of Cuatro Ases at the ready to bid welcome. The other members stood in a semicircle around Miguel Ángel. Kicks. Punches. The crunch of bone. Four … five … six … Outside of the semicircle were the second-class spectators, the other neophytes who would soon get their own turn to be pounded. The rite of passage always follows the same form, according to Gennep. Seven … eight … nine … Miguel Ángel was quick. With the agility of a cat, he was able to dodge most of the fists. He sparked one way and then the next. He covered his head. And then Chepe Furia stopped counting. "Three more, change over," he ordered. Three fresh kids stepped in. Kick, kick, kick. Rib crunch, blood, airless lungs. Ten … eleven … Symbols are important, Gennep wrote. They give the ritual meaning. Twelve … gasping … thirteen. "Alright, dog, welcome to the Mara!" Chepe Furia announced. He offered his hand to Miguel Ángel, who, hearing the magic number, fell to the ground, to the dirt. All the other home-boys raised their hands and signed the Salvatrucha horns. They welcomed their new brother, congratulating him: *"¡Órale!"*

"I was hallucinating. My whole face was swollen, and I could feel a cracked rib. But Chepe Furia gave me his hand, and then I felt like I was a part of something really awesome," Miguel Ángel would remember eighteen years later. He had been jumped into what would be his family for the next thirteen years.

With rare exceptions, you don't get to choose your first gang name. Your new name is picked by the group. And it's usually unflattering.

Miguel Ángel has a clownish face, with an outsized mouth and eyes slightly farther apart than normal.

On May 3, 1996, as people across El Salvador were sticking crosses in the ground to commemorate the Cross of May, Miguel Ángel Tobar died and a new man came to life. The newest member of the Mara Salvatrucha: El Payaso, or the Clown of the Hollywood Locos Salvatrucha.

Xipe Totec, Our Lord the Flayed

Xipe Totec was a popular precolonial deity worshipped from what is today El Salvador to Central Mexico. The legend goes that at the beginning, when the first humans came into the world, Xipe Totec took pity and offered them his own skin for sustenance. This is why corn is associated with renovation, with the death that gives us life. Something must die so that something may live and thus, in an infinite circle of death and life, the ancient Mesoamericans understood their world. The priests of Xipe Totec skinned enemy warriors and dressed in their skins as an offering to the generous god who had given food to their ancestors. The bloody side of the skin faced out, and the hands, still connected by strings of flesh, hung loosely from the priests' wrists.

In homes and temples, Xipe Totec was represented by clay figures. A being that rose out of the scales of old skin. When the old skin sloughs off, a new being is born. And he is born into suffering.

With the arrival of the Spanish, the priests of a strange new god banned these practices. Human sacrifice was prohibited and nearly all native holidays were replaced by Christian ones. But people always combined some aspects of both faiths. In the case of El Salvador, instead of paying homage to Xipe Totec, people started worshipping the Holy Cross. Every May 3, instead of a priest donning human skin, wooden crosses are set out and hung with fruit in thanks for the rain and the renovation of the earth and its plenty.

But the Indians, in a wink to their ancestors (and to Xipe Totec) make their crosses with wood from the mulato tree, which constantly sheds its bark, its skin. And so every May 3, as El Salvador prays to the Christian cross and venerates the sacrifice of the Christian God, at the same time we are venerating another god who also offered his skin to save our ancestors.

Xipe Totec, Our Lord the Flayed.

9
Mission Hollywood 1:
A Cleanup in the Clique

Marbelly has learned an amazing hominoid skill: putting one foot in front of the other to move forward. She practices walking constantly, and, at two years old, grabbing at anything she can and is nearly always at the point of tumbling into the dirt. Like any father, Miguel Ángel has taken precautions. A curious child in this home, however, runs risks different from those she would face in most homes around the world.

Miguel Ángel has a grenade. Not a homemade bomb. Not a Molotov cocktail. An M-67 industrial grenade—the type that the soldiers and guerrillas would hurl at each other in the mountains during the twelve years of civil war. To Miguel Ángel, it's a kind of life insurance, although it's really more like death insurance. Aware that Marbelly wants to explore every nook of their home, her father has put his grenade on top of a high beam so that she won't one day find it, pull its rusty pin, and blow them all to pieces.

"This piece is a little sensitive. If I pull the pin and let it drop, the balloon pops … It pops and I'm a goner, but I'll take whoever's around with me," Miguel Ángel says as he pulls out the pin and, after a moment, secures it back into place.

His life has always been so close to the edge of the abyss that trusting in a little rusty ball of metal doesn't seem out of the ordinary. Not to him or to Lorena.

Sometimes it's worth pausing a moment. There are details—but are they just details?—that powerfully capture complex realities in just a few words. Miguel Ángel and his family, knowing that the Mara Salvatrucha wants them dead, sleep next to a grenade. Miguel Ángel understands death, and he prefers, for his and his family's sake, that they die by grenade rather than by the Mara Salvatrucha.

He's gotten skinnier. You could see his ribs before, but now it's worse. The basket of provisions the Salvadoran state sends him is just enough to eat frugally for a week. Detective Pineda sometimes—*sometimes*—supplements the basket with a few dollars from his own pocket. The rest of their income comes from selling the marijuana Miguel Ángel grows outside their shack, or from asking for "donations" from Coke or Pepsi delivery drivers. They shell out reluctantly. When an ex-gangster, even if he's retired, asks for money in the street, it'll always have a whiff of extortion.

Lorena serves up a plate of boiled chayote flavored with lime and salt. Marbelly shows off her newfound talent and toddles toward her parents. She takes a piece of chayote and sticks it in her mouth. It's hot, but she eats it anyway, giggling.

Miguel Ángel takes a piece and swallows it. He's sitting on a half-buried tire in the yard in front of the shack. His past comes to him in waves. As it turned out, he explains, he hadn't yet proved enough that he wanted to become a soldier of death. Shortly after killing for the Beast for the first time, she asked for more. This time she wanted the blood of a friend.

Miguel Ángel kept an M-67 grenade hidden above a ceiling beam, intending to use it on himself and his family if they were cornered.

"What happened was that the barrio forced me to fuck up this *loco* from the Gauchos who didn't want to join up with the Mara. He was my homeboy, but a Gaucho, not a Hollywood. Because the *loco* didn't want to follow MS-13's rules," he says, sitting on the tire.

No Place for the Timid

The majority of new gang members didn't need—and still don't need—to be forced or threatened in order to join. Poverty in Central America pushed them right into the gang's arms. The general hardship, lack of opportunity, violence, and quasi-medieval living conditions, turned joining up with MS-13 into a completely logical choice. It's a choice between being nobody and being part of something. Between being a victim or a victimizer. Being Miguel Ángel Tobar or the Clown of Hollywood. In those years, however, just before the turn of the millennium, Chepe Furia couldn't wait around for poverty to do its convincing. Barrio 18 was arming itself. A war was looming.

With the clique already established, mostly by former members of neighborhood gangs, Chepe Furia needed to make clear to the kids already jumped in, as well as to future members, that joining the Mara is not always an option. For the kids who belonged to rock-throwing, chicken-stealing gangs, there was only one path that didn't lead to MS-13.

"So they threw us a line. The thugs who didn't want to accept the two letters, that didn't want to be part of the big MS-13 family … you got to drop them flat. *Bam!* They finished El Pollo. Cut his throat. You couldn't defend anybody in those days, because they'd just say, 'Hey, are you with the Mara or not? Are you blue or not?'" [Translator's note: Blue has multiple connotations in this context— it refers to the traditional color of Southern California gangs, the blue of the Salvadoran flag, as well as the blue of tattoo ink.]

It brought home to them how things were changing, how nothing would be the same again.

And the strategy was effective. Nobody messed with the Mara Salvatrucha 13. It wasn't a group you could join for a while, have some fun with, and then leave. It came and it took over. MS-13 doesn't nibble, it devours. And the boys understood, they got it, but they also understood that the Mara is a competitive space, where everyone's after prestige and honor, status and perks. Everything was permitted, even eliminating rivals for the most trivial infractions, so that everyone was as blue as you. It was a time for building character, preparing for what was to come.

Those who didn't get the message were done for. A kid confused about the complex gang argot accidentally called himself "*bicha*," which is most commonly used to refer to members of Barrio 18. "Done for," Miguel Ángel remembers. Another kid, an aspiring gangster blazed on marijuana, committed a similar error: he referred to himself as a female. Instead of saying he was *pedo* (high), he used the feminine form of the adjective, *peda*. "Done for." Wiped out. Young kids who were just developing into teenagers as they became members of the Mara Salvatrucha were settling their differences by machete. The toughest of them survived. Chepe Furia was letting them weed themselves out, purifying the ranks. And he had a name for the purification. He called it Mission Hollywood (though he would also use this name for a massacre that would prove fundamental in the gang's history and formation).

Only the most brutal survived: those ready to kill for the pure fun of it, or to obey an order. Those fateful mistakes and confusions, committed by youngsters who often didn't even know how to write, were so trivial that Miguel Ángel has practically forgotten them—even though, back when he was the Hollywood Clown, he was in the thick of the drama. Because it wasn't important, because nobody was waiting for those kids to come home, because they lived in *destroyer* homes in the San Antonio neighborhood and ended up rotting on the banks of the river. Maybe that's why he barely remembers the details. So many murders were still to come, so many gruesome, sadistic deaths, that maybe these early deaths were buried in his memory beneath the avalanche.

Everything moved quickly. The Hollywood Locos Salvatrucha de Atiquizaya was growing. The police started following their trail.

And the nascent clique was beginning to get into skirmishes with their Barrio 18 enemies.

In neighborhoods like Chalchuapita, Centro de Chalchuapa, La Periquera, and others around Atiquizaya, Chepe Furia's cousin, Moncho Garrapata, had started to organize other kids on the street, under a different banner: Barrio 18.

In the last years of the 1990s, these two men, who both came of age during the Civil War, founded a kind of cultural movement based on the most disturbing values. They steered the young toward a dark abyss. An extremely violent whirlpool in which these young sought respect and status. In order to stop being nobodies and become feared men, they made a deal with the Beast: I'll give you Miguel Ángel Tobar and you give me the Hollywood Clown of the Locos Salvatrucha.

With both sides armed and ready, it was time for the game to begin.

10

Threats from Prison

February 2012. Everything in this tropical heat is damp. The police officers of El Refugio in their dark blue, long-sleeved uniforms are a pitiful sight. Nobody would fault them if they suddenly tipped over in a faint. Inside the tiny detectives' office, a fan lazily spins the hot air as Detective Pineda reviews documents on his ancient computer.

"This was a big week," he says enthusiastically.

Chepe Furia remains a free man because the judge believed—*did he believe him?*—that he would not go into hiding for a second time if he was released. And yet, the secrets that Miguel Ángel spilled didn't come to nothing. Forty-two gang members from the Hollywood, Parvis, and Ángeles cliques are facing charges of homicide, extortion, and illicit gang affiliation. All thanks to information delivered by Miguel Ángel.

In El Salvador, criminal investigations overwhelmingly depend on witness statements. A corpse, and a witness who tells what she saw about how a person became a corpse, is enough for prosecution. If there's no witness, a lot of prosecutors simply chuck their cases onto the trash heap, what they call the "overspill," a chasm of archived cases from which very few files ever reemerge. Cases rot, just like the bodies. "Without a witness, all there is is a body. Period," a homicide prosecutor told us in February of 2016. "Without a witness, we don't even open a file," another prosecutor said. The first prosecutor was in charge of 500 homicide cases, disappearances, and attempted homicides. The second prosecutor couldn't even remember how many active cases he had open. He only knew that, so far that year, still in February, he had received seventy-eight new cases, eighteen of which were homicides. Homicide cases don't officially go cold for fifteen years. They pile up on top of the prosecutors, bringing them to their knees. With luck, they can close a couple of cases a year.

El Salvador is a good place to commit a murder, or a whole string of murders.

A statistical aside: the probability that you'd be indicted by a judge after murdering someone—not convicted, merely charged—is less than one in ten. In 2015, less than one out of ten murder cases ended in a conviction. This means that if you're a corpse, there is less than a 10 percent chance that the person who turned you into a corpse will be brought to justice. This is according to the statistics from El Salvador's most violent year of the century, which racked up numbers worthy of a war zone: 103 homicides for every 100,000 inhabitants. Remember, in the United States there are typically about five murders for every 100,000 inhabitants.

Pineda tells us that he "captured a gangster set on killing the Kid."

Inside the shack, the days seem to have come to a standstill. Miguel Ángel is smoking pot, sitting on one of the tumbledown chairs on his small covered patio. Lorena is tending to Marbelly. A mountain of dishes sits in the cement sink.

Miguel Ángel seems to enjoy our visits more and more.

"Hey, what's up," he says as we settle in. "Hell yeah, we're gonna talk today. I've been thinking about a fucking ton of hits I'm gonna tell you about."

Not a word about the recent attempted hit on himself. It seems to be just another day in his shack: hot and slow.

Miguel Ángel starts explaining how it's a good time to kill if you smell horses. But if you smell a goat, "you better split, because that's a sign that the Beast is tracking you down." It's not just that you'll smell the goat, he continues, but the hair on your arms will stand on end. He's a gangster, but a rural one. His points of reference aren't hip-hop, rap, or Nike Cortez. His imagery concerns animals, the smell of cattle, and rubber boots.

Just days after they tried to kill him, he's willing to rattle on about almost anything. We interrupt Miguel Ángel's spiel about the goats and the horses: "Hey, so did they try to kill you this week?"

"Oh, yeah. A crazy guy with tattoos on his face."

We have to drag it out of him, a few words at a time. "Wow, and what happened?"

"Nothing, they nabbed the homeboy when he stopped to smoke a joint in the woods, right over here at the turnoff."

Some stories aren't worth dressing up. They're better told dry. Dry like a hammer against wood. Mara Salvatrucha assassins tried to kill Miguel Ángel earlier this week, and Miguel Ángel—no big deal—just chatting away about the smell of goats.

"So I already know these *locos* are looking to off me. It's not the first time they've thrown shit my way. I know they're coming. And they're only coming to throw down."

Miguel Ángel is sure that the whole gang knows that the witness they call Yogui, who shows up in court to spill secrets with the voice of a mouse, is Miguel Ángel Tobar, the Kid, previously known as the Clown, from the Hollywood Locos Salvatrucha of Atiquizaya.

Death hovers all around him. To the Kid, the sicario was just another sicario—one of so many—who want to see him dead.

Death has always trailed the Kid. In his own mythological terms: you need to be strong and steady when you get a whiff of the goat. The scent of the Beast.

Detective Pineda supplies details of the arrest: "We received information that a strange man was prowling about the area. We sent out patrols. An officer finally spotted this man in the brush. It was late, getting dark, and he only saw him when the ass-hole's tattooed face popped up to take a hit of the joint he was smoking."

The sicario is known as the Crime. He's a gang member, about thirty years old, and the tattoos all over his face set him apart from a rank-and-file MS-13. When the police searched his bag they found an M-16 rifle, four rifle cartridges, and a 9mm pistol with eight cartridges. The careless sicario—as if he were carrying any old thing in his bag—stopped to get high before his kill. Later, he'd confess that two other sicarios were on backup, but that they must've split when they saw the cops. He said that the other two were war veterans. "Cobras," he called them. Former killers who found work doing what they knew best: killing. A lot of people in El Salvador had graduated in weaponry during the war, and when so-called peace came about, they couldn't forget their training.

Detective Pineda says that they're still trying to get more information out of the Crime, who is currently being held in police headquarters.

Back at the shack, Miguel Ángel keeps wandering through his memories, occasionally losing himself in a haze of marijuana. When he's really high, he takes long pauses as he talks, filling his sentences with onomatopoetic clatter: "I was walking with a rifle, and *crack*, I heard this noise," he says, posing as if holding a rifle in his arms. He freezes, eyes darting all around.

Today, however, it's hard for us to hear stories from this murderer without worrying about the murderer getting murdered.

"That's how it is, those dogs aren't going to rest until they have me counting stars," Miguel Ángel says. "That's all they're thinking about in prison."

The Smell of Pine

"Don't send sheep to hunt a wolf, because the wolf has claws and teeth, assholes, and they're sharp, so stop fucking around," The Hollywood Kid told the prisoners on the other end of the line. The call came in from a Salvadoran prison. It was early 2012, just after the Crime's arrest. It was the first time his homeboys had told him directly that they were after him.

The prisoners on the other end of the line were trying to get a word in, but the Kid wouldn't let them. To every threat he had a retort at the ready, as if he'd been waiting for this call his whole life.

"We know about you," the prisoners snarled, "and soon you'll be smelling pine trees."

They were referring to the wood of coffins, but Miguel Ángel knew more about coffins than they did. "Sons of bitches, they don't even make pine boxes here. They make them out of caro-caro or mango wood. You don't even know what kind of wood they use, and you don't even know what pine smells like. You all going to be smelling like smoke, because there's an M-16 waiting for you here motherfuckers."

Miguel Ángel was bluffing about the machine gun.

"*Bicho* ass-wipe! The Beast is gonna ..."

The Kid interrupted again: "The Beast don't control me! I control the Beast!"

Who knows if the Kid really believes he controls the Beast. Sometimes he says he does, and sometimes he says nobody controls the Beast. What's certain is that the Beast is stalking him. In 2010, long before the Crime's arrest, Detective Pineda received a confidential memo about a plan to attack the detectives and their protégé. Prison informants said the plan was to shoot up both the police station and the Kid's shack with an M-16.

At this point, there's something we should highlight: the gang knew that the Hollywood Kid was a traitor. Which means that the state failed to protect their informant's identity. And the gang knew where the Hollywood Kid was hiding. Which means that the state failed to appropriately hide him.

After the Kid dropped that line about controlling the Beast, all he could hear on the other end of the line was breathing.

"You already tried sending someone to take me out. That didn't get me shaking. There's thirty-five bullets waiting for you," he told them, reminding them again of his imaginary M-16.

The Kid didn't want to end his diatribe without making perfectly clear that he'd once served them well, that he'd been an exemplary messenger for the Beast, that he was who he was.

"If the barrio's got thorns," he told them, "I'm the barrio's thorn. If the barrio's been poisoned, I'm the barrio's poison. You sons of bitches. The hurt is waiting for you. If you want it, just try to fuck with me."

—◄—

What Miguel Ángel Says about the Beast:

- If The Beast takes you away, you'll know why.
- Those taken by the Beast are adored by the Beast, spoiled by the Beast.
- He's dead now, the Beast took him.
- The Beast's horns are made of gold.
- You die the death the Beast wants you to die.
- I saw the whole Beast, with all her seven horns.
- I could feel the Beast breathing down my back.
- The Beast's still in control here.
- They know I've got their back, that if anyone lays a finger on them, the Beast will come out.
- I've lost everything to the Beast.
- The Beast is following me, waiting for me to mess up.
- I turned and told him: It's for the Beast, you fucking son of a bitch, then *pop, pop*.
- He's part of her now, already part of the Beast.

The Shack

Miguel Ángel is nervous. He feels cornered. The Beast, once again, has her claws around his neck. After the Crime's failed attempt, there have been more, always with a new strategy. These gang members are from the Hollywood Locos, but they're not high-ups. Sometimes they're not even members, but aspiring members, who come like nineteenth-century bounty hunters seeking glory in exchange for trophies. If killing is a meritorious act in the MS-13, killing a traitor who has embarrassed none other than Chepe Furia will, in western El Salvador, be like cashing in on a Most Wanted flyer.

"Just the other day this guy came by who was just a baby. He came round here, the son of a bitch, all threatening, hanging with some woman. The next time I go to get tortillas I bump straight into him again. There he goes, walking with the same old hag. 'Oh yeah, homeboy, what's up?' I say to him. He's all, 'Easy, easy.' I whip out my grenade. 'Tell the homeboys I've got this waiting for them,' I said to that mountain monkey, and he just shit his pants, the asshole."

Today Miguel Ángel plays the loner with no friends. But there's also something fierce and furious about his gaze.

Miguel Ángel still has one foot inside the MS. A lifetime of being a hitman in the savage world of gangs left him with a lot of contacts. They've confirmed there's a pricetag on his head. The *mara* who kills him will gain a lot of respect. He'll be honored as some mythical, invincible son of the Beast. The hopeful upstart who successfully kills a traitor will be immediately received into the gang, skipping over an initiation process that requires four or five murders to earn the title of *homeboy*. Chepe Furia knows that the only true incentive for his lost boys is not money, but respect.

"Whoever kills me only has to score one goal. It'll be like winning the Balon d'Or," says Miguel Ángel, in a better mood now, landing soccer references.

The MS is after Miguel Ángel. Those who know him, because they want to avoid the long sentences in rotting prisons that his testimony will bring them. Those who don't know him, because they can't allow a traitor to go unpunished. But these aren't the only two groups who want to kill him. In the eyes of the Barrio 18, he's nothing but a piece of *mierda seca*. A killer of Eighteens.

Miguel Ángel tells us what happened to him a few months back, in November 2011.

El Refugio had exploded into celebration. Hundreds of people from the village and its environs had congregated on the main road that runs between Miguel Ángel's little plot of land and the police post. All the towns, hamlets and villages of Mesoamerica celebrate the day of their patron saint. Here, appropriately enough for Miguel Ángel, the patron saint is Our Lady of Refuge for Sinners, one of the most revered invocations of the Virgin Mary in the Catholic world.

But only the elderly and the occasional young believer care about such details. The rest of the town celebrates the blowout pagan style: with a lot of Cuatro Ases and hours of cumbia and reggaeton, along with marijuana and machetes. The mayor's office supplied the DJ, some large stackable speakers, a tower of metal tubes that spit out a swirl of flashing lights, and a fog machine that pumped multicolored steam through the constant clamor. A ramshackle, dusty version of the US Latino disco clubs of the 1980s.

El Refugio is controlled by Barrio 18. Although Miguel Ángel's street doesn't have a heavy gang presence—thanks to the nearby police post—the neighboring suburbs do. And everyone from the surrounding areas comes here for this party. It's the event of the year. Miguel Ángel knows it, the police know it, and Detective Pineda knows it. But, even so, they thought it was safer to keep Miguel Ángel here than to move him to an MS-controlled area.

On the feast day of Our Lady of Refuge for Sinners, the DJ made a blunder, one that almost cost him his life and spoiled the party for everyone: he played the wrong song. A song by the Colombian cumbia musician, Aniceto Molina, who made his career in El Salvador. His songs were smash hits there. Most of them were full of double entendres. The track the DJ played told the story of a Salvadoran hairdresser (*"un peluquero salvatrucha"*) who had a two-story salon with a sign out front that read "Services offered upstairs and downstairs." The problem was that Aniceto used an old word to refer to Salvadorans, one coined in the nineteenth century when Honduran and Salvadoran armies ousted the filibustering American adventurer William Walker (who'd sought to annex the isthmus to the Confederacy and enslave its people).

General Florencio Xatruch was charged with expelling Walker. And so, since 1855, in honor of the general, Hondurans have been known as Catrachos, and because of a consonance between the two nicknames, Salvadorans became known as Salvatruchas. The names were well liked in both countries until, more than a century later, Salvatrucha became associated with the MS.

The song that played in El Refugio that day was "The Salvatrucha Hairdresser." The refrain goes like this:

> We cut hair, upstairs and downstairs
> We braid hair, upstairs and downstairs
> We paint lips, upstairs and downstairs

When the song started, a group of Eighteens climbed onto the DJ's platform and forced him to turn off the music at knifepoint. For a few minutes everyone was silent. In their world, *salvatrucha* means only one thing. The heroism of General Xatruch was too far into the past to matter.

Miguel Ángel saw everything from his little shack and did nothing. He saw the Eighteens triumphantly jump off the DJ platform, almost right in front of his door.

"They say a piece of shit witness lives here, that he was a fucking madman," one of them said.

"I hope he comes out. I'm not scared of a shriveled little piece of shit," another Eighteen said, as another cumbia song started up. Miguel Ángel remembers the burn of rage he felt. He opened the door and thrust his grenade in their faces.

"And this turd doesn't scare you? Fucking monkeys!"

The boys ran off. Away from the cumbias, away from the party. Far from Miguel Ángel.

It didn't take long for the detective and his men to hear about what had happened. The town is small, the main road only a mile long. Everyone knows everything.

Miguel Ángel tells this story with pride. As if to convince us that he'll never be easy prey. At least not while he's got his grenade.

11

Mission Hollywood 2:
Killing Eighteens

The war between the MS-13 cliques of Atiquizaya and Ahuachapán and the Barrio 18 cliques of Chalchuapa and Santa Ana is the Salvadoran equivalent of the family feud between the Hatfields and the McCoys of West Virginia and Kentucky in the second half of the nineteenth century.

El Salvador is a very small country, spanning barely more than 8,000 square miles, and the boundary lines between the different departments are nebulous. Borders are demarcated by a conocaste tree, a curve in the road, an old piece of property or a historical marker. At least the Hatfields and the McCoys had a river to separate them. Here only the fear of the others keeps people on their side of the line. But the patriarchs of both gangs, the ringleaders of each clique, felt their people were unjustly cramped. They started to send their youth out to expand their territory, to try to drive out the other side, those who were actually just a mirror image of themselves.

Atiquizaya is about five miles from Chalchuapa. All that hatred stirred up by deported gang members, for years, was only five miles away. Not even half of a half-marathon separated these children of no one from each other.

Chepe Furia was an expert at starting new gangs. He had an eager group of hitmen, ready to prove themselves. The younger and weaker had succumbed, almost all of them at the hands of their own comrades in that purge called Mission Hollywood. Chepe Furia only needed the right tools to light up his vision of hell.

"Shit, we had a double-barrel .357, some bombs that had never been seen around here, a nine-millimeter with three clips, and a police-issued CZ, a real one," Miguel Ángel said from his shack, when the second part of Mission Hollywood was little but a distant memory of a few dozen murders.

Chepe Furia outfitted the Hollywood Locos Salvatrucha with a small arsenal for a bunch of kids who'd been used to rusted guns and machetes. The ex-national policeman went to Guatemala at times without telling his lost boys. He didn't have to explain himself to anyone in Atiquizaya. The arsenal was wondrous to those boys used to knifing and kicking their way to the top. A world of opportunity fanned out before them. Beyond the small-time pistols, Chepe Furia had a G3 automatic rifle. Equivalent, in historical value, to America's Remington shotgun. It's a heavy rifle with a lot of ammunition, able to fire 600 bullets a minute and dismember a person with only one. It was used by Salvadoran security forces in the '70s and continues to be a symbol of authoritarian power and cruelty.

Chepe Furia had a G3. A war rifle transplanted to a new war. He also had a 12-gauge shotgun, a .30-30 carbine, and plenty of ammo to feed them both.

Members of the Hollywood Locos Salvatrucha had the equipment to start the war, but above all they had the will to do it. The

Eighteens, led by Moncho Garrapata, knew this. They'd already lost plenty of members at the hands of Chepe Furia's young hitmen. One of them was the alleged sorcerer whom Miguel Ángel had decapitated in order to earn his gang name. Sooner or later it was going to be their turn to bleed.

Los Palmas were three members of the Barrio 18. Unusual for the area, the brothers lived with their dad, Óscar Palma. The older man was unable to quell the terrible anxiety he felt for his three boys who he knew were desperate to gain the respect of the Barrio 18. To prove their bravery, they'd murdered a member of Chepe Furia's clique. But in doing so they also acquired some powerful new enemies.

Chepe Furia was a skillful leader. He couldn't continue to watch from afar as his kids died out in the field. He had to show them by doing.

"Chepe ambushed the eldest Palma," Miguel Ángel said. "He smashed him on the head with the butt of a rifle."

The two remaining Palma boys, just like the McCoys, sought revenge. They ambushed the Killer Whale of Hollywood. They trapped him as he was crossing Barrio 18 territory on his way to buy crack. They knifed him across the neck and jaw and left him lying in a dirt road, bleeding out. But Killer Whale didn't die. In a sort of irreverent gesture toward death and in honor of the Beast, weeks later, Killer Whale got a tattoo over his scar. It read: Hollywood Locos Salvatrucha.

The Hollywood boys were ready for this challenge. They held a *mirin* and decided that the Palma family had to suffer.

The clique's strongest men were El Stranger, Two Faces, El Delinquent, Fly, Francis Tamarind, Víctor Maraca, Troublemaker, Lethal, Killer Whale, El Hollywood, and of course, the Clown.

They only had to decide which of them would carry out the revenge.

Killer Whale volunteered. He was eager to go further than a neck tattoo to prove his loyalty.

They stalked the second Palma boy and, just as he was opening his front door, Killer Whale shot him in the head with a 12-gauge shotgun. Chepe Furia watched from his pickup.

"He popped his coconut. Totally unrecognizable," remembered Miguel Ángel.

It's hard to stop a stampede of horses. Especially if something keeps chasing them. Hatred was spinning into a frenzy in this country. Death filled life with meaning.

The third Palma boy, mourning the loss of his brothers at the hands of the Hollywood Locos, decided to lie low. He stopped hanging out with the Eighteens, and kept close to his dad. But MS-13 was unstoppable. The last Palma brother also died at the hands of Chepe Furia and his foot soldiers, and the old man was left completely alone.

Fallen warriors from both camps. Funerals on one side, funerals on the other.

Víctor Maraca was walking down the street when he saw another one of Moncho Garrapata's underlings, another child of the Barrio 18, whom they called Matata. Víctor had nothing against murder. He'd killed before, and prior to joining the MS-13, when he was in another, smaller street gang, he'd committed assaults and hold-ups alongside his brother. With rusty .38 calibers, they'd robbed laborers on payday and delivery trucks on the road. But his murderous instincts and impulses were usually channeled into making money, rather than earning respect. Víctor Maraca let the Clown lead the mission.

"It was Víctor Maraca's idea," Miguel Ángel said, sitting outside his shack. "'Get ready,' Víctor told me, 'he's coming this way. He's just dropped off a load [of drugs] and he's strapped [with money].' *Bam*! On a bike. And it was just me on a street corner when the guy comes around. Money in his hand. And *bam*! The sucker comes up, *pop, pop, pop* ... And, see, he's from here to the cot [about two yards away], gave it to him right in the coconut, I even got splashed with his juice, and the son of a bitch, the money still in his hand, he was done for."

The Hollywood Locos wanted to wipe the area clean. Chalchuapa and Chalchuapita were both claimed by the Eighteens, Comanche territory for the MS, and they had to wipe them out of there. This was Mission Hollywood, killing under the name of their own gang. Chepe Furia was good at creating a sense of gravity. He infused meaning into their lives: hating and killing someone who, without even knowing you, hates and kills you.

At the height of Mission Hollywood, the Clown was sent to steal a taxi in Santa Ana, the closest and third wealthiest Salvadoran city. War needs a steady stream of resources. Santa Ana was important during the coffee craze, and even today it's one of the few department capitals that can be called, with an almost straight face, a genuine city.

Killing in hamlets and rural barrios such as Las Pozas, San Antonio or La Línea is relatively simple. There are few police and they have few resources. The landscape is rugged, covered with rocks and vicious, thorny underbrush. It's also sparsely populated, which means it's less likely that there'll be witnesses. And there's always a quick escape from the crime scene into the nearby hills or woods.

Santa Ana is different. There are street lights, a couple of malls, restaurants, paved roads, sidewalks, public telephones, a theater, a cathedral. It was, by the end of the 1990s, a small city, though with many desolate zones and, even then, multiple paths into the hillsides. Still, the city had a defined downtown. Practically a metropolis, less than a half-hour away from Las Pozas.

In Santa Ana—a sign of its urbanity—there were taxis.

"The idea was, we'd steal a taxi and kidnap the driver."

The Clown cased a taxi parking lot. A young man passed him and caught a glimpse of the crude tattoos the Clown had on his hand, though he wasn't close enough to read them. The Clown, though, was able to make out one of his tattoos: Eighteen, right across the neck. An enemy.

The man walked off. But as the Clown staked out the taxis, the same man, accompanied by two others, came back.

"Hey *bicho*, son of a bitch, lift up your shirt," the Clown ordered. The other responded in kind: "Lift your shirt, you *bicha*."

"So you want to see my papers? You'll be surprised if I lift my shirt, because I am what you are."

"You're numbered as well?"

"Nope," the Clown responded as he took out the 9mm they'd lent him for his special mission. *Pop. Pop.*

He put two shots into the first guy.

Pop. Pop.

And two shots into the second guy's back as he fled.

Pop. Pop.

The third got away.

"See, no, we're not the same," the Clown said scornfully to the Eighteen bleeding out on the pavement before him. He then got into the taxi he'd been stalking and, at gunpoint—with the extra determination of one who's just committed murder—told the driver to step on it. He'd hijacked a taxi and killed in the name of MS-13. The Clown was winning s. He was up for anything. In those days, he had only one thing to lose: his gang's respect.

But it wasn't all a victory dance for the Beast and the Clown. In the remaining months of their mission, members of the Hollywood Locos also died, as did members of the Parvis Locos, their sister clique. One of the boys who died at the hands of the Barrio 18 was the one who'd been with Miguel Ángel during the killing of the sorcerer, that first murder that initiated Miguel Ángel into the MS-13 and transformed him into the Clown. The boy had been called El Hollywood, an enviable name, eponymous with the entire clique. Now he was gone.

The MS-13 mourned its deaths. Hate united them, but so did grief. Sharing a mission sealed their pact. The boys mourned with a Salvadoran claw thrust into the air as their brothers' coffins were lowered into the ground. As the war progressed the gang members redoubled their loyalty, and their hate.

While the Salvadoran state looked the other way, a pact was sealed in the streets that later, countless deaths later, would become much more difficult to dissolve.

Killer Whale, having executed the second Palma brother, was arrested and convicted of homicide. The clique didn't only lose members by death, but by arrests and in the form of deserters who realized too late that the game wasn't really a game.

And the conflict boiled on. All of them wanted to keep climbing the ladder. Climbing it together. The war reached a climax when Chepe Furia's men started going after family members.

César Garrapata, Moncho's older brother and a Barrio 18 patriarch of Chalchuapa, left his house one day and, noticing something odd, quickened his pace. What he'd seen was the Clown signaling to El Stranger. César never reached his car. El Stranger and the Clown each emptied at least three clips into his body.

"And that's how the myth was born that gangs will empty at least three clips into a body. It's a way of saying: See, you sons of bitches, this is so you'll feel the Beast and learn that war is war," Miguel Ángel explained, years after unleashing that storm of bullets.

Before Moncho Garrapata had time to react to the attack, Chepe Furia himself went to look for him at his house.

"'Come out you asshole and let's kill each other off!' Chepe screamed. But Moncho, angry as hell and armed, wouldn't come out," Miguel Ángel described.

Chepe Furia decided to call off Mission Hollywood after Barrio 18 had been kicked back to Chalchuapa and Chalchuapita, far from the MS home turfs. Sure, Barrio 18 was still around, but, at least for the moment, they were more concerned with staying alive than organizing attacks. They weren't trying to expand anymore, and only wanted to stop losing territory. It was time to move on. It seemed to Chepe Furia that his ship was armed and packed with provisions, and his crew had proved itself to be loyal and worthy of the Beast. His crew no longer needed him. And wouldn't for a long time to come. Chepe Furia, without warning or explanation, disappeared without a trace.

March 2012. Miguel Ángel is a caged animal.

He's furious at the authorities. He's also scared, though he won't admit it. The basket of provisions from the National Victim and Witness Assistance Program hasn't come in a month. In any case, he complains, "Sometimes it comes without the goddam bags of rice or only with a little bit of oil."

He's been living in this dump for more than two years, and his desperation is palpable. Being a traitor seemed like a good idea in the heat of the moment. But now the situation has cooled and turned to shit. A life of misery, enclosure, constant boredom, and endless waiting. His whole existence dependent on others, never on himself.

Miguel Ángel thought it would be a speedy process. "One nail drives out another," he once said. That's how he thought it'd be, brisk, abrupt, hammer in hand: one nail goes in, another comes out. He rats on a few ex-homies and the detective and the prosecutors forgive his life of crime. But that's not how it works. The justice system of the most murderous country in the world operates on old machinery, rusted clunkers that are missing screws and in need of oil. Chepe Furia is still free thanks to some of those rusted or missing screws. Judge Salinas believed—or did he?—that Chepe Furia wouldn't jump bail. The corrupt police and many of the gang members have yet to be charged. And now there are new cases circulating in the court system, like the case of the well in the neighboring municipality of Turín, where Miguel Ángel claims to have dropped a body, in the company of other MS members. The slow and clumsy justice system is always behind. A person can spend two years in jail in El Salvador without a conviction, waiting to know his fate, while the machinery spins its rusting, clanking wheels. Two entire years in a jail overpopulated by 400 percent.

The detective won't allow Miguel Ángel to leave until he tells the judge all of King Furia's secrets.

For years Chepe Furia was the chain binding Miguel Ángel to the Mara Salvatrucha 13. Their fates were intertwined. The life of that one-time national police officer cast a shadow over the life of the son of the alcoholic *miquero* who regularly gave his daughter to a foreman. A campesino child had stepped into the backwash of the

United States. They say one beat of a butterfly's wings alters the world. But in this story, it's out of place to talk of butterflies. It's better to say that the eruption of the Beast left no one unscathed.

Miguel Ángel is so bored that he's started writing. He has a schoolboy's spiral notebook. The cover bears little multicolored numbers in front of a black backdrop, and the word 'Mathematics' written in red block letters. He awkwardly announces that he's started to write his life story, but when he opens the notebook and reads aloud, it's only disconnected phrases.

He reads with the fluency of a six-year-old.

"Wh ... whe ... when I ... got to kn ... know ... the ... mara ... it was be ... because ... of Chepe Furia, an ... old ... bas ... tard... from the ... north."

He reads a few more phrases about El Farmacia, about Gauchos 13. It's not a story so much as a series of catchphrases. Ever since he was a kid, El Farmacia "had the mind of a psychopath." Gauchos 13 were founded by deportees who had "nobody on their side."

Some phrases give you goosebumps. They're written in big, barely legible, shaky letters, and plagued by spelling errors. One line reads the Spanish equivalent of "The gang nows the vise of kiling or spiling blud ober the earth."

Miguel Ángel enthusiastically shows us his notebook and tries, despite the stumbles, to read with dramatic flair. He raises his gaze every few syllables to see if we're impressed. He says he'll go on writing until the whole story of 'The Kid and the MS-13' has been told. On the inside cover of the notebook, Miguel Ángel has drafted various ways of writing MS; some in gothic handwriting, others in block letters with dashes between each letter. There are also several 666s (the number of the Beast) scattered throughout, and a small drawing of what looks to be the head of a demon with several chins.

They're as badly drawn as the tattoos on Miguel Ángel's arm.

On his left forearm, you can just make out: *"Mi vida loca."* The d *in vida* is hardly legible. The *l* in *loca* looks like a *b*. If the phrase weren't so predictable, one would think the tattoo read *"Mi vida bola,"* my drunken life.

He puts his notebook away and asks to talk in a corner beside the shack, behind a dried-up tree. He wants to get as far as possible from the guard watching TV in the house next door.

"These sons of bitches are fucked. Last week a cop came by and offered me a thousand dollars to keep my mouth shut about the police who handed Rambito over to the gang. They want to break me, they want me to disappear," Miguel Ángel says, huddled on the ground, glancing nervously toward the guard.

Rambito, the vegetable seller from Atiquizaya who ended up tortured to death and left on the side of the road, is the key to Chepe Furia. Since the body appeared in November 2009, 120 miles from Atiquizaya, the public prosecutor's office has pushed for the trial to take place elsewhere, far from Judge Salinas and his strange inclination to grant bail to a man who always runs. It was two police officers who ordered Rambito's arrest and who took him from the subdelegation office without signing the log book. It was Miguel Ángel who'd seen Rambito pass by in a car with the two sergeants, Tejada and Hernández. It was Miguel Ángel who, hours later, saw Rambito get into a pickup with two colors of rope in his hand. It was Miguel Ángel who saw Chepe Furia, El Stranger, and Liro Jocker in the car. Miguel Ángel, the clique's star hitman, against Chepe Furia, the Brain. And two cops who allowed the events to unfold.

The starved and bony Miguel Ángel admits the offer was tempting. That he really considered it.

"I could've taken that thousand and gotten the hell outta here, to Guatemala. Disappeared. And none of these fucks would've ever heard about me again, and everyone would've gone free out here, cops would've had to arrest the Hollywoods in the streets, one by one."

But something didn't smell right to Miguel Ángel. The promise smelled rotten. He suspected the police had a trick up their sleeve. Because if he left with the money, they'd know. It'd be so easy for them to contact a gang member and blow his cover, tell them that the traitor who was putting the Hollywood Locos behind bars was now freely walking down the streets of Atiquizaya, or perhaps hiding among the rows of coffee trees.

Miguel Ángel, an ace at gaining time, at dodging the charging bull, didn't give a straight answer.

"I'll think about it. I'll let you know," he said to the sergeant.

12

The Hollywood Soldier

Mission Hollywood had left the Clown and his clique exhausted. The Eighteens of Chalchuapa knew how to shoot back, and many MS members died during the war. Both gangs' territory became more and more defined. Atiquizaya was mostly MS-13. Chalchuapa was mostly Barrio 18. That division continues today.

The police of Ahuachapán, backed by the local forces of El Refugio, Turín, Chalchuapa and Atiquizaya, launched an operation to capture gang members.

The Hollywood Locos Salvatrucha weren't only losing members to death, but also to jail.

By 2000, the gangs weren't yet plainly at the center of El Salvador's national security debate. Newspaper headlines mostly reported armed assaults and kidnappings of upper-class children.

El Salvador was violent. In 2000, it was, if we apply United Nations standards, epidemically violent. At the turn of the century this small country had a rate of 45.5 homicides for every 100,000 inhabitants. Pretty bad. And yet, the five-year period between

2000 and 2005 would be El Salvador's most peaceful period in the twenty-first century so far.

Peace in El Salvador is another country's extreme violence.

The police were hardly *investigating* the cliques, their leaders, or their members. They weren't even documenting any piecemeal investigations they were conducting. In 2008, Detective Pineda had to start from scratch because his colleagues hadn't kept any data. Instead, they'd gone out like hunters, looking for the easiest prey. The average age of a clique member was about eighteen, and many were already getting face tattoos. The police's plan was to scare everyone and hunt down whoever let their guard down. The cases they had against gang members were weak. Accusations of assault, homicide, attempted homicide, battery—all without much in the way of evidence or witnesses. Proof of the police's incapacity to properly deal with the gang problem lies in the fact that many of the most infamous gang members of the moment would land back in the streets just a few years later. Officers hoped they could stem the tide by decommissioning some of the young warriors for as long as possible, which wasn't very long.

X, the child gang member dazzled by the recent deportees who danced to Tavares in 1993, was successively detained in several jails around that time, just as Mission Hollywood was coming to an end. X was first locked up in July 1999, and not released until a decade later. Right around then the government decided to imprison members exclusively by affiliation, in secluded prison wings (or "gang universities"). This practice marked the rise of the national MS leadership behind bars.

If the bloody war between lost boys marked the gang's infancy, its young adulthood was marked by the imprisonment of homies and recent deportees.

X recalls that the gangs didn't yet control the jails in 2000. In fact, he himself would shake his cell bars begging to be let out of La Esperanza (better known as Mariona or Miami). X knew that La Raza ruled the prison, and that he was in the minority. The prison guards had to hit X's fingers with a club to get him inside his cell. X remembers one guard's parting words: "We lock you up at night so we won't have to find your body in the morning."

X was sent to cell 27, ward 2. He was greeted with a question and a slap with a machete. "And you, injun, what's up with you?" barked a member of La Raza before hitting him with the flat face of his machete. "Look what happens to troublemakers," and he lifted a sheet hung as a curtain.

"Two were giving it to El Spider de Apopa. One forcing Spider to suck him off and the other banging him from behind. Spider was eighteen years old," remembered X in June 2017, a grimace darkening his face in the small interview room of an immigration detention center in Texas. He was waiting for a judge to review his petition under the United Nations Convention against Torture. Given the blood he shed in El Salvador—and hounded as he was by the Salvadoran police—X isn't eligible for asylum, but he can try to avail himself of the convention. To do so, however, he must show that if he is repatriated there's a greater than 50 percent chance that he'll be tortured. If his judge only knew what El Salvador is like. If his judge only knew what it means to desert the MS-13. If his judge only knew the long history of the gangs. If his judge only knew that if X stepped one foot in El Salvador, the MS-13, the Barrio 18, and the police would know. And they'd all want to get a hold of him.

X says El Spider died of AIDS, years later. He remembers the prisons eliciting only two things in a gang member: anger and fear. The next morning X was attacked by a group of inmates and taken to a place within the prison known as El Pepeto. When they arrived, five Emes, of the Mexican prison gang, were lined up like children in trouble, surrounded by members of La Raza. They were being interrogated by an infamous prisoner known as Macarrón, right-hand man of Bruno, the Raza leader. X was lined up next to El Panther, El Fool, El Pirate, El Dragon, and El Shaggy, and then clubbed in the chest, the back of the legs, and the back. They ordered him to lift a dumbbell with powdered-milk cans, filled with cement, hanging off either side. The circle of men with machetes was closing in. X understood that if he bent down to lift the weights he'd be attacked, so he jumped up onto the tabletop and ran. The other five Emes followed, trying to escape La Raza's machetes. They reached the cell bars X had rattled in desperation the day before, begging the guards to let them out. Most of the guards only laughed. But one, named Carballo, opened the door and the Emes were able to escape what would have been yet another massacre in the Salvadoran prison system. The chase yielded two machete wounds, one on Pirate's hand and the other in X's abdomen, where he still bears a scar.

As has happened again and again throughout the history of these gangs, a space that was supposed to rehabilitate them, offer them an alternative, only pushed them into further violence. The gangsters jailed in Salvadoran prisons in the twenty-first century confronted the same questions as the migrants who'd reached California in the 1980s: What are you capable of doing to save your life? Can you fight? Are you willing to kill? Will you be the hunter or the hunted?

The six MS-13 gang members, still shaking with fear, were taken to the Island, the cell for targeted inmates. There were three other Emes there: Spuky de Viroleños, Cuchumbo de Novena, and El Diablito of Hollywood, who, currently, and at least since 2008, is the most celebrated MS member in El Salvador as well as the face of La Ranfla, the gang's national leadership, formed by incarcerated members in 2002. Through collective decision making, La Ranfla has established many of the general norms that Salvadoran gangs abide by. If we were to conduct a survey asking who is the leader of the MS-13, most people would answer El Diablito. He'd already done several stints in prison, having been repeatedly taken out of one and locked up in another to save his life. He was sentenced to thirty years for premeditated homicide in July 1998. And yet, despite being in prison, he would be tried a further six times for conspiracy, threats, illegal possession of war weapons, and homicide.

El Diablito, unlike Chepe Furia, joined the Hollywood Locos Salvatrucha after having only spent fifteen years on the streets of Los Angeles. In the early '90s a man named Sandoval jumped him in and gave him the gang name Diablón (Big Devil), though in the Salvadoran prisons where he'd remain until 2017 he was known as Viejo Bigotudo (Old Mustaches) or Sam Bigotes. Diablito, real name Borromeo Henríquez Solórzano, came back from the United States as a teenager. He was welcomed by a gang legend, Ozzy de Coronado. Following Ozzy's lead, he refused to recreate the Californian cliques in El Salvador, founding new ones instead: Harrison Locos, Sanzíbar Locos, Criminal Mafiosos, Big Crazys and Guanacos Criminal. That's to say, Diablito did not create Hollywood Locos in El Savador. It was Chepe Furia, despite having been a member of the Fulton in Los Angeles, who created Hollywood Locos.

This would have its consequences for Chepe Furia, but not until much later.

Back in 2000, X found Diablito in the isolation cell, scared, covered in bruises, and with a broken hand. El Diablito is now one of ten Salvadoran MS members on the US Treasury blacklist, but back then, alone and angry in his cell, he was part of a generation of gang members itching to enact their revenge against the "civilians." They'd arrived at a place where they were not victimizers but victims. And they didn't like that role. The gang members who were jailed in those years, like all who were arrested in the west after Mission Hollywood, would die, serve life sentences, or emerge from jail after having earned a ton of street cred.

Those in prison—around 8,000 people in 2000—were going to taste the gangs' wrath. The system, until then exclusively controlled by the civilian mafias, was about to get a makeover. The prison massacres would continue through the decade.

The Hollywood Locos who remained outside of prison were part of a clique that was drastically starved of members by 2000. Only five were left, including the Clown. Chepe Furia had disappeared once again, and the Clown was sure that their leader was hiding in Guatemala.

Only sixteen years old, the Clown had already come full circle. Born into war, recruited into the MS-13 by an ex-military officer, he decided it was now his time to hide. The Clown presented himself at a military barracks and asked to sign up.

Record no. 38 of the Transmission Support Command of the Armed Services of El Salvador states: "On the sixth day of September 2000, before the witnesses, Sergeant Sabino Flores Martínez and Deputy Sergeant Jorge Alberto Martínez Bonilla, Miguel Ángel Tobar, of Salvadoran nationality, son of Jorge García and Blanca Rosa Tobar, measuring 5 feet 2 inches, with previous employment as a day laborer, brown eyes, dark skin, and a scar on his left eyebrow, and without any legal documentation, enlisted under oath."

That day, he pledged to the flag of El Salvador after being read to from the Military Justice Code, warning of the impossibility of pardon in cases of desertion and other offenses or crimes. Below, between the signatures of the two military officers, are the poorly written letters, *M* and *A*, and two fingerprints attesting to the Clown's decision to join the army.

On the same page is the Clown's photo. His head is shaved and, though the image is in black and white, thanks to the style and the patches you can tell he's wearing the classic olive-green uniform. A son of war clad in war garb. The look on the Clown's face reminds us of Detective Pineda's theory about the gaze kids have before and after they kill for the first time. This isn't the gaze of a child. It's the gaze of a broken man. It's the impassive, severe, stony gaze of someone who's seen too much. Who has seen, and done, terrible things. At the time the photograph was taken, the Clown was already a seasoned murderer.

One word appears next to the Clown's face: deserter.

That word would weigh heavily on Miguel Ángel Tobar's life.

Miguel Ángel was born on January 4, 1984, according to the ID card he would acquire years after joining the military. When he presented himself at the barracks, he was barely sixteen. He had no military experience, but he did have four years of experience as a member of MS-13.

In those days you didn't have to take a polygraph test to rule out gang membership. State security forces didn't yet fear being infected by what was still a relatively obscure virus. The minister of defense in 2017, David Munguía Payés, acknowledges that "minors were often accepted in the military back then. People would bring in their misbehaved kids and beg us to take them off their hands, as a favor." And this despite laws banning recruits under eighteen.

The Clown received his military training at the Transmission Support Command in San Salvador. The Salvadoran state first trained the Clown in basic soldiering skills: marching, the use of military-grade weaponry, military regulations, and how to handle and maintain radio communications equipment. During his first three months in service, the Clown, funded by Salvadoran tax dollars, perfected his use of the M-16 rifle, the M-60 machine gun, and M-67 grenades.

And Miguel Ángel, who only thought of the military as a safe place to hide, started to scavenge. Every two weeks he'd take whatever M-16 ammo fit into the left pocket of his olive-green uniform. He'd trade the ammo with other cliques around the country for ammo that was useful to the MS, or he'd sell it off to criminals. Into his right pocket he'd sometimes slip an M-67 grenade, like the one that years later would keep his family safe at night. Once, after seeing how poorly the military warehouses were guarded, the Clown stole three grenades in one weekend. He

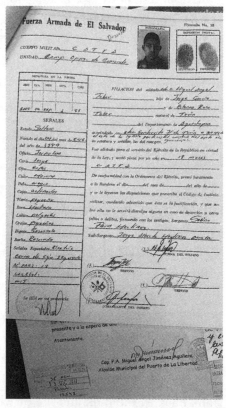

Miguel Ángel signed up for the army aged only sixteen, too young to enlist legally. Written to the left of the photo is the word "deserter."

was disappointed to find, once he got to Las Pozas, that he'd mistakenly taken three smoke grenades. More successfully, Miguel Ángel stole dozens of bullets that would later carry death throughout western El Salvador.

There's a major pipeline between military arsenals, gangs, and drug traffickers. Between 2010 and 2017, the public prosecutor's office prosecuted more than two dozen military personnel for stealing grenades, rifles, and machine guns. The M-60 machine guns, which can fire up to 550 bullets per minute, have been sold on an MS-13 clique for $3,000 each.

When the Clown went on leave, he was visited by the four members of the Hollywood Locos who'd been left stranded in El Refugio and Atiquizaya. Sometimes Ángeles Locos members came around, and, less often, members of the Parvis Locos. "So many fucked-up little *bichas*," the Clown would think to himself. The Hollywood Locos still had the G3 rifle that Chepe Furia had given them as a seed weapon, as well as a .357-caliber gun and some 12mm rifles. The Clown took care to keep track of all the weapons in his clique's possession. But, as time went on, the clique's cohesion eroded, and the new recruits no longer came to meet him. The Clown felt he was seeing the death of Chepe Furia's creation.

After receiving seventeen checks from the military and spending almost eighteen months as a grunt by day and a gang member by night, pledging to the flag while contributing to extra-official violence and crime, the Clown deserted. It was a military offense that could land him six months in prison. On February 28, 2002, the Clown stopped presenting himself at the military barracks and slunk back to the rank and file of what had always been his true regiment: the Mara Salvatrucha 13.

13

Chepe Furia's Fall

"Did you hear?"

Miguel Ángel is on his cell. It's 9 p.m. on March 10, 2012.

"I heard. The *bicha* is down," Miguel Ángel responds.

He says this while waiting for a police officer from El Refugio to give him more details, staying out of his little room, and keeping his eyes peeled on the barren stretch of his front yard. He has his grenade in hand, as well as a machete, and plans to stand guard all night. Lorena and Marbelly are sleeping.

"Shit's about to hit the fan. There's about to be a whole fuckload of murderers coming for the Kid," Miguel Ángel says. There's one more police officer standing guard, he says. Two now, instead of one, in charge of his protection.

"What do you think is going to happen?" we ask him.

"There's only two ways this can go. Either he gets the judge to let him off again, or all shit breaks loose in the court and the Kid has to come deal with it all. Because dropping the charge for Rambito's murder would be epic, even with all the connections the motherfucker has."

Today, José Antonio Terán has been captured for the second time.

He's Down

Chepe Furia's captures were never as spectacular as his escapes. Indeed, in terms of drama they fell flat.

On December 24, 2010, when they first captured him, it was a group of soldiers on their routine patrol through the neighborhood of San Antonio who happened to see him outside his storefront with his dad. The second time, two public security police officers just got lucky. Neither Detective Pineda's bloodhounds nor any specialized intelligence unit seemed able to locate him. Even though there was ample intelligence placing him exactly where he was captured, no search was ever conducted.

On March 10, 2012, exactly one year after Detective Pineda received the court order to recapture Chepe Furia, overruling Judge Salinas's baffling decision, a pair of police officers saw something strange. They were making their rounds when a man spotted them and then bolted. If the man hadn't run, the agents would later tell their unit, they wouldn't have noticed him. After all, he was just a nondescript guy with graying hair, a graying beard, and zero attributes pegging him as a gang member.

The police gave chase and stopped him before he was able to enter the house where he'd been staying. It was in Bella Santa Ana, a middle-class suburb less than thirty minutes from Atiquizaya.

The man, looking momentarily confused, said it was just a misunderstanding, he was only in a hurry. He spoke in a friendly manner, with a smile on his face. The police searched his wallet for identification. That's when they discovered that they were holding

Chepe Furia, nervous, dazed, but smiling. The most wanted man in western El Salvador.

The officers handcuffed him and called for backup. Having captured him flagrantly avoiding arrest, they had the right to search the house as well. Inside they found a 30-30 carbine with seventeen cartridges, two 12-caliber rifles and ammunition for a .25 pistol.

The house wasn't in his name, or in the name of any gang member or known associate. It was under the name of a businessman who owned a floating restaurant on Lake Coatepeque, a two-story barge with elegant tables and waiters who dish out shrimp cocktails, barbecued meat, and beer.

Chepe Furia was taken to a windowless cell in the Santa Ana police post.

When he found out about the arrest, the chief of police of all of western El Salvador, Douglas Omar García Funes, visited his cell. He wanted to meet the mythic boss in person.

"It's incredible how smart he is," García Funes would say, months later. "When you hear him talk, he almost convinces you he's just a businessman. He's polite and courteous. He draws you out. He told me we were colleagues, reminding me that he'd been an officer in the national police force."

Chepe Furia was sent to San Francisco Gotera Prison, in the department of Morazán, on the opposite side of the country. An officer from the Central Investigative Division assigned to prisons told us, anonymously, that Chepe Furia was being brutalized by the leader of that prison, Walter Antonio Carrillo, a forty-year-old known as El Chory (El Shorty) of the Fulton Locos Salvatrucha. According to the public prosecutor's office, El Chory's connections reach as far as Maryland, where he's also coordinated criminal activities. El Chory was a national gang leader, and one of the most powerful men in western El Salvador. His clique boasted more than forty members, carried automatic rifles, and maintained relationships with drug trafficking organizations dealing their product into Guatemala through what is known as "The Little Path," a well-trodden shortcut for traffickers who want to avoid moving through Honduras. The most important area for the Fulton Locos was Nueva Concepción, a municipality some fifteen miles from Atiquizaya.

Detective Pineda defined Chepe Furia's new situation like this: "Apparently, every time Chory sees him he beats the shit out of him."

Pineda and two of his investigative officers affirmed that the gang's problem with Chepe Furia was that he'd led the Hollywood Locos as if they were just a bunch of hitmen. "He didn't report any earnings to the gang, let alone to the greater network of western cliques," said an agent of the Center of Investigative Policing. "It was a bitch going after him while he was on the streets, because Atiquizaya and all its surrounding areas were his turf, but everything changed once he was in jail," an official of the police's Elite Division against Organized Crime told us.

But Chepe Furia had a hope of escaping this new situation when Judge Salinas, once again, tried to release the man who'd already slipped from the authorities twice. On August 20, 2012, four months after his recapture in Bella Santa Ana, Judge Salinas ruled that there wasn't enough evidence to prove that Chepe Furia was a leader of the Mara Salvatrucha, and acquitted him of all conspiracy charges.

And yet, this time, the judge's suspect decision did not lead to Chepe Furia's release. Detective Pineda had convinced the specialized prosecutor's office to investigate Rambito's case. After all, the facts of the murder of Rambito—who was a police informant—incriminated two police investigators. The public prosecutor's organized crime unit took up the case and charged Chepe Furia, El Stranger, and Liro Jocker with Rambito's murder. But because the body had been found 118 miles from Atiquizaya, the charges were filed on the other side of the country, in the Specialized Court on Organized Crime of San Miguel.

But that's not all. Judge Salinas's ruling seemed so bizarre that the Specialized Court on Organized Crime reversed it yet again. And this time emphatically. The court reminded Salinas that, according to the witness at the heart of the case, Miguel Ángel Tobar, Chepe Furia "distributes weapons, is the brains of the organization, has many ties to the police, [and] constantly travels to Guatemala to make more contacts for weapons and drugs." The court also reminded Salinas that the witness "had been part of that organization, which implies that he has first-hand knowledge of the events [about which he's testifying]." The court ordered Judge Salinas to rescind his ruling in favor of Chepe Furia.

Chepe Furia remained in prison, facing charges of conspiracy and aggravated homicide.

Miguel Ángel Tobar's role became more important than ever.

In 1917, in the heart of western El Salvador, Ernesto Interiano, the Legend, was born. As with all good Salvadorans, we know a lot about his mother, but about his father we only have street-corner gossip. Some stories make him a Guatemalan pharmacist, others, a military man. No one knows for sure. When Milagro Interiano, Ernesto's mother, could no longer hide her growing belly from the needling eyes of the small, bourgeois plantation elite of Santa Ana, her father decided to lock her up in the back of his mansion, among the servants and stable boys.

And so the young Milagro lived out the rest of her pregnancy, like a princess in a medieval story: cast out like a family ghost to the darkest depths of that great house. That's where she gave birth to her son, her only son. Ernesto Interiano was held in the callused, arthritic hands of the servants and celebrated with shots of guaro.

And there he grew up, until his grandfather, finally moved to compassion, let them both move into the main quarters of the house, returning to the arms of the Interiano family. Due to the years of punishment, however, the family's honor had dwindled.

Back in the house, Milagro was able, once again, to wear French fashions and eat dainty food at mahogany and cedar tables. But Ernesto couldn't let go of what he'd seen and absorbed in the servants' quarters. His whole life he was drawn to pungent language, to streets and brothels. As a teenager, he'd hand out meals to the panhandlers and widows in the central plaza. They say his first words were taught to him by his indigenous nana, Teresa Pushagua. Nahuatl words. Forbidden words in those years.

Beggars Loved Me *was the title of a biography of Ernesto by Carlos Consalvi.*

From early youth, Ernesto was always in trouble with the law. The National Guard poisoned his dog, Satanás, which affected him for life. Days later, he gathered the bodies of dead dogs and laid them in front of the National Guard's offices, shouting: "Let's see if the dogs will eat dogs!"

He'd have problems one day and worse problems the next. They accused him of many crimes. He made enemies of those he defeated. He was a good shot with a pistol. But his last skirmish was against an enemy that was too big for him.

In 1943 Ernesto was driving when he cut off his longtime enemy, Samuel Álvarez, a scion of one of the most powerful and moneyed families of El Salvador. Riding with Álvarez were two personal guards of the coup dictator Maximiliano Hernández Martínez, who'd ordered the extermination of El Salvador's indigenous people in 1932.

A shootout. Ernesto killed one of the guards and fled into the mountains. The government turned him into a Salvadoran John Dillinger, designating him "public enemy number one."

In several standoffs in the coffee plantations of Santa Ana, he outsmarted the National Guard. Before going into hiding he picked up his two great loves: his mistress, Clara Tobar (unrelated to Miguel Ángel), and his daughter, Miriam Interiano. With his woman beside him and his little girl in his arms, he vanished among the coffee trees on the outskirts of Atiquizaya.

Despite all the checkpoints and raids, they could not capture him. The dictator turned to the same hunter he'd used to exterminate indigenous people in 1932: General Calderón, his attack dog. The general was able to find Interiano's weak spot. It was his mother. His solitary and remorseful mother. General Calderón surrounded Milagro's house and didn't let any food or supplies in. If Ernesto didn't appear, his mother would starve to death.

But Ernesto did show up one night, proud as he was, with his leather boots and his revolver on his hip—or so the legend goes. He wanted to jump the fence around his house to get to a dark alleyway, but a bullet from Félix González, El Salvador's Olympic shooting champion, reached him first. Félix had been hired specifically to kill the infamous bandit. Ernesto, mortally wounded, managed to kill his assassin, leaving the Olympic team without their best marksman, and the police officers and national guards who were there desperately trying to shield themselves from Ernesto's wrath before he died.

Ernesto's body was shot to shreds by the dictator's guards. His face alone bore sixteen bullet wounds. Before the burial, his mother and her faithful servants plugged the holes in his body with rose petals and cedar chips.

The dictator had won. The panhandlers wept. Military order was imposed in the Salvadoran West. But the state hadn't been counting on the dozens of beggars, thieves, prostitutes, and market vendors who flocked to clean up Ernesto's blood with their rags, make altars, invoke him in séances, light candles in the middle of the night and ask him for favors in exchange for offerings of drinks and bullets.

In western El Salvador, not even spirituality is detached from the lore of shootings and bandits. This region had been watered in blood, and so it blossomed.

Ernesto's daughter, Miriam Interiano, the child who'd fled with him, grew up to be a hippie. She turned into a symbol of youthful rebellion, capturing the heart of the most ruthless army officer of the 1970s, General José Alberto "Chele" Medrano—credited with founding the fearsome paramilitary group, ORDEN. After meeting the daughter of Ernesto Interiano, El Chele Medrano left the military and dedicated himself to the bohemian lifestyle. When he was murdered by guerrilla forces in front of his own house, he was raving in the throes of a drug-induced hallucination.

It seemed Ernesto's spilled blood had cursed the great Salvadoran army and marked the beginning of a tradition that still lives on in our nation's spirituality.

Today, people still light candles in the middle of stormy nights, invoking and asking impossible favors of the most beloved bandit of the Salvadoran West, Ernesto Interiano.

One day in May 2012, Miguel Ángel asks us: "Do you know what it means to see a black he-goat at midnight?"

"It's Satan. It can't be anything but Satan. It's the Devil. And there's something he wants," Miguel Ángel says confidently, pacing and rolling another joint. He's shirtless. He looks vigorous and strong, despite protruding ribs and some white blotches on his chest, a sign of malnutrition.

Miguel Ángel has delegated ears all over the region. His spies are men who admire the gangster lifestyle and see him as a special figure within the MS world, a heroic traitor, a man who rebelled against the Beast and yet, somehow, has managed to stay alive.

One of those ears is El Topo, a former member of the infamous clique of Victorias Locos Salvatrucha, whose turf is only a few miles from El Refugio. He's not the brightest bulb. He lacks Miguel Ángel's uncultivated mental agility. El Topo speaks slowly and rarely. His years in the gang never erased his campesino ingenuousness. He's around thirty years old, dark-skinned, taller than Miguel Ángel, with a Gothic-style "MS" tattooed on his arm. He retired twelve years ago. The gang seemed to have tolerated his departure, and he claims he hasn't participated in any recent missions; but there are rumors among the police that he's become the object of a green light, the gang's irrevocable death penalty. Because he's a coward, who sought a quiet life for himself.

El Topo often stops by Miguel Ángel's shack. They smoke dope, eat tortillas, and talk about the Beast, about how she's always chasing them. El Topo's visits leave Miguel Ángel haunted by esoteric gang culture: demonic goats, devils, fog, omens. He doesn't like these visits, but he doesn't care enough to stop them. At most, he throws El Topo a couple of contemptuous looks. What would be a scandal in the United States—an ex-gang member visiting a protected witness who's putting MS-13 leaders behind bars—is unremarkable in El Salvador.

Every year, the National Victim and Witness Assistance Program (UTE, for its Spanish acronym) deals with about a thousand people who've been given some type of state protection: "white" witnesses, who saw a crime take place but were not involved; typically angry witnesses who've decided to testify in the most homicidal country in the world; and traitors, like Miguel Ángel. This last category is the minority, and accounts for around fifty cases a year, but these witnesses are the most useful to the public prosecutor's office. These witnesses didn't just see a crime, don't only know how it was planned, but also know about the perpetrators who didn't themselves pull the trigger. The witnesses participated in most of the crimes concerned. The relationship the authorities have with these confessed criminals, as we've seen in our visits to Miguel Ángel's shack, tends to be arm's length, to say the least. A monthly basket of supplies and little more.

"Sometimes I have to hassle the visiting doctors to donate a little milk," Mauricio Rodríguez, the UTE director, told us in June 2013 when we asked him about their budget. According to him, they once received training from a member of the United States Marshals Service, in charge of the US protected witness program. The marshal explained that the US program included moving a witness and his family to another state and funding at least a year's training in a new trade, as well as board and lodging, a monthly stipend, and a full change of identity. Rodríguez imagined having those resources and smiled. In El Salvador, by law, the UTE can't give money or change anyone's identity, and only in very rare instances can they continue to offer protection after the court process is over. In most cases, once the court process has stopped, so has the protection, and so has the meager basket of provisions. "Off to the streets to eat shit, to survive any way you can," summarizes Detective Pineda in his no-bullshit manner.

Dozens of still active plea-bargain witnesses have been executed in El Salvador due to the pathetically inadequate safety measures.

An example. In May 2016, we asked the judge in charge of specialized sentences to remember how many cases he'd had to shelve because the protected witness had disappeared. The court he presides over is high-risk, specializing in organized crime, and is located in the main tribunal of El Salvador, Isidro Menéndez. It's the mecca of Salvadoran justice, where the most complex cases go, and is protected by elite units attached to the police and public prosecutor's office. The mecca of Salvadoran injustice, someone with a flair for sarcasm might say. After three days the judge came up with seven case files, including twelve protected witnesses who had disappeared over the last five years. The vagueness with which the disappearances were recorded speaks volumes about the lack of care for those who are promised protection in exchange for betrayal: "impossible to locate," "unable to locate witnesses," "no one able to give information on their whereabouts," "not located," "his whereabouts are unknown," "dead," "did not show up," "location never found."

Many rejoice in the fact that Viejo Lin, a national leader of the Barrio 18 Sureños, is behind bars, but few remember Luis Miguel, the witness who gave him away. For many Salvadorans it's a relief that El Chino Tres Colas, another Barrio 18 leader, is locked up, but few know about Zeus, Apollo, Orion, Aries, and Neptune. The trial against the thirteen gang members known as the Packagers, accused of twenty-two homicides in Sonsonate, made national news when gory details leaked out about how they would pack dismembered victims into black bags. But no one ever thanked

Raúl; nor did anyone thank Zafiro and Topazio for resolving the massacre of Las Pilitas; or Daniel, for explaining how the gang of Los Sicarios, with a high police membership, operated in western El Salvador. Who knows how many lives have been saved thanks to the incarceration of most of the Hollywood Locos Salvatrucha, but almost no one, apart from Detective Pineda, worries about the safety of Yogui, Miguel Ángel Tobar. Plea-bargain witnesses live in the dust. They're used as a trial progresses and are then discarded, resigned to a miserable confinement among the police, many of whom hate them.

"Just hearing them talk gives me diarrhea. Those fuckers. I'm not going to look after a bunch of hobos," a police detective in charge of obtaining confessions from plea-bargain witnesses told us in 2013.

Miguel Ángel explains how what the detective had foreseen ended up coming true. A few days earlier, El Topo paid Miguel Ángel another visit. He had a shifty look on his face and refused to make eye contact with Miguel Ángel.

Miguel Ángel boasts of his familiarity with the world of the occult. He says he knows something about witchcraft, and that he once saw the "Black Book," a legendary book in this town, and supposedly the antithesis to the Bible. A mix of indigenous traditions with Catholic culture is common in these parts. Some people invoke the spirits of old bandits, or famous witches of the past, asking them favors in exchange for an offering. These same people go to mass and consider themselves fervent Catholics. But Miguel Ángel dispenses with the Catholic side of the syncretic mix.

"Hey, Topo, I see you have something splitting your soul, something eating at you. Come on, I'm gonna give you a candle test," said Miguel Ángel to the crestfallen gang member.

He led him into his room, lit several candles, and said a few words while looking fixedly into El Topo's eyes.

"The candles don't lie, Topo. You have something going on with me. Speak," Miguel Ángel told him.

El Topo confessed that the Beast had told him to spill his blood. He said that El Mafioso, an MS member of the Pride Gangster Locos Salvatruchos, one of the few MS cliques left in Chalchuapa, had given him the order.

Miguel Ángel didn't attack El Topo. He merely told him to be careful. He declared that he could see these things before they happened; he could anticipate them. His advice to El Topo was, keep talking to the MS and tell them everything. In just a few words, he deftly carried out a classic counterespionage tactic.

The gang had failed again.

When Miguel Ángel Tobar has to put on a show, he proves himself to be an astute, ingenious, and determined man. An expert con, a tamer of beasts—capable of getting the truth he needs to survive, of walking seasoned assassins to their deaths. Walking men to their deaths is something that marked the arc of his life. It's how he betrayed his gang to avenge his brother. And how he landed in his own private prison, in what would be his last home.

14

Here Lies the Hollywood Kid

March 2004. The hottest month of the year. Two more months and the rains will start. With them come mosquitoes spreading disease: chikungunya, dengue, zika. But in March there's only heat. It's a crushing, humid heat, like a hellish burst of hot steam.

The Clown was twenty years old and an important member of a clique that hadn't only grown, it had also cozied up to a lot of other cliques in western El Salvador. In those days, MS-13 cliques were working through a very difficult problem.

One of the Hollywood Locos had been murdered. Cirilo, a long-time member from the lost boys generation, had been shot dead. Along with a fellow MS, named El Horse, Cirilo had been sent to kill an Eighteen from Chalchuapita. But only El Horse came back from that mission, unscathed. He said they'd killed an Eighteen, a *chavala*, and, without a word about Cirilo, El Horse walked away. A body turned up in Chalchuapita. Days later, MS members found out it was Cirilo.

The leaders of the various cliques came together to confer.

Others from western cliques reported they'd lost members in a similar way, always shortly after being seen with El Horse. Luckily, especially for the young rural gang members, taming El Horse isn't too hard. The MS-13 intelligence apparatus feeds off gossip. They started asking around. They put eyes on El Horse, kept their ears pricked.

That's how they found out that a hitman was hiding among them, a player on both teams, who killed on one side as much as he killed on the other.

This man had crossed a dangerous line. It wasn't double agent work, but something closer to madness. He had MS tattooed on his chest and 18 tattooed on his thighs. As if he'd been split in half by opposing forces. This sort of double-dealing had been unthinkable in those first years of the Salvadoran gangs. El Horse had warred from both sides of the battlefield. When all the face tattoos looked like little more than decorations, and gang life itself looked like a violent children's game, one player had wanted double the decorations and to take two turns in the game.

El Horse had killed Eighteens. He'd killed MS. Everything pointed to this truth. But truth wasn't even important. The two competing tattoos, at that point, were all that mattered. The decision had been made. The Clown didn't know how the gang had found out about the tattoos, but he didn't care. He was a faithful soldier. The Beast had emitted its orders, and the Clown was ready to obey.

We'll never know if El Horse was scared out of his mind or simply insane. It's unclear how he started this dark game in which he bled for two families at once, for two Beasts. All we know is how it ended.

The young Clown of the Hollywood Locos, Chepe Furia's star pupil, was in charge of the job. At twenty years old, he'd honed his skills and tricks. Mission Hollywood had taught him a lot. The clique trusted him to kill. To the Clown, this was an honorable mission. The honor of his homies was in his hands.

But the brief wasn't simple, either. His victim was a seasoned killer. And everyone was watching. This time, he had to show off more than his knack for violence. He had to show off his smarts.

The Clown began slowly—gaining El Horse's trust. He'd have him over to his house. There, the Clown had a small bakery, a modest outfit, something to distract the authorities from the stench of the gangs, something to get him a bit of spare change. He offered El Horse fresh bread, marijuana and Cuatro Ases. Hours passed, the two of them alone, talking in the midst of the weed smoke and cloying heat.

El Horse's strategy to dispel the homeboys' suspicions was to sign up for every single mission, and never decline a hit. Killing had become a vice with him, and that vice would be his downfall.

"Look," the Clown said, "we have information on where two bastard *chavalas* will be later today, El Viejo and Raddish."

It was a clever lie. The Clown knew El Horse was friendly with those two gangsters. Once before, MS-13 had sent El Horse to kill Raddish, but he'd failed and had left Raddish with barely a few scratches. The Hollywood Locos were upset about El Horse's mistake. And they were furious when they realized it wasn't a mistake. The Clown didn't just have orders to kill, but to teach a lesson, to create a precedent.

El Horse accepted the mission to finish off what he'd started with Raddish. The Clown gave him a .38. and told him that members of the Parvis Locos would join in on the hit, bringing the ammo. They walked together toward Atiquizaya in silence. And then the Clown turned a corner.

"The *chavalas* will be coming this way," the Clown said.

El Horse looked nervous.

"Tsk, tsk," said the Clown.

They saw more than five members of the Parvis Locos, the sister clique of the Hollywood Locos from Park View, Los Angeles. All bearing machetes.

"Gimme the cannon, it's got no bullets," the Clown said to El Horse. El Horse checked, a last desperate hope, and then obeyed.

The ritual began.

They took hold of El Horse, calmly at first, like a priest about to offer communion. El Horse didn't resist. They taped over his mouth and made him kneel on the fertile Salvadoran ground, ground that had already absorbed so much blood.

First, the Clown cut off his ears, spraying El Horse's face in blood.

"Today you'll tell us how many homeboys you've hit, you son of a bitch," the Clown said, committed to his ceremonial role.

They put tourniquets on El Horse's arms and legs. It's amazing what young gang members know about human anatomy when it comes to torture.

They hacked off his arms.

They hacked off his legs.

It's called the vest cut.

But the Beast wanted more.

"Come on, homeboy, give it to me in the head," begged what was left of El Horse, the tape having been removed for the next step.

"Who said we're your homeboys? You're going to die like the Beast says."

They cut out his tongue.

They gouged out his eyes.

The piece of meat that was once El Horse swung in and out of consciousness. The former sicario was writhing but could no longer beg for mercy.

The Clown was deep in it, invoking the Beast. He had one body in front of him, but thousands of possibilities. Blades slipped in, organs came out. What the first *maras*, the stoners, did with dead bodies exhumed in Californian cemeteries, the Clown did with the living body of a traitor.

The rest of the sicarios had taken a few steps back and now watched in silence. It was only the Clown hacking into a chunk of flesh. Some of the Parvis Locos left: this went beyond killing. Some stayed to watch the final act.

The spoiled remains of El Horse awoke, or so it seemed. With no eyes, he could no longer see. With no tongue, he could no longer speak. But he snored, a throaty whistle, a choppy groan. Life is strong and stubborn, and resists being stamped out.

The Clown slowly slid in his machete, carefully feeling the heart beating through the blade. He slid it further in. A clean cut above the abdomen. He pulled out the machete and slipped in his hand. His fingers curled over the weak, fragile heart.

"That's how they're born and that's how they die. I gave him an operation, like bringing a child out of a womb. So from now on I'm no longer the Clown, this is where the Hollywood Kid is born," exclaimed the Kid, staring at the heart in his fist.

From that day until his death, Miguel Ángel Tobar would be known as the Hollywood Kid.

15

Blood in the Turín Well

In his book *Sapiens: A Brief History of Humankind*, Yuval Harari explores what defines us as a species. Our clearest advantage over other early hominids, he argues, was our ability to create fictional figures, to invent lies and believe them collectively. A group, for example, is a fictional entity. It has nothing to do with its members—these can always change—or with a place, which can always be destroyed. Harari claims that our success as a species was rooted in our ability to generate ideas, complex ideas that gave rise to states, religions, warfare. This is how we came to rule the world. This is the advantage that allowed our ancestors to survive the blows of history. Ideas of this kind allow an individual to align himself with a cause and, therefore, with other people he doesn't know and will never meet.

Neither the Mara nor the Beast actually exist, of course. They are complex ideas that encourage some people to harm other people. They are creations. History is plagued with such creations. Pushing individuals to attack each other mindlessly, motivated by a belief in something that simply does not exist, that has no material nature. They attack, and they attack in very disturbing ways.

Miguel Ángel is one of those rare individuals who does reflect, who bravely asks himself why, why, why? Or at least he's asking himself questions now, now that he's confined to this shack. And, in mid 2012, he has ample time to think. He's been locked up here for close to three years. Miguel Ángel sits outside smoking pot at night, studying the stars and the darkness, sometimes crouched like a cat atop the outer fence surrounding his shack, feeling a fresh breeze that smells of burning sugarcane. Inside the tiny hut sleep his wife and little girl. Miguel Ángel reflects, he asks himself why, as he looks up at the stars. Why so many had to die by his hand. He hardly knew any of them. Not enough to truly hate them. He wonders whether what he did to El Horse was justified, why he shot an unknown taxi driver in the head, why he shot that prostitute in Atiquizaya. His mind takes off and ties itself in knots. He smokes. He knows that that fictional construct, the MS-13, now seeks to kill him, and, despite being merely an idea, its impact on reality, its ability to murder and torture, is all too real.

"The Barrio has a thorn in its foot, and I'm the thorn," he once said to gang members who were threatening him from Ciudad Barrios prison.

Without having read Harari, Miguel Ángel knows he's as much the owner of that fictional idea as the hitmen who threaten him. And that's why he sometimes convinces himself that, despite everything, he's still a member of the MS-13 and eternal enemy of the "*diecihoyo*" (a portmanteau that turns "eighteen" into "eight-hole" to avoid naming them explicitly).

The questions, after thinking around and around the dizzying circles of his life, sometimes turn into answers and offer some explanatory key: the Beast, the Mara, the frantic war with Barrio 18. "The fuckers," as he calls them, "the eightshits, the faggots, the eightholes."

"The neighborhood's fate," he says, with the conviction of a Tibetan monk who, after much meditation, has found the path to Truth, "is a bitch. The Mara was the beginning, we brought with us the name of the Devil, Satan, all of us marked by the MS-13 are marked by the Devil. We're souls delivering over other souls, all of us tangled up in the same knot." Pursuing the eightholes is an end without end. That's gang warfare. It'll never end.

He expounds all this in the certainty that he's understood his life and that he can explain it clearly. He speaks with open eyes, head tilted up toward the sky, gaze lowered to the ground. His sentences are halting, filled with dramatic pauses. He utters them as one would utter a sacred truth.

Stripped of their dark mysticism, the conclusions he reaches reveal a cycle, the cycle of violence, something that will never end because it has no way out. It's taken decades for academics studying gang violence to understand this. Miguel Ángel the assassin, however, understands it intimately.

It's winter 2004 (Central American winter is approximately May until September). In other words, it's raining. After a long string of hellishly hot days, it's finally raining. The Hollywood Kid moves through his world as an aimless gang member. His clique grew after both phases of Mission Hollywood. In the first phase, they eliminated those they saw as lukewarm and cowardly, kids who didn't want to get on the MS-13 bandwagon of death. In the second phase, they stormed the strongholds of Moncho Garrapata in the center of Chalchuapa, Chalchuapita, and Periquera. This phase caught the attention of the police.

In response, the police launched Operation Hollywood. The idea was to rein in a burgeoning clique that was moving beyond small skirmishes and the occasional murder. The operation captured some of the clique's heavyweights. One of them was Guillermo Solito Escobar, once part of the Meli Meli 33. His gang name was El Stranger, and he was Chepe Furia's right-hand man. For all practical purposes, he was the leader of the Hollywood Locos Salvatrucha of Atiquizaya whenever Chepe Furia was away. Dozens of others were also captured in the police sweep.

The Kid pushed those who remained into the Beast's line of vision. He brought back the rule of law. To the police, it was more important to stop the MS-13 than Barrio 18. Their boys were more bloodthirsty. Their leader knew how to stir them up. There were also more of them. And, after so many police operations and arrests, the clique's control had finally been diluted. The ex-soldier and ex-Clown, Miguel Ángel Tobar, had become the Hollywood Kid, and the laxness he saw astonished him.

An Eighteen from Chalchuapa, for example, a warrior during the last war, came, on horseback, to buy his pot in Atiquizaya.

"Thinks he's so cool," thought the Kid, indignant, hardly believing his eyes.

He summoned the other youngsters, and together they waited for the rider to pass them. When the Eighteen appeared, the Kid shot him. He fell off his horse and the boys swarmed him, hacking with the machetes the Kid had bought them to win their support. Little by little, the rules reestablished themselves. This was MS-13 turf. That over there was Barrio 18 turf. Whoever trespassed on enemy territory had to abide by the rules of the game: kill or be killed. The lost boys had a new mentor.

Unlike the other cliques, members of the Parvis Locos of Ahuachapán had remained strong even after the Barrio 18 and police strikes, but they were still a clique of inexperienced boys, most of them recently jumped in. This was no longer the booming heyday. The Kid, by far, the most experienced killer in the area, would do with these boys what Chepe Furia did with him and the generation of lost boys in the early 1990s.

More cycles in the life of the Kid.

His years in the MS-13 taught him that all pacts with the Beast are made with blood.

Anthropologist Arnold van Gennep, as we've seen, explained how rituals allow people to transition from one state of social being to another. And yet, rituals also serve to strengthen sociocultural values and prevent undesirable behaviors. Through symbolically meaningful participation, people forge the arc of their lives. These actions are also channels of communication.

In the world of Salvadoran gangs, death is a form of group communication. The gangs leave messages, complex messages, when they kill. A lightning mission that leaves a body riddled with holes says something. It's like when a boy kicks a ball over to another boy. He's saying: Want to play? If a head is left in a public plaza, the message is for the state—and it also communicates certain ideas to the public at large. If the eyes are gouged out and the tongue and ears cut off, the gang is saying: ver, oír, y callar, see, hear, and keep quiet. If they go at an enemy body for hours, penetrating its anus with knives and bats, and then leave the remains in enemy territory, the message is directed at the enemy: We're winning. A symbol of humiliation in the gang world.

An enemy's body is a blank canvas.

That's why, when the Kid, in full murderous rage, chose his next target, he didn't merely want to kill him. He wanted to write a message on his body. He wanted his disciples to read it.

His name was Ronald Landaverde, and he was the brother of a youngster who'd briefly been an Eighteen before he became an evangelist and left the gang for good.

The Kid spoke to whoever was left in the regional cliques: Hollywood Locos, Parvis Locos, and Ángeles Locos. He told them that they were going to hit a *chavala* in order to sign a pact over his body.

The Kid knew of a dry well in the municipality of Turín, on land that had been abandoned after the railroad used for coffee exports fell into disrepair. The site of Ronal Landaverde's murder is riddled with metal spikes crusted over with dirt and intermittently poking out from the overgrown brush. Beyond the abandoned tracks is a neglected cornfield. Then, a widening expanse, a yawning, open plain. In the middle of that expanse a concrete structure stands a meter high. The well.

This is where the Kid took Ronal Landaverde. He told him they were going to get high with some other potheads. Years before, perhaps, Ronal would have declined, but the Kid had always been simpatico, an entertaining talker, and the Kid had been out of the area for a couple years, and besides, the war between gangs had loosened its grip over western El Salvador. Smoking a joint with the Kid seemed like a fine idea.

Gathered around the well were kids from all three of the cliques. Ronal Landaverde tensed up when he saw all the human piranhas that had been summoned by the Kid. But it was too late.

"See, you son of a bitch, you're the brother of that *bicha*, El

Gringo," the Kid said to him, not at all simpatico anymore, hissing his brother's gang name like it was a threat.

"Yeah but, look, my brother's out of it now. He's retired. You can talk to him if you want," begged Ronal Landaverde.

"Nah, our beef isn't with him. It's with you," said the Kid, tying a rope around his neck and pulling it tight.

The Kid ordered another teen to grab the victim's arms. He looped the rope around and gave the two ends to two kids on either side. He ordered them to pull in opposite directions. This time he wasn't there to kill, but to watch others kill.

He made everyone join in. Over Ronal Landaverde's body they sealed their new pact, their new foundation. His body was written on and then locked in a safe: the Turín well.

They didn't want any blood on the outside of the well, and so they used rope and not machetes. The Kid had decided that they'd let him down little by little. With the same rope they'd used to asphyxiate him, they started lowering him into the well. But Ronal Landaverde performed one last act of rebellion.

The rope had bitten into Landaverde's body. The nylon sawed into his neck and instead of going down smoothly into the water, his body spun uncontrollably, spraying blood all over until he finally fell on top of a pile of other bodies.

According to the Kid and other plea-bargain witnesses, other bodies would be thrown in turn on top of the body of Ronal Landaverde, chucked into the Turín Well in the following years. Eventually, the well's excavation would become a gruesome national spectacle.

With just that one act, the Kid had reanimated the cliques, kick-started the game, and riled up the players.

→←

April 3, 2012. Miguel Ángel is sitting in his shack. Once again, he's circled back to his killing of the prostitute. Every so often, he comes back to this crime. It affected him. He never understood why he killed her. He knows why he killed the others. For most of them, it was simply that they were Eighteens. But he has no idea why, in 2004, he fired three bullets into a woman's chest as she was sitting quietly in an Atiquizaya brothel.

"That day, I swore I'd never kill a woman again."

After a short pause, he continues: "Unless she did something to taint the honor of the barrio, unless she owed something, but just like that, for no reason, that's fucked. I mean women are tasty, and then just like that there's one less to go around."

He says this without a hint of humor.

It's how he reasons. He likes women. He reckons that if he kills them, there will be fewer left for him to enjoy.

Then he starts ruminating about what's really bugging him, this feeling he can't shake: that he was deceived.

"I have no fucking idea why Chepe wanted her dead. Some private business he had. Must be. Maybe he rented out that brothel himself. Maybe she had some dirt on the fucker."

Throughout the evening Miguel Ángel keeps mulling it over, tormented by doubt. When he speaks of these murders, he does so naturally, without lowering his voice, just a few yards away from Lorena, who pretends not to hear. Sometimes, if we turn quickly enough, we can catch her looking our way. But when we look straight at her, she lowers her gaze, settling it on whatever she's pretending to do.

It's four o'clock in the afternoon and Lorena serves us coffee so weak it tastes like a coffee-flavored tea.

Less than two miles away, a man is celebrating because he's

finally gotten the go-ahead to exhume the bodies of the Turín Well.

This man is Israel Ticas, and he's standing next to the well, talking on the phone to an official of the Ministry of National Security who has promised to help him exhume the bodies.

Israel Ticas has a grim job. But he enjoys it as much as if he were manager of Disneyland.

This man, familiarly called "Ticas" by every student of Salvadoran crime, calls himself the dead man's attorney.

He's the only forensic scientist employed by the attorney general's office. A forensic *criminologist*, he often has to correct people, though he isn't even a forensic scientist by trade. He studied civil engineering, and, after many zigzags in life, learned how to exhume bodies. He's been working for the public prosecutor's office for twelve years now. Joining the force in 1989, Ticas was a police officer throughout the last years of the war. After the peace accords of 1992, he joined the Scientific and Technical Police Division of the newly formed National Civilian Police, which was, in reality, neither very scientific nor very technical. Everyone contributed whatever they could as international experts strove to retrain these veteran soldiers and ex-guerrilla members. Ticas was bright and stood out. In 2000, he was put in charge of opening clandestine graves for the prosecutor's office. He went on to attend specialized courses and workshops to further progress in his peculiar interest.

In sum: Ticas is the single person authorized in El Salvador to take bodies out of the earth. The one and only authorized forensic scientist in the office devoted to prosecuting murders in the most murderous country on the planet. It's worth emphasizing "authorized," because many other people do dig up bodies in this unhappy country. There are prosecutors who, to advance their cases, grab a shovel and dig wherever a witness has told them they'll find a corpse. "Sometimes," a prosecutor from western El Salvador told us, "we damage the bodies, but at least we come up with something, a bone or a skull with which we can prosecute these crimes. Remember, in this country if there's no body there's no case."

Ticas is dark and wiry. He tends to twitch his mouth, roll his eyes, click his jaw, and he blinks often and quickly. The dead have left their mark on him. Ticas claims to have lifted 703 corpses from the earth, twenty-seven of them from wells, like the one in Turín, where he's working now.

Fifteen months ago, Ticas descended into the well for the first time. He went down in a harness, an orange rope, an oxygen tank on his back and a mask over his face. The Turín well is deep, the deepest Ticas has ever scavenged. That first time, in December 2010, he descended fifty-five yards. At the bottom he lit his lamp and saw scraps of clothing, many bone fragments, and several torsos. He came up with proof to back what two witnesses, including Miguel Ángel, had said: that there are bodies down there.

In January 2011, they had decided on a strategy to reach these bodies. Descending and then digging was not an option. The well is narrow and far too deep, and the structure could easily collapse. To get to the bodies Ticas would have to dig a tunnel about 100 yards from the well. The tunnel would slope down until it reached the base of the well, where they would cut an access door leading to the bones. By January 2011, Ticas had everything he needed: an electric shovel for digging the tunnel, two trucks, and a tractor for hauling the dirt. Ticas was pleased. But by the end of that January, two cold fronts had swept over El Salvador. The Ministry of Public Works, which owned the machinery, demanded its return. They promised to lend it out again, only needing the machinery to finish up some unnamed projects before the weather got any colder. Ticas had only excavated about ten yards by that point. For the next fourteen months, nothing happened. Summer passed, then winter, then summer returned. Ticas posted a call on Facebook for someone to lend him machinery so he could proceed with the excavation. It's now April 2012, winter is soon coming, and Ticas is happy for the first time in a very long time. The armed forces and the Ministry of Public Works have given him back his electric shovel, three dump trucks, a loader, and even a tractor with which to smooth out his tunnel.

"We'll get there, before they take it all away from us, before October," says Ticas excitedly.

He means that if, by October 2012, he doesn't manage to remove the bodies, the six alleged gang members who've been arrested thanks to the testimony of Miguel Ángel and one other witness will be released. In October, the two-year maximum time that a person can be jailed without a conviction will be up. The prosecutor's office believes that there are more bodies in Turín, as Miguel Ángel and the second plea-bargain witness have talked about other victims of the Hollywood Locos and allied cliques. What is more, in line with information given by other informants, the prosecutor's office believes the well was used by many western cliques: the Fulton Locos, the Prindin Gangsters, and the Acajutlas Locos. And by a now disbanded group of kidnappers, as well. Prosecutors say that a former member of that group told them that when they reach the bottom of the well, "[they]'ll be surprised."

Ticas giddily gets off the phone, ready to get back to the labor of excavating.

Miguel Ángel is sitting in his shack on April 3, 2012, as Ticas begins to excavate what he once threw into that well. Meanwhile, Miguel Ángel keeps asking himself why he killed that woman.

16

A Murdered Prostitute, a Burned-Out Car

Chepe Furia turned up again in late 2005, but he didn't stay for long. Seeing him depended on whether he wanted to be seen, not whether you wanted to see him. Chepe Furia had become increasingly inaccessible to his followers. He'd changed. The gang war was no longer his main focus, and he seemed to have delegated the Kid and other veteran gang members to conduct the gang rituals, to "walk" rivals, to make sure Atiquizaya remained a bastion of the MS-13.

President Francisco Flores's iron-fist tactics had borne fruit. Rotten fruit. The murder rate shot up after the first national security operation against the gangs. The homicide rate for every 100,000 inhabitants was 36.6 in 2003, the second lowest in the century; in 2004 it was 48.7; in 2005 it was 63. This latest dose of medication only aggravated the symptoms of the deadly Salvadoran epidemic. And yet, the same medication was prescribed again and again: the iron fist was followed by an even heavier iron fist. The strategy continued from 2003 to 2009. Six years of senselessness that turned

El Salvador into the most murderous country on the planet: 71 homicides for every 100,000 inhabitants.

The prisons had been handed over to the prisoners. Gang members who were jailed at the turn of the century finally stopped being battered victims of the system, stopped being the vulnerable ones. Little by little, as the police turned their attention to those recently deported from the United States, and as those same deportees were pushed to the most impoverished neighborhoods of El Salvador, the jails became flooded with people whose bodies showcased tribal markings: 18; MS.

Between the year 2000—when Operation Hollywood was rolled out throughout western El Salvador—and 2006, the inmate population almost doubled. According to the Institute of Public Opinion at the Jesuit University of El Salvador, it shot up from 7,800 to 14,682.

Most gang members lived a nomadic life, in constant migration from jail to jail. They were sent to new jails in an effort to save their lives. Clobbered, stabbed, sometimes hardly alive, they were transferred from a prison controlled by La Raza to another where La Raza's tentacles strangled all the same. X, that gang member who had clung to the bars of a Mariona prison cell in 2000 as he begged the guards to let him out, would remember, seventeen years later, that the MS's exasperation finally boiled over on February 19, 2002.

Several gang members who'd been locked up for years were transferred to Apanteos. El Diablito of Hollywood arrived sometime after his arm had completely recovered from the beating he'd suffered in Mariona. Then came El Crook of Hollywood, a bearlike hulk addicted to exercise and better known as the Thief or the Bitch, who, years later, in 2015, would be added to the US Treasury's blacklist. At that time, he was serving a sixteen-year sentence for kidnapping a shopkeeper on the western coast. Then came Skinny de Stoner, Western Tail, and Skinny of Francis. La Raza was losing its influence in Apanteos. They no longer controlled all the sectors of the prison, and the veteran gang members sought to take over even more. There were 150 MS members throughout the prison, and around 400 members and supporters of La Raza. X remembers that a *wila* circulated among the MS, a message encrypted in gang language: "Break the criminal."

The plan was to take advantage of a sporting event organized by the prison director, Óscar Rivas, who had had the absurd idea of organizing a soccer match between the MS and the common criminals. Those who'd been raped, extorted, and beaten for years would play against their rapists, extortionists, and assailants. The warden had picked a ludicrous moment to implement his idea of healthy recreation.

The MS would honor the *wila*. They trained for the soccer match by preparing "magic machetes," hiding machete blades inside table legs, and collecting knives they'd smuggled from outside the jail. Proud of his innovative methods, the warden invited the head of the Santa Ana Police Department, Commissioner Pablo Escobar Baños, representatives of the Office of the Ombudsman of Human Rights, and even the inmates' families to come see their beloved sport play out in Apanteos prison.

The game only lasted a few seconds.

It made headlines in the daily newspaper, *El Diario de Hoy*: "According to reports from the National Civil Police, the inmates were invited to participate in a soccer game at 10:30 in the morning ... In a matter of seconds, the MS took out chains, knives, daggers, iron rods, and sharpened sticks, which they had made themselves to attack their opponents. On seeing the danger, some of the common criminals ran the other way; others brandished handmade weapons and wounded several gang members. Inmates punched and stabbed one another with their sharpened knives and rods, leaving the grounds covered in blood."

The warden was fired a few days later.

That day, it took a platoon of the Public Order Maintenance Unit to lock the prisoners back up. Fifty of the wounded were returned to their cells, and two others, identified as MS members, were discharged from the prison as deceased. They were José Alfredo González, twenty-two, known as El Devil, who was inside for possession of a weapon of war; and Jimmy Alexánder Sáenz Mojica, twenty-three, convicted of counterfeiting money. José Rosario Cruz, a prison guard, was also seriously injured, with multiple stab wounds to the abdomen.

The ferocity of the MS, after years of humiliation, as well as the advantage they gained after their premeditated attack, forced the other inmates to retreat. By offering up the lives of two of their members, they obtained what the juveniles of the gang had achieved years ago: to have a space for themselves, away from the other prisoners.

The idea to separate inmates from rival gangs had been suggested a year earlier, on February 28, 2001, after twenty-five MS members attacked eight Barrio 18 members. After the incident, most MS were gathered into two prison sectors free of Eighteens, but they were still held with the common criminals—that far-reaching tentacle of La Raza. After the attack of 2001 and the bloody soccer match of 2002, the state decided to completely cordon off the MS, to isolate the beasts.

The gang members were reunited in sectors four and six of Apanteos Prison. Only them. No one else. "It was the first time we were all together again," remembered X.

These kinds of attacks would not stop until the gangs were transferred to entire prisons exclusively reserved for their members. No longer just sectors, but entire prisons. "Gang universities," as X described them.

The older gang members, who would later become infamous throughout the country, first met each other in those prisons, where they were free from the attacks of the other mafias. They soon created a new group that initially bore several different names: *El Pichirilo*, *El Curro*, *La Ranfla*. The last of these names is still used today in reports about the MS-13, including FBI reports.

X claims that the purpose of this new *ranfla* was to create a plan of control for the new prisons. "There were too many homeboys wanting to do what the civilians did." MS members stealing drugs from fellow members, raping their homeboys' visitors, extorting the weakest or poorest members as if they were mere indigents devoid of homeboy honor. "There were trashy people, walking around like beggars, without cutting their hair or nails and stinking all the time," explained X in 2017, as he was waiting to hear a decision about his immigration case in the United States.

At first, the *ranfla* only intended to regulate two sectors of Apanteos. In doing so it established three ground rules: keep clean, respect each other's drugs, and respect each other's visitors. It was necessary to punish some rebels. To make an example of them, El Rambito de Teclas Locos, El Zarco de San Cocos Locos, and El Sharky de Quezalte Locos were all given beatings.

This remained the *ranfla*'s strategy throughout 2002: keep running the gang from inside the prison and raise it to the level of the other prison groups. But the creation of the *ranfla* meant, for the first time, the creation of an organized party leadership. Leaders of cliques steering the leaders of other cliques. Little by little, leaders making decisions on the outside started consulting those in the prisons. Gang leaders, accustomed to living under *ranfla* rule in Apanteos, started to defer to them even after being released. X was a member of the *ranfla* in early 2002, when the Fulton Locos in Sonsonate were a rising clique. Deportees from California were streaming into Sonsonate, and they asked the leader of the Fulton Locos in El Salvador, El Chory (the same guy who, years later, would beat up Chepe Furia in the Gotera prison) if they could keep their name. Chory consulted the *ranfla* in Apanteos, and the *ranfla* asked the new Fulton Locos a favor in return for their blessing on the use of the name. There was a prison guard, Officer Laínez, who had been abusing gang members in sectors four and six. To officially get permission from El Chory and the *ranfla* to establish their clique in Sonsonate, the aspiring Fulton Locos had to kill Laínez. They fulfilled their end of the bargain a few days later, X recalled, and the Fulton Locos of Sonsonate became a clique under El Chory's leadership.

As the *ranfla* started taking control of outside operations, one gang member saw the potential in the new structure. El Diablito of Hollywood made two moves that would define him as the face of the *ranfla*, and the person with the most important contacts. First, he got a gang member known as La Súper Abuela de Arce, or the Super Grandma of Arce, to bring in a cell phone in December of 2002. A small Siemens which was smuggled into the prison, in pieces, hidden in Súper Abuela's anus during a visit. X remembers the exact date—December 31, 2002—because that day, after three years inside, he was allowed to talk to his wife for one minute. El Diablito kept hold of the phone. The second move he made was even bolder. Earlier that year, El Diablito had asked for a transfer to the Quezaltepeque facility, where other street-famous MS leaders were serving time, including El Fool of San Cocos Locos, El Tangle of Stoner, El Crime of Adams, and El Negro of Harvard.

Who knows what tricks he'd had to pull, but somehow El Diablito managed to get himself transferred.

A few months later, in early 2003, according to X, El Diablito returned from Quezaltepeque to Apanteos. And he returned with a new right-hand man—El Crook of Hollywood. They explained, as if it were already official, that in Quezaltepeque there was a *ranfla* as well, and that the two of them, along with all the homies in Apanteos, were part of that *ranfla*.

El Diablito, still armed with the Siemens that rode inside Súper Abuela's anus, was able to connect the two *ranflas*. And he was their connection.

Then came El Diablito's last move. The gang member jumped in by the Hollywood Locos of Los Angeles asked for two deported gangsters on the outside to be included in the *ranflas* of Apanteos and Quezaltepeque. The two were Ricardo Adalberto Díaz, El Rat of Leward, and Rubén Rosa Loco, El Goat of Centrales, who, together, controlled the city center of San Salvador: managing clandestine brothels, drug sales, extortions, and robberies. They both happened to be close friends of El Diablito. Gradually, without anybody questioning the transformation, El Diablito was turning the *ranfla* (originally created to control homies in two wards of a single prison) into MS's national leadership committee. He had learned the technique from the Mexican Mafia, the Eme, in California: if you control the prisons, you control the streets. The message to the gang members on the streets was clear: one day you're going to be on the inside, and it will be better for you if you're on good terms with the leaders behind bars.

The *ranfla* had become La Ranfla.

The Mara Salvatrucha 13 took over two sectors of the Apanteos prison between 2001 and 2002. Imprisoned members were enrolling in the gang university and graduating as gangsters. MS-13 was thoroughly organized: it had both laws and leaders, an established hierarchy, and a standardized system of punishment and execution.

By 2005, when Chepe Furia (who had never yet set foot inside a Salvadoran prison) returned to Atiquizaya, the Hollywood Locos Salvatrucha clique he had founded was filling out with recently released, or graduated, gang members. They included El Stranger, who would become second-in-command, and El Whisper, who, years later, after getting sent back to prison, would threaten the Kid with being left smelling of pine.

It suited Chepe Furia that other MS generals were taking charge of the fight against Barrio 18. His interests lay elsewhere.

Chepe Furia, the Kid recalls, was spending a lot of time in Guatemala, but he never told anyone where he was. He came and went as he pleased. Chepe Furia wasn't even leading any *mirins* anymore, nor ordering hits against Eighteens. It seemed, to the Kid at least, that the war wasn't that important to him. Chepe Furia was only coming to the Kid to order the occasional hit, which often had nothing to do with the gang war.

The first of these was against the prostitute. Though the police weren't yet seriously investigating the clique, they'd opened a dossier and drawn up a list of murders tied to MS-13. The police thus had photographs of the crime scene, in which she appears lying on her back on the floor. The pictures show a large, dark-skinned woman. Her arms are folded over her head, hiding her face. She's wearing a tight white shirt, with blue sequins and the word "Ángel" on the front, soaked in blood and revealing folds of her flesh. Her sandals are also bloodstained. The photos were taken minutes after the Kid shot her three times in the chest.

Chepe Furia showed up earlier that day in the San Antonio neighborhood. As usual, he took a seat in his little store, ready to play cards with a group of old men. When the Kid, whom he'd sent for, came around, they walked together toward the soccer field. He told him he had a mission for him, which he should complete at sundown. He gave him a .357 pistol with three explosive bullets. He wanted to be sure his target would die.

The Kid was to kill a woman who worked in a brothel off a main street in Atiquizaya. The Kid knew this was a dangerous mission. The street ran through the center of town, not far from the restaurants of the central plaza. This wouldn't be like walking another gang member, or making a hit in rural pastures or near the Turín well. He was being asked to make a hit in the heart of the city, and early in the day, too, not under the cover of night.

Above all else, one question clouded the assassin's mind. After almost ten years of being an MS-13 faithful, after almost ten years of blindly following the orders of his leader, the Kid, for the first time, asked himself: "Why?"

Why kill this woman?

Why did Chepe Furia want her dead so badly, so immediately?

Why couldn't he wait until it got dark and then walk her?

Why did it need to be that very day, right around sunset?

Why her?

What was this all about?

The Kid, who had been in the clique from the very beginning, rising through the ranks, could count all the times Barrio 18 had crossed the Hollywood Locos Salvatrucha. He knew, even better than Chepe Furia, the names of all his enemies, and the names of the dead homies that needed avenging. This prostitute wasn't on any of those lists.

So why?

He asked himself that question the rest of the afternoon. But his loyalty to and admiration for Chepe Furia vanquished his doubts, and he never said anything. He took the gun his leader gave him. He said, "Hell yeah," and he went off to set up the murder with four other gang members, who would be his scouts making sure there were no police in sight when the time came.

"Shit, I don't want to kill her," the Kid remembers thinking as he left San Antonio.

"I don't want to kill her," he told himself again as he got ready to head out.

"Shit, if I kill this lady I don't know what I'm doing it for, what she did wrong," he thought as he walked toward the center of Atiquizaya.

"Maybe one day she'd even lend her snatch to me," he said to himself, before calling the lookouts to start the mission.

He was hunting, for the first time, for some excuse to not do the only thing in life that he knew how to do, and do well, better than anyone else in his clique: kill.

For a moment, he thought he'd found the perfect get-out. He was casing the brothel, a shabby little house with a red lightbulb outside and a garbage bin in front, when he saw some policemen walking by. He hid behind a fig tree, called one scout and told him, "Hey, there's a couple cops walking by, up by the salons, I'm not going to execute the mission." The scout responded, "No, man, they're just some rural cops, and they're already gone. They turned down the road to San Lorenzo." He had no more choice. Either he had to admit that he wasn't going to do it because of his conscience, or he had to do it. The Kid took a long slug from a small bottle of Cuatro Ases, sucked on a joint and went to do his job.

He ran, ran past two of his scouts, and crossed the alleyway. He stepped through the door. Three women sat at the bar. He knew which one he had to kill. "Hey," he said. All three of them turned to look, quickly raising their arms in defense. The Kid extended his right arm, dropped his cheek to his shoulder to get a sight line along his extended limb. The visor of his cap was pulled down, covering his forehead, leaving just a sliver of vision for him to aim and fire three shots into the woman's chest.

Pop. Pop. Pop.

And then he ran. He ran a long way. He scrambled up a hill, jumped a few fences, and came to a creek. Using a piece of plastic, he scooped up the water and poured it over his face and into his mouth. He drank and drank. He went into a field and hid. He slipped back into the world he belonged to: the outskirts, the edges, the margins. He hid in the scrub to finish his *guaro* and his joint. He thought his heart was going to burst. He felt like he'd never felt before, like he was about to die of asphyxiation. He was used to killing, but not to this feeling.

Six years later, already a traitor to his gang, he would tell Detective Pineda about that murder. The police included it in the document they handed over to the prosecutors, but they never actually charged Chepe Furia. Without specifying, the prosecutors said there were "some inconsistencies" in the story. Detective Pineda would remind them that the Kid could describe exactly what the victim was wearing, what position she was left in, and how many times she was shot—all without seeing the police report. Detective Pineda would say that something smelled off about the prosecutors' decision. The other possibility was that, in a country as murderous as El Salvador, the prosecutors simply saw it as a bygone crime, with a forgettable victim, in a system that typically leaves these bodies for the worms.

The Kid never asked Chepe Furia why he ordered him to make that kill. Chepe Furia rewarded him with treats, as if he were a dog: *guaro*, marijuana, and a few slaps on the back. The Kid slipped back into the gang's daily life.

A few months later Chepe Furia came looking for the Kid again. This time, the mission was even stranger than blasting a prostitute who had nothing to do with the MS-13. Chepe Furia asked him to torch a double-cab pickup truck.

He had two lookouts go along with him. They bought the gas, spilled it out in the bed of the truck, splashed it on the windows, doused the interior, and then torched the lot. A brand-new truck.

The Kid, with his assassin's mind, thought: "Why not kill the owner instead of burning the ride?" It was the second time that dangerous question bounced around in his head. His second bout of: *why?*

It didn't take long for the grapevine to broadcast that someone had burned Viejo Oso's (Old Bear's) new truck. Viejo Oso was a large, burly man with a reputation for violence.

The Kid's doubts lingered. Turns out that Viejo Oso was a friend of Chepe Furia. The Kid had often seen them throwing back drinks and betting on cards in San Antonio.

This time, the Kid took his doubts a step further.

He started asking around the petty thieves who worked with Viejo Oso. He questioned some of the local drunks that liked to make bets with Chepe Furia. He found out that two months ago, Chepe Furia and Viejo Oso had planned a robbery together. They robbed Viejo Oso's own sister. Viejo Oso gave Chepe Furia all the intel: the day, time, place when his sister would have a lot of cash on her. Chepe Furia, with a couple of his bandits, carried out the robbery and gave the money to Viejo Oso to hide.

The Kid kept digging. He found out that a few weeks later Chepe Furia was complaining about Viejo Oso—that he wasn't answering his calls and was basically avoiding him. Viejo Oso kept his distance but sent Chepe Furia a couple of small installments of the money, which the Kid referred to as *piscachitas*, little pinches. Meanwhile, here was Viejo Oso suddenly driving around in a new Toyota pickup.

Chepe Furia, the leader of the Hollywood Locos Salvatrucha, the western bandit, ex-member of the National Police, had been swindled by his friend. And so he decided to burn Viejo Oso's truck. Get him back.

The Kid remembers seeing Viejo Oso actually crying afterward.

"Oh man, Chepito, they burned my new truck," he griped to Chepe Furia.

"We'll investigate, don't worry, we'll investigate. And when we find out who did it, we'll set things right," Chepe Furia said.

A couple of days later, Viejo Oso delivered what was owed to Chepe Furia—close to $7,000.

The Kid was there that day when Viejo Oso had come around whining. And after he left, Chepe Furia laughed at Viejo Oso, and threw the Kid another treat: a few bucks to buy pupusas, stuffed tortillas. Later he'd give him the rest of his wages: twenty dollars.

It was the first time the Kid thought something wasn't right about his relationship with Chepe Furia.

It was the first time in years that he didn't feel part of this all-important organization, MS-13, the mega, the Beast that ran the world. He was starting to feel instead like Chepe Furia's lackey.

He felt bad about himself, just like he used to feel before joining up with the Hollywood Locos Salvatrucha.

The Kid had never asked for money before. He never tried to get out of doing a hit. He never complained about being sent on dangerous missions: walking an Eighteen, killing an ex-*compañero* from the neighborhood, or decapitating a witch. Killing was never a problem for him. Money was never important. As long as it was all in the name of the Beast. But the woman and the burned truck were another matter. They weren't about the Beast. They were about humans. They were about the world. About a man. About José Antonio Terán.

17

The Murder of Wendy

Marbelly wobbles around the shack, and Miguel Ángel finishes tending to his small marijuana garden before sitting down to talk. It's August of 2013. Miguel Ángel has been living in the shack for almost three years as a protected, plea-bargain witness. Following our usual pattern, we talk over multiple cups of coffee. Very weak coffee. Café Listo, it's called, instant coffee that comes in cheap little packets. It's the worst of the crop—stuff you could never export. The best beans head out in ships from Acajutla and Unión, and the worst beans, or rather the bean chips, stay in El Salvador. It's what the poor campesinos drink, those who dedicate their lives, entire generations, to cultivating coffee. Drinking a few sips of this awful brew in western El Salvador, the world's coffee cradle, is enough to understand the curse that has ravaged this land since the arrival of the white man: you have to surrender all that's good and get used to garbage. It's as if grape growers in California only knew the sourness of the worst boxed wine.

Miguel Ángel drinks the stuff every day, along with Lorena, and even Marbelly.

Something big has happened since we last talked. Something of critical importance in the history of the Hollywood Locos Salvatrucha. But Miguel Ángel only responds to our pressing questions with two words: "Don't know."

Chepe Furia, José Antonio Terán, the former National Police officer, the former migrant, the maestro of Miguel Ángel, the man who appears and disappears, has been sentenced to twenty years for the murder of Samuel Menjívar Trejo, the twenty-three-year old vegetable vendor who worked in the Atiquizaya market and was found 120 miles away from where officers Tejada and Hernández had taken him in to the station on November 24, 2009. El Stranger and Liro Jocker were the other two passengers in the truck, along with Samuel, familiarly known as Rambito.

The charges were brought on December 6, 2012. Detective Pineda's strategy, along with the prosecutors specializing in organized crime, was to prosecute the case away from the west of the country, far from the jurisdiction of Judge Salinas, the judge who'd liberated Chepe Furia twice before. Weeks before the final verdict, Miguel Ángel testified that he saw the three gang leaders get in the car with Rambito on the same day his body was discovered. The trial took place in a specialized court for organized crime in the eastern part of the country, eight months after Chepe Furia had been recaptured. On the day of his sentencing, the mythic gangster was wearing a white t-shirt with gray details. He had a three-day stubble (though he was usually clean-shaven), and short hair (slightly longer than he wore it when people referred to him as Don Chepe, the garbage magnate of Atiquizaya).

The judge believed the prosecutors that the gang members had tricked the police informant, Rambito, by pretending that they were going to the funeral of a murdered MS member. The prosecutor's office explained in a press release: "The victim's cell phone confirmed the information that the victim had relayed to the authorities. The information pointed to the imputed 'Chepe Furia' as the subject who planned criminal actions and received money from extortions." The five-paragraph press release also, without compunction, spread two lies. The first: "The accused (Chepe Furia) is the head of the Fulton and Hollywood Locos Salvatrucha cliques." Chepe Furia did business with the Fulton, but he never headed it. The head of that clique was El Chory, who would be the bane of Chepe Furia's life in Gotera prison. The second lie: "The detention and trial of the gang leader and various other members has reduced the incidence of crime in the region."

Gangs don't wither when a leader goes to prison. The violence they plant puts down roots. Decades of bad decisions made by politicians were glossed over in this trial. Chepe Furia had long stopped instigating his own murders, or dealing with the gang war head-on. Spilling blood cost him too much money. Though he acted like the village capo, there was nothing he could do to stop the bloodshed he'd helped unleash throughout the region.

But the authorities would learn this in the years to come. According to police statistics, in 2012, the year they captured and sentenced Chepe Furia, there were ninety-eight homicides in the department of Ahuachapán, including the towns of Atiquizaya, El Refugio, and Turín—centers controlled by the Hollywood Locos. The following year, 2013, there were ninety-five. In 2014, there were 130. In 2015, there were 199. In 2016, there were 201. In 2017, there were 219. More and more murders. More than double the number in 2012.

The gang, once grown to maturity, doesn't wither just because you cut off one of its roots.

The police didn't say a word to Yogui while they toasted the number of years Chepe would be locked away. Yogui just kept rotting away in his shack, surrounded by wasteland, with hardly enough to eat, drinking horrible coffee, and haunted by the memory of having killed that woman.

Miguel Ángel is only kept on in his shack because he's useful. Or more necessary than useful, at least as the prosecutor explains it to him. There's still the Turín well. And the cops who handed Rambito over.

When asked what he thought about Chepe Furia's conviction on that hot August day, Miguel Ángel replied, "Don't know." A more honest response might have been, "I don't give a shit." Chepe Furia was old news. A well full of bodies, a whole clique turned against him, years of being confined to a shack, hunger, assassination attempts, death threats from gang members, threats from prosecutors. Chepe Furia's sentencing would have been a life event for any normal person. Or even for any less than normal person. But the life of Miguel Ángel is much worse. It's something degraded. Death, its constant presence, that grenade that rests above his head, the memories that eat away at him every night—they don't let go, don't let him rest. What happened, happened. In order to survive, only what is happening now can matter.

Chepe Furia is in jail. For Miguel Ángel, death doesn't stop with Chepe Furia. Life goes on. And yet, death hovers. The Beast prowls.

Lorena pours more coffee. It's so weak you can see the bits of sugar dissolving at the bottom of the cup.

Lorena is young. In other circumstances, she would be considered a child. But living her life with Miguel Ángel, no way can she be considered a child. She's a woman, and a tough one. She's seventeen years old. They've been together since she got pregnant at fourteen.

There's a complicity between them, one that doesn't play out in direct conversation. Miguel Ángel talks and, though it seems she's not paying attention, she's ready to corroborate with a date or confirm some anecdote with a monosyllable uttered toward her partner. She's bright, with eyes, like Miguel Ángel's, always on the alert, always flitting around the shack. Miguel Ángel has taught her to recognize the sound of a pistol's safety being clicked off and to identify the distinctive gait of a gang member. He talks to her in back-to-front gang code, and she understands.

"*Rramo, otra torra nepo feca rapa trosono y tocipan,*" he says. If you're not familiar with gang slang, his request is incomprehensible. There are only two words in the sentence that would appear in any Spanish dictionary: "another" and "and." But Lorena understands and brings him another cup of that wretched coffee and some sweet bread.

Miguel Ángel doesn't put his arms around Lorena, he doesn't give her kisses, or hold her hand. And she doesn't seem to miss these signs of affection. She's never known them. In the campesino way of life, they're not expected.

When asked if he sometimes tells his wife and child that he loves them, Miguel Ángel responds: "No, I mean, since I was little that wasn't really in my vocabulary, you know. The thing is that they know I'm strong for them, that if anyone touches them the Beast'll come out."

This declaration, pronounced in the presence of strangers in a small shack in Barrio 18 territory, is probably the sweetest thing Lorena will hear from Miguel Ángel. It is, without a doubt, a declaration of love in the midst of death.

At some point in our conversation, we ask Miguel Ángel a question he may not have heard before. "Can we talk to Lorena alone for a bit?" He doesn't answer. He widens his eyes and stares. He seems disconcerted, tense. He doesn't say yes, but he doesn't say no.

"Do you feel in danger?" we quietly ask Lorena. Miguel Ángel is only about ten feet away, watching us.

Not kissing is as common among campesinos in this part of El Salvador as is assuming that a woman would never speak about anything personal with any man besides her husband.

"Well," Lorena murmurs, "a little while ago they went and shot at my dad's house. At like four in the morning. The dog started barking. A man was standing outside for like ten minutes. In the morning we found a nine-millimeter shell." As she talks, her gaze flits between the floor and Miguel Ángel.

Lorena's father's house is in Las Pozas, one house away from where Miguel Ángel grew up, and where his mother and his sister still live. That's where Miguel Ángel did his courting. Lorena has three brothers and three sisters. She studied until fourth grade and can barely read or write. When she reads aloud, it's hard to understand her. Her parents are both campesinos: her father working in the bean fields, and her mother pounding corn into masa. Since she was a kid, Lorena always preferred to go out to the fields with her father, because her mom would make her pound corn, make tortillas, and take care of her little sisters. She found the bean fields were less demanding.

"Do you know what he's mixed up in?" we ask.

"Yeah. Yeah, I don't even want him to leave here at all, but they're not going to keep him here forever ... *mjijijijiji*." She laughs that peasant laugh that seems to be asking for forgiveness, expressing shame at what was just said. She covers her mouth and giggles quietly. *Mjijijijiji.*

"Are you going to follow him wherever he goes?"

"Yes. How could I stay here?"

"How do you imagine the future, Lorena?"

"I don't know. See my girl grow up. *Mjijijijiji.*"

It's hard to be optimistic about the future of their daughter, Marbelly. The present clouds any vision of the future. It's like trying to see where you're going while walking under an umbrella in a torrential downpour. At two years old, Marbelly Lisbet knows how to say *bottle, mama, come here, pigeon* (there are a lot of pigeons roosting in the trees surrounding the shack), and she also knows how to say *gunshot*. Lorena says that Miguel Ángel taught his daughter to recognize the sound of a gunshot. Which is why when they shot at Lorena's father's house at four in the morning—where they were staying the night—Lorena only realized because her toddler woke her up and pronounced two of the five words she knows:

"Gunshot, mamá."

Wendy

The Hollywood Kid never liked killing women.

It wasn't an ideological position toward gender, or even an ethical one. He just didn't like it. He thought such murders were pointless. Killing Eighteens made sense—part of the system of reciprocal aggression, a sort of potlatch, to borrow a concept from Marcel Mauss: an interchange of violent gifts. Even killing an MS member made sense in the Kid's logic, as long as they were traitors, or had committed a serious fault against another homeboy. The clique and the mara are spaces of constant competition, vying with each other to fatten the Beast with young flesh, with homeboy meat. But killing women didn't fit into either logic. It was like dirtying his hands or debasing his weapons. It went against his purpose of being.

Wendy was a sixteen-year-old girl who didn't know anything about this savage world of codes, machetes, hidden graves, wells full of cadavers, traitors, and beasts. She didn't understand, and the savage world swallowed her. The Beast engulfed her. Spellbound by the gang members, Wendy slept with an Eighteen, a kid without rank or status in his clique, a "puppy." At the same time she was hanging out with the Hollywood Locos.

Wendy hadn't a clue. She had no idea these weren't times for playing around, not when the Beast had been growing in El Salvador for almost two decades.

It's interesting that the deaths of tough gangster grunts belongs to a lady, the Beast.

Wendy didn't take precautions or use prudence—two traits not typically associated with sixteen-year-olds, but absolutely necessary for anyone who approaches the Mara Salvatrucha 13. One time she told the Kid that he should tattoo his chest with an "18," because "MS-13" was too long. Those words in the mouth of any man would have been enough, with luck, with a lot of luck, to get him hacked to death by machete. But to the Kid, Wendy didn't deserve his machete or his gun. She didn't merit his barbarity. She was a chick, a babe. He didn't pay her much mind.

But cliques contain multiple interests and attitudes, and MS-13 isn't exactly known for letting offenses slide or for respecting the lives of women. Wendy kept on letting her tongue loose, dropping foolish insults at the feet of the gang members. Until a few of them got fed up.

A group of Hollywood Locos took Wendy to the cemetery one afternoon, telling her they were going to get high. Instead, they killed her. The gang member who practically decapitated her had previously retired from MS-13 but was now courting them again like a prodigal lover. For him it was more important to make his case, to leave clear messages, just like the Kid had done on multiple occasions. The gang member saw the girl as a blank slate he could write his message on.

The Kid didn't participate in the murder, but he watched. He didn't like to write on that kind of paper. He preferred the roughened sheets of the bodies of Eighteens, or even other MS members. And so he put himself in a secondary position, as lookout. He hung back as the machete sliced into Wendy's face.

They didn't rape or torture her, though that often happens when the cliques decide to kill a girl or woman. Wendy only suffered two machete hacks. The first, probably aiming for her neck, struck her on the chin right below her lower lip. The blade was sharp, and the arm that swung it was strong. The hack broke through the mandible and reached the back of her head, almost lopping it right off. The second blow was vertical, hitting the top of the skull and cracking it lengthwise, splitting it open, cutting off locks of her hair. Wendy died quickly. They then dragged her body to a ravine. It had rained the night before and there were puddles. They pushed her head, which was barely hanging on by a few strings of flesh, into the mud, and left her. They didn't bury her, or even cover her with sticks.

That was how a group of campesinos found her. Among them was her uncle, Héctor, who happens to be the father of Lorena, the Kid's wife. Accompanied by the local police, Héctor inspected his niece's body. He turned it over, careful with the head that was barely attached to the body of a girl who had never understood the savage world of gangs. He was the only relative who had the courage to confront the barbarity written on Wendy's body.

The Hollywood Kid had been the lookout at the murder of his wife's cousin.

Family relations at the bottom of an abyss.

Even in the inferno of Salvadoran violence, a murdered sixteen-year-old with her head almost off was likely to cause a scandal in both police stations and newsrooms. In the middle of 2009, Sergeant Pozo, under the direction of Detective Pineda, took on the case and discovered that amid the Hollywood Locos clique there was a piece that didn't quite fit, a piece that was increasingly likely to become a blank sheet of paper for his homeboys to write on. It was then that Pozo began his hunt for a ruthless and slippery gang member known as the Hollywood Kid.

The Kid learned that he was the police's primary target. He knew of a detective named Pineda. He also knew, because the police had been planting information among collaborators and low-ranking gang members, that they were accusing him, and him alone, of Wendy's murder. And for a simple reason.

Detective Pineda had been profiling the members of the Hollywood Locos. Twelve years after the birth of the clique, dozens of murders later, the state began finding out who was who. The Kid's profile ticked several boxes: he was one of the oldest members, close to Chepe Furia, smoked a lot of dope, and had a young girlfriend named Lorena. Lorena and Wendy were cousins. Simple deduction, based on intuition rather than evidence, pointed to the Kid as the perpetrator of the crime. Perhaps there was something in that family relationship that had become a motive for the murder.

Detective Pineda had another reason to believe he might be able to flip the Kid. At the beginning of the year, he had ducked out for a while. He'd abandoned his homeboys for another group in the area—one that would let him keep the status he'd worked so hard to acquire. The Hollywood Kid, the tough sicario, had turned to evangelism.

During the first months of 2008, the Kid started attending one of those rudimentary evangelical churches that were sprouting up in countless villages and backwood communities. He sang fervent Pentecostal songs and listened to the histrionic predictions of humble men who went to school just long enough to learn to read the Bible. The Kid dressed in buttoned-up long-sleeve shirts, khaki pants, and dress shoes. He began quoting the Bible and acting like a repentant gang member.

But the church wasn't really a revelation for the Kid. Jesus hadn't called him. It was just another strategy. Years before, he had hidden under the skirts of the state by joining the army; now he hid behind the word of God. But only for a little while. Later, he would sarcastically say that he became *"evangi-loco"* in order to hide from the police.

By the end of 2008, he'd given up being a sheep and turned back into a wolf.

And yet the Kid's strategy to escape the police became another sign to them that he was someone they could convert into a traitor. Under Sergeant Pozo, the search continued.

A number of times the Kid had to take off running. Once, if it hadn't been for Pozo being so fat, the Kid would have been caught. He managed to hop over a series of fences and disappear like a fleeing deer.

The Kid came close to firing at his pursuers more than once. He never knew that Officer Pozo had come pretty close as well, but Detective Pineda didn't send out his men to bring in bodies. He wanted snitches. Once, Pozo got a patrol of soldiers to detain the Kid and let him go after he promised he'd talk. They didn't want to kill him, they wanted to break him.

After months of hunting, Sergeant Pozo walked into that dilapidated house in Atiquizaya where the Kid had sought refuge. Knowing that he needed to bring him in or he wouldn't see him again for months, Pozo opened the metal door with extreme caution. He saw the twenty-seven-year-old assassin smoking his fifth rock of the day, and he flipped the safety off of his 9mm. The Kid's trigger fingers were hooked around a .357 and a .40. Sergeant Pozo took a deep breath. He steadied his nerves, and, still pointing the gun at the Kid's head, said, "Hey, take it easy. I can see you're armed."

They met at the war's end.

Both of them came from the United States, and after they arrived their destinies would be interlaced forever. They were strangely alike.

The evangelicals came first. Much earlier. The first church was called Mission Central America, and was built in western El Salvador at the end of the turbulent nineteenth century. They didn't get much of a welcome—the coffee elite was profoundly, aristocratically Catholic. The landowning elite persecuted the intruders as if they were heretics. When they held their services, their histrionic and ululating cults, they were stoned by the Ladino campesinos who had been taught to hate them. The first missions made few converts, though their hallelujahs and visions were accepted by a few indigenous people in the area, and the first local group was formed on the skirts of the Santa Ana volcano. They hunkered down, discreet, like a recessive gene in the Salvadoran DNA just waiting for the right moment to express itself.

The moment came at the end of the 1970s. Many more evangelicals were flocking from the United States. They were founding churches, seeding their Protestant beliefs in every corner of the country, above all in shanty towns and remote hamlets. For, like the first wave of evangelicals, they were only accepted by the poorest of the poor.

Today, when night falls in El Salvador—typically around six in the evening—in the roughest neighborhoods and villages of the most violent country in Latin America, in back alleyways and putrid backwaters, in zones abandoned by the state and abandoned by the world, even in the overcrowded prisons, you will hear the singing, the clapping, the shaking of tamborines. "Hallelujah! Praise Be to God!" Prophesying and speaking in tongues, breaking the silence of the night.

"*¡Ay! silabás, silabás, silabastei, silabastei, ando rama silabari, ando bari silabaste.*"

When the civil war was over, the others came.

Tattooed all over, hardened by California prisons, the gang members also went into the roughest neighborhoods and villages. They too were welcomed by the poorest of the poor.

It was in those slums and backwoods that the two groups got acquainted. They understood each other. Both felt rejected. They realized that they were brothers. Preachers and gangsters, heroes and villains, but brothers when all's said and done. The evangelicals were the only ones not to spurn the gang members, and the gang members were the only ones who didn't hate the evangelicals. Since their first encounters after the war, they've stayed close. Since the early '90s both groups saw themselves as reigning over the margins, as giving direction—though by very different means—to the lives of those neighborhoods and villages where the state represents nothing but a distant threat.

When gang members tired of serving the Beast, they looked for the pastor, who accepted them, who came into their homes, who helped and protected them. The gangs didn't mess with the evangelicals. Hundreds of men, the Beast tattooed on their bodies and faces, sang out praises in the broken-down temples of God. The dominion of the Beast ended at the threshold of the temple. Her hatred stopped at the door.

18

Little Piñata

Miguel Ángel has run out of minutes on his phone. He sends a text instead. It's noon, December 14, 2013. The text (corrected for multiple spelling mistakes) reads: "What's up, bro? Just wanted to say my old man is dead. The Beast scored one on me. The Kid."

The Kid's father had hanged himself the night before.

At sixty-seven years old, Jorge García, in his umpteenth suicide attempt, succeeded in hanging himself from a beam of his house.

After drinking enough Cuatro Ases to get himself good and soused, Jorge García went back to the house he shared with Rosa Tobar, the mother of Miguel Ángel. He tied one end of a rope around his neck and the other to one of the patio beams. He climbed onto a chair and then knocked it over. The beam he was hanging from broke. His wife, found him on the ground, humiliated, with the rope still around his neck.

The insults resounded through the darkness, the back alleyway filling up with curses.

"You old, useless, godamned son of a bitch! You old shitbag! You can't even kill yourself!"

The neighbors woke up. Héctor, Lorena's father and next-door neighbor, quickly realized what was going on. It was García's fifth suicide attempt in the last two years. There may have been more. It always happened at night, always when drunk, and always with a rope around his neck looking for a beam to hang himself from. And Rosa Tobar always reacted by hurling insults at him. You old piece of shit. You stupid idiot. Old son of a bitch. But, until that December night of 2013, Jorge García had always failed.

After hearing the first beam crack, Héctor told his oldest son to poke his head through the wall—which is made of tin cans—separating the two homes to see what was going on with the old man. After her fill of insults, Rosa Tobar locked herself back in her room. The neighbors heard the door slam and the shouting stop, but somebody was dragging something across the ground. Héctor's son saw the old man, a few yards away, trying to hang himself again. He set up the chair, he tied the rope back around his neck, and he looked for another beam. This time he found one made of iron. The central beam over a metal-roofed patio littered with old junk. He tied the knot, climbed up on the chair, and stepped off.

"Papá, I think the old man killed himself," the boy said to Héctor.

Father and son went and pounded on Rosa Tobar's door.

"Doña Rosa! It's your husband! He's hanged himself. Open up! Doña Rosa."

"Let the old shit hang himself. Let him get it over with."

But Héctor and his son insisted, and Rosa Tobar in her faded robe finally opened the door. Disheveled, pale and tiny, her deeply wrinkled face betrayed a long, sad life. She opened the door and shuffled back into her room.

Héctor and his son walked out to the patio where they found Jorge García's body hanging from the iron beam.

Héctor thought the body looked like a piñata. A small swinging bag of dark flesh.

Jorge García, the *miquero* with the disfigured arm, swung from the iron beam.

The father who had loaned out his daughter's body swung from the iron beam.

The father who drank while his daughter was raped swung from the iron beam.

The father of the Hollywood Kid swung like a piñata from the iron beam.

Miguel Ángel answers the phone. He says he won't go to the wake or the funeral. The police don't want him to be so visible. He'll deliver some plastic seats that El Refugio's mayor's office loaned to him and his family, and then he'll go back to his shack to wait out the trials of the Turín well.

Jorge García was a condemned man. His hopeless life had condemned him since he was a child. But there were a few particular moments that hurt him so bad, he lost the will to live. Years before he finally took his own life, the Beast had sunk her fangs into Jorge García. And now the Beast had swallowed her meal.

As Miguel Ángel explains, the Beast, his father's personal Beast, has taken what was hers.

The Beast's Massacre in Horeb

A common story in El Salvador: a family relocates to start a new life, away from the gangs.

On February 25, 2012, this family arrived in what they thought was going to be their new life. Fleeing Atiquizaya and the Hollywood Locos Salvatrucha clique, they were moving fifteen miles away into the department of Santa Ana, to rent a humble house in the middle of a dusty lot with overgrown weeds. Six of them arrived that day to see the new house and arrange the rental contract. Although the neighborhood, Horeb, was in the municipal district of San Sebastián Salitrillo, which was controlled by the Mara Salvatrucha 13, family friends had assured them that there wasn't a heavy gang presence, so that they would live in poverty, but in relative peace. The family wasn't worried about the future, but about the gang they were fleeing.

One of the six, the youngest woman, about twenty years old, had told her boyfriend in Atiquizaya that she was breaking up with him. The boyfriend didn't take the news well. It all might have ended normally, maybe with a brief public scene, some yelling, and a drunken night listening to ranchera music—except that the dumped boyfriend was David Antonio Morán Rivas, El Lunático, of the Atiquizaya Hollywood Locos Salvatrucha clique.

In those days, even the youngest members of the clique had already racked up their kills. The Kid had been Yogui, the protected witness, for two years now, and he didn't know all of the new gang members.

A Mara Salvatrucha 13 commando crew was waiting for the family outside of Horeb. Two fifteen-year-olds, one twenty-year-old, one thirty-five-year-old, and the jealous ex-boyfriend, El Lunático.

As the family was leaving their new house, the gang members blocked their way and, without a word, started shooting. The shells collected at the scene by police belonged to 30-30 carbines. Three of the family were killed: María Galán, Jorge Galán, and Juana

Elena Flores. The other three survived, including the former girl-friend, but in critical condition.

According to police statistics, it was the fifth massacre of 2012, only two months into the year. Throughout the country there would be twenty-two massacres that year, claiming seventy-two victims. That made it, according to the police, a relatively good year. The year before saw forty-one massacres in this tiny country, resulting in 137 fatalities.

Juana Elena Flores, one of the victims of the Horeb tragedy, was the Kid's aunt. His father's sister. María Galán was the Kid's cousin, the daughter of Juana Elena. And the last victim, Jorge Galán, was María's husband.

Two years later, in February of 2014, Salvadoran prosecutors would put out a press release celebrating the conviction of two of the attackers in the Horeb massacre. Melvin Antonio Linares Mencus, El Danger, and William Ernesto Castillo Delgado, El Blue, were sentenced to 138 years in prison for three murders and three attempted murders.

The police explained that they caught El Danger attempting to flee the scene of the crime. But they never included El Lunático or either of the fifteen-year-olds in their inquiry. Meanwhile, the remainder of the traumatized family had fled again, dispersing across the country. The Kid, from his shack, did a little investigating of his own and was able to reconstruct the crime better than the police. He pinpointed the motive, and he knew who the perpetrators were before they were brought to trial. The Kid informed the detectives in El Refugio, but the case didn't interest them—there were already two men captured and sentenced, and, in El Salvador, that counts as success.

Jorge García, the Kid's father, never even heard about that

massacre. The ex-*miquero* had sunk into the most profound alcoholism. He tried to wash away his memories in guaro, but some memories wouldn't wash away. Jorge García started trying to kill himself, and kept on trying until that December night in 2013 when he found a strong enough beam to escape his rotten world.

A year and ten months after El Lunático and his crew committed the massacre in Horeb, the massacre would take its fourth victim, an ex-*miquero* swinging like a piñata fifteen miles from where the rifles spat out their shells.

19

"There Aren't Any Other Options"

Miguel Ángel is no longer frustrated; he's desperate. An incident in August 2013 makes his new situation perfectly clear.

Without explanation, three months ago, the basket of provisions sent by the state stopped coming. Just stopped. Miguel Ángel remains a protected witness, he meets his obligations, and he attends whatever court dates the prosecutors demand. The state, however, only partially meets its obligations: though it's not bringing charges against Miguel Ángel for his multiple crimes, it has forgotten the other commitment, to provide him with scanty but regular supplies.

A few days before, hungry and worried about feeding Lorena and Marbelly, Miguel Ángel slipped outside the fence around his shack. He walked about 200 yards away from the police outpost, over the main street of the tiny village of El Refugio. Near the few little stores, the onetime MS-13 member took off his shirt in the middle of a plaza dominated by Eighteens and waited for a soda or snack delivery truck to pull up, so he could bother the driver for a dollar.

In El Salvador, gang extortion, known as *renta*, is so pervasive that some multinational and transport companies have contracted ex-military and ex-police officers to work as gang liasons. They don't even try to avoid paying up. They just want to pay a reasonable *renta*. Some companies, with the misfortune of being based in between MS and 18 territory, have to pay both gangs. The monthly fees range from the ten dollars expected from someone who sells vegetables on the street, to the 5,000 that a company with delivery trucks, such as Coca-Cola, might have to pay.

As part of the 2017 investigation, Operación Jaque (Check Mate), state prosecutors intercepted communication between incarcerated gang leaders who asked their forty-nine MS-13 "programs"—federations of cliques brought together under a common leadership—to hand in all the money they'd made in the past seven days. The total came to $600,552. If you take this as the weekly average, that would mean that the gang pulls in—mostly through extortion—a total of $31.2 million dollars a year. The sum is surprisingly low: if the gang distributed all its funds equally among its estimated 40,000 members, each member would receive only $64 a month. MS-13 is a mafia, but it's a mafia of the poor. The bulk of that money goes to lawyers, funerals, weapons, and unofficial pensions for the widows of dead or imprisoned homeboys. The MS-13 economy is barely a subsistence economy.

In 2013 a desperate Miguel Ángel was standing shirtless at a crossroads in El Refugio, waiting for a truck to pass by. He knew that the sloppy tattoos on his body—the small "MS" on the back of his left hand, the scrawled *"mi vida loca"* on his forearm— would make any truck driver take his request for charity a lot more seriously.

But not one delivery truck passed. Instead, a pickup rolled by with a couple of prosecutors on their way to the police station. They recognized him, and, concerned, asked what he was doing in the street. Miguel Ángel, furious and glaring, responded: "Standing here shirtless looking to make a buck so I can get something to eat!"

The prosecutors threw him a frightened glance and drove off. After a while, Miguel Ángel gave up and went back to his shack.

Today, Miguel Ángel is ranting against the prosecutor's office, against the UTE, against the police, against the whole world. He's at the end of his tether. He's thinking of leaving the shack, dropping the whole legal process, escaping, turning into an outlaw.

"I'm not scared of anybody. All I need is my papaya orchard in some quiet spot, my family, and whoever comes around to fuck with me is gonna taste almonds, 'cause I'll have my beans all lined up and ready for them."

Metaphors and onomatopoeias for bullets: beans, nuts, seeds, explosions, *pop, pop, pop*.

Nearby, the Turín well is completely flooded. The criminologist Israel Ticas has called off the excavation. The heavy machinery arrived after the start of the Central American winter, too late to do any digging or make any progress toward recovering the bodies. And yet, Ticas, literally swimming in a stew of death—the muddy pool at the bottom of the well—was able to pull up a few femurs, craniums, and foot bones that belonged to four different murder victims, including a woman. The authorities have come to believe that there are more than twenty bodies in the well. Ticas had estimated, two years previously, at the beginning of the excavation, that there were at least fifteen bodies. But other, anonymous sources have told us that they couldn't be sure there weren't even more bodies. Ticas and his assistants excavated what they could, but had to stop due to the danger of a collapse. They used different colored ropes when descending so that in the event of a collapse, rescuers would know what bodies they were digging out. Ticas always used the red rope.

Because of the lack of machinery, they've only recovered a handful of bones after two years of work. Since October 2012, the six gang members arrested and accused of dumping their murder victims into the well have walked free, released because they couldn't legally be held any longer without charge. One of their few conditions was to periodically report to the court. But they weren't stupid. They never showed up.

Miguel Ángel still hasn't testified for the case, and when he does, it'll be in a courtroom with no defendants present. Justice in the most murderous country in the world is bad theater, with pathetic, vulgar, and sometimes absent actors.

All Miguel Ángel and his family have left to eat is a few vegetables, some tortillas, and a couple packets of dried soup. Eventually, some police officer will donate something. They're living like beggars, waiting for justice from a kangaroo court. And Miguel Ángel has a tense relationship with the prosecutors, who have gone as far as threatening to accuse him of the same murders he denounced. He's convinced that some police officers have tried to walk him. Something is going to blow. He's exasperated with the Salvadoran state, which has condemned him to a life so miserable it's intolerable.

He keeps talking about his plans to escape.

"I'm thinking of arming up and just taking care of myself. I gotta have cat-eyes. Go into hiding. Because where I'm going, there are Eighteens."

Miguel Ángel has reached such a boiling point that, at the prosecutor's office a few weeks ago, he pretended to have forgotten everything he'd told them, refusing to recognize a member of his former clique who was being charged with racketeering.

"I showed the prosecutors I didn't give a fuck. I let some *bicho* from Atiquizaya go free, so that the prosecutors could see just how few fucks I gave. They lost their shit. But I don't give a fuck. I'm getting out of here. I'm gonna split."

Sometimes Miguel Ángel goes months without seeing the prosecutors, who are bogged down with dozens of cases and barely have time to prepare their witnesses. They usually talk to the witnesses on the eve, or the very morning, of a trial. Sometimes prosecutors who don't know Miguel Ángel and don't understand the case show up at the shack. He's had to explain everything from the beginning to multiple prosecutors.

Miguel Ángel squats down on one of the half-buried tires in the yard of his shack. There's weak coffee and sweet bread. We broach a topic we've never talked about till now.

"When it's all over, Miguel Ángel, then what?"

"As far as I know, soon as the process is all over, they're going to leave me with nothing. The prosecutors say they'll give me some money from their own salaries to go work somewhere else, plus a bit of money for my woman to come and visit me once a month. No house, no food, so I got to just figure it out."

"Do you feel used?"

"In this whole thing, the one who's gotten least out of it is me. All the honchos in high society, they got what they wanted. How much was Rambito's murder worth? Chepe paid eleven thousand dollars to walk Rambito. I got nothing out of it."

"Is there any guarantee that you won't become a hitman again when the state lets you out?"

"There aren't any other options. There should be some job

program. I should get a chance to make a clean sweep of things in the courtroom. I haven't gotten rid of my tattoos because they haven't offered me a thing, and the tattoos at least protect me on the street. The information I've given them is worth something. I told them what I did, who I shot, and everything that the others did. That should be worth something."

"Can you rule out that you won't go back to doing the same?"

"No, I can't. If they offered me other opportunities ..."

"Do you feel that the people of this country owe you something?"

"I risked my life. I quit the streets and I brought a fuckload of sicarios off the streets with me. I mean, that's why there's a fuck-load of people who want to kill me now. Cops, gangsters. I don't know who works for who here. It's a thing they call organized crime. I don't want to be in danger, I got my little girl. Society doesn't care that she's threatened, they only care that the witness made his statement."

He raises his voice. He opens his hands and shakes them as if he's waiting for something to fall from the sky. He stands stock-still and lowers his gaze. And when he looks up again, there's fury in his widened eyes. He throws his head back and stares down without blinking. Like he must have stared at El Horse before ripping the heart out of his chest. But he only says: "If they stopped and thought about it, they'd probably say, 'Hey, things could go badly for this *bicho*. He's got a daughter, he's got a wife, we could at least give him a job.'"

A phrase that Miguel Ángel has used and that seems to sum up not only his life, but the life of so many other children of war in this country: "They didn't give me no other choice."

Part III

Abyss

20
Traitor

treacherous [adj.]: 1. Of one who commits betrayal.
2. Said of an animal: of unpredictable reactions.
3. Something more damaging than expected.

The Kid doesn't know it yet, and nor do we, but this will be our last interview in the shack.

It's late afternoon, January 14, 2014. Dusk.

We've been visiting the shack for two years. In all that time the Kid only got mixed up once, when he was telling, with much verve, the story of one particular murder. In all that time, he never seemed nervous. Having the temperament of someone who has committed multiple murders and would willingly have committed many more, nervousness doesn't seem to be part of his makeup. We've seen him fed up, tired, dejected, furious, but never nervous.

Today, though, he seems nervous.

He keeps darting glances at the door. He responds to our questions hurriedly, in short bursts, and has stopped following the thread of the conversation. He won't hold a gaze more than a split second before glancing again at the door.

Tomorrow he's going to testify against officers Hernández and Tejada, the alleged accomplices of Chepe Furia in the murder of Rambito. A group of police will pick him up from here and he'll ride with them across the country, to accuse two of their colleagues of aggravated homicide and organized crime. The Kid has already said that he saw them in a patrol truck with Rambito on the day of his murder. He's already explained that hours later he saw Rambito get into Chepe Furia's car with two lengths of rope. But this was at the pretrial hearing. Tomorrow, he must repeat it in the sentencing hearing, in which the two officers may be sent to prison for twenty years or more.

The Kid is listening to our questions about what's going to happen tomorrow, when suddenly his eyes widen and his body tenses. A police officer from El Refugio walks into the shack with his right hand on his holstered gun. There's a whole new group of detectives working the case since Gil Pineda was transferred a few months ago. He's gone to another of the violent departments of El Salvador, as the new chief of homicide.

The police officer who has just walked in pauses to survey the scene. It's the first time an officer has interrupted one of our interviews with the Kid. He seems irritated, asks to see our documents and press credentials, occasionally glancing angrily at the Kid as he checks our papers.

He tells us to leave.

"Not until the Kid asks us to," we respond.

The Kid makes a call on his old phone to the chief of the police at the outpost, Detective Pineda's replacement.

"Yeah," the Kid says, "they just want my life story, who I am, where I'm from … Yeah, I know you have to be careful talking about some of this … Yeah, I know I could be digging my own grave …"

He hangs up. He's pale. Lorena watches the tense scene and sends Marbelly waddling over to say two of the five words she knows, to distract the officer so he'll let go of his gun.

"Here … pidgey," Marbelly says, pulling on the officer's pants, trying to get him to turn his attention to an imaginary pigeon.

The angry officer turns and leaves the shack, promising to come back after talking to his chief.

"They're nervous about tomorrow," the Kid tells us, looking down.

A prosecutor from Ahuachapán, who asked to remain anonymous, revealed that he had seen some police officers pressuring the Kid, offering him money to keep quiet, threatening him with death if he testified against their colleagues.

We ask the Kid if we should leave them alone. Seemingly humiliated, he nods.

Lorena is standing at the door to the street, watching for the officer to come back. She opens the door for us and steps aside, smiling.

In the San Miguel Specialized Court for Organized Crime, where the sentencing hearing takes place, the Kid becomes Yogui.

Yogui is wearing a dark blue police uniform, without badges or insignia, that is about three sizes too big. He's also wearing a black knit balaclava, and just imagining putting this on one's head is suffocating. San Miguel is the hottest department in the country, where it's not rare for summer highs to hit 105°. Yogui walks into the courtroom with his shoulders raised and tense, as if he were wearing a metal back brace.

It's nine in the morning. The two prosecutors, a man and a woman, are looking grave. The defense, two lawyers who also defended Chepe Furia in his trial, are joking around. They whisper and laugh at their desk. The accused police officers are in the back of the room, their backs to the judge, sitting behind a screen that lets them hear but not see what's going on. They sit very still. They close their eyes periodically, seemingly in prayer.

The judge, with his wrinkled, sharp-featured face, orders the witnesses to stand.

The prosecutor calls the first witness, Yogui, to the stand. It's a formality, however, because there is no stand in this courtroom— just a few plastic seats. Yogui walks forward and sits on one of them.

"Good morning, Yogui," the prosecutor begins.

"Good morning, sir," Yogui answers in a voice that sounds like the Beast itself. As a protection measure, they distort the voices of the protected witnesses. They've made Yogui's voice sound like it's coming straight from the tomb, and it's hard to distinguish his words between the cavernous echoes.

"What are you going to testify about today?" the prosecutor asks calmly and formally, flipping through his notes.

"I don't know," Yogui responds.

Silence in the courtroom. The prosecutors lift their heads, and the defense team lets out a muffled chuckle.

The Kid rips off Yogui's mask, the black balaclava. Miguel Ángel Tobar, the Hollywood Kid, sits with his eyes wide, staring at the prosecutor, almost challenging him. It's obvious that today, like he did almost four years ago, he's come to rat on someone, and the air crackles with expectation. Maybe he's going to rat on somebody unexpected. Maybe it's not going to be the police or the gangs getting foiled.

The Kid still has the voice of the Beast, even with his face exposed. With no air conditioning in the courtroom, he's perspiring. Beads of sweat drip down his face.

"I don't know," he repeats in that deep, booming voice.

The prosecutor stands up, clears his throat, and asks the judge if he can modify the Kid's voice since you can hardly understand what he's saying. He asks, as well, for the judge to order him to put the balaclava back on. It seems he's trying to gain time to understand what's going on. Maybe he hopes that if they change the Kid's voice, the meaning of the words will also change, and he won't be left standing in the middle of the courtroom looking quite so ridiculous.

"You say put it on, but it's not you whose face is itchy, who's practically suffocating," the Kid says, now with the voice of a mouse.

He raises his eyebrows and stares fiercely at the prosecutors.

The prosecutor cautiously alludes to the first testimony the Kid provided.

"Do you remember? As you testified in 2011 —"

The Kid interrupts: "I remember that the first prosecutors made me say a bunch of things. I don't know shit about what's written in those reports."

The defense team doesn't hold back their laughter. The accused officers, eyes shut, continue to pray behind the screen. One of them has dropped to his knees. The lead prosecutor is dripping. The sweat will soon soak through his white shirt, and then his dark jacket. The seated prosecutor is also sweating. She lowers her gaze, not wanting to look at her partner, who shuffles some more papers on the desk. It's an absurd scene. It's obvious he's buying time, dripping sweat onto the pages, trying not to seem completely lost.

"Have you been threatened?" the prosecutor asks, in a voice even quieter than a mouse's.

"No," the Kid says.

"Did you receive any visitors before coming to testify?"

"No."

The prosecutor—voice now trembling—warns the Kid about giving false testimony, laying him open to perjury charges.

"Okay," the Kid says.

The prosecutor, deeply embarrassed, keeps trying for another five minutes. His partner doesn't make a move. The Kid, to the delight of the defense team, continues responding in the style of his wife: monosyllables and short phrases. The courtroom has turned into a sauna.

They finally give up. The Kid is taken back to the waiting room. The prosecutor whispers to his partner, gets to his feet, adjusts his jacket, and asks the judge for an adjournment to be able to step out and make a phone call. The judge denies the request. The prosecutor asks to speak to the witness privately. As if they hadn't been humiliated enough, the judge glares at the prosecutor and reminds him that they've had years to prepare the witness, and a few more minutes shouldn't make any difference. The prosecutor sits down and nervously starts bouncing his leg. He shuffles through his papers again, as if he could find something useful in there, or maybe he's wishing he could turn back time, figure out a way to spend more time with the witness, make sure he receives his basket of provisions, or stop the local police from threatening him.

"I request permission to go to the bathroom," the prosecutor says to the judge. The judge drops his head and, exasperated, puts both hands on his forehead. The prosecutor looks like a scolded child. The defense attorneys chuckle openly. The judge reluctantly grants the request. The prosecutor rushes out of the room, as if it were only his bladder, and not his whole being, that was suffering.

The Kid is a murderer. He's a multiple murderer. He's also a traitor to his gang. He is undoubtedly a man who could kill again. Nevertheless, without the Hollywood Kid, the state of El Salvador in this courtroom is nothing. Or worse than nothing: it's a prosecutor pretending he needs to pee.

The prosecutor comes back into the courtroom a few minutes later. The expression on his face makes clear that he got nowhere—the Kid didn't give in.

The hearing goes on for another four hours. It's an experience the prosecutors will struggle to recover from for a long time. One by one, the other witnesses—mostly policemen—will deny knowing anything, just like the Kid. All of the police witnesses who previously admitted to seeing their fellow officers take Rambito to the Atiquizaya police station—even the one who had confirmed that the officers had failed to fill out a police report—say they don't remember. All of the police witnesses, without exception, repeat the same phrases: "I don't know," "I don't remember." They all hang their heads and keep their gazes on the floor as they deflect the questions of a prosecutor who's melting into a puddle of sweat on the floor.

The defense team, meanwhile, spends the day earning the easiest money of their lives. Watching with obvious delight, they hardly even need to cross-examine. The judge, finally deciding that the show has gone on long enough, advises the prosecution to throw in the towel and refrain from calling any more witnesses. His tone of voice shifts sympathetically, drawing out the vowels in a sort of sing-song, like a soothing friend: okay, okay, that's enough. One of the defense lawyers, cruelly rubbing it in, asks the judge to let his adversaries continue.

There seems to be something masochistic compelling the prosecutors to go on. The hearing continues. They call the next protected witness: the woman who worked at the store where Rambito bought the ropes that would be used to tie him up. Everybody in the courtroom knows that the woman creeping like a dark specter into the court, using a cane and wearing a black balaclava, is the store clerk from Atiquizaya. She's a secondary witness.

"This is going to be good," one of the defense attorneys says to the other. "I want to see what the hell they're going to ask her."

The questions are absurd. Did she see the ropes, does she remember who bought them, what kind of rope was it? Her testimony serves only to support the Kid's testimony. The poor woman has spent hours dressed as Santa Muerte for nothing. Or maybe just for the amusement of the defense team. The state prosecutors, after almost four years of investigation, have managed to prove that one day a woman sold two lengths of rope to a young man she did not know.

A case that seemed as good as won has unraveled into nothing. Police officers were told to arrest a man. Some witnesses saw those same officers in the street. The man was later seen with gang members. The man was later murdered. The police acted oddly and didn't want to provide records or justify their arrest. That was all the prosecutors needed to show. Chepe Furia, Liro Jocker, and El Stranger—the gangsters implicated in the murder—have already been convicted. They were the killers. The police, the other actors in the crime, were those who had the victim in their custody before the gang members took over. It should have been an open-and-shut case. But it turned into a pathetic comedy.

That afternoon, officers Tejada and Hernández are declared innocent of Rambito's murder.

We call the Kid at six in the evening of the same day, just after he's returned to his shack on the other side of the country. What happened in San Miguel? When did you lie: today, or when you first told us what happened? Did you see the police with Rambito, or was it all made up?

"I saw them with Rambito," the Kid says, "and I saw Rambito head out with Chepe and the others ... The thing is ... I didn't want to say it myself. I'm already carrying a lot of crosses, don't want to pick up another."

The Kid has done it again. He turned his back on his first gang when he betrayed a couple of members of the Mara Gauchos Locos 13, obeying Chepe Furia's order to purge the weakest. He turned his back on his second gang, the MS-13, when he killed his brother's killers. He turned against the letters tattooed on his own body when he decided to become a protected witness and testify against his homeboys. And now he's turned yet again, this time on the prosecutors, who forgave his crimes in exchange for his testimony.

Betrayal is the exit the Kid takes to change his path in life.

And yet, the Kid was never the first to break faith. The Gauchos betrayed him first, when they tried to run with MS-13 and then repented, thinking the Beast would understand. His MS homies betrayed him first when they killed his brother, El Cheje. And Chepe Furia betrayed him over and over, abandoning the Kid when the clique was going through its worst time, ordering him to kill a woman and burn a pickup truck, violating the creed he had taught him in one of the first clique *mirins*: barrio first, barrio second, and barrio third. Truth be told, the MS-13 made a lot of promises to the

Kid, and it was he, Chepe Furia, who jumped ship time and again when the seas got rough. And then there was the state prosecutor, who not only promised to expunge his history of violence, but also to take care of him, protect him, give him something to eat even if it was just a meager basket of basics, and protect him from police threats.

The Kid is a traitor who gets back at traitors by betraying them.

Today, the Kid turned the attorney general into a laughing stock. The news spread fast: prosecutors in other parts of the country heard of the fiasco and mentioned that their colleagues might take legal action against the Kid. It was time for betrayal to change direction once more. It was time to move.

21
Outlaw

outlaw [noun]: 1. A criminal on the run from justice.
2. A man living in exile, having been
forced out of his country or home.

Old man Jorge is dying on his cot.

A mixture of pus and blood oozes from his leg. His wife, just as old and worn as he is, tends to the wound. The pink juice running down his calf smells so bad his wife can hardly eat. She says that she's constantly breathing the smell of decomposing flesh. The old man isn't going to last long. It's a March afternoon in 2014, a warm, muggy day full of clouds of buzzing insects. The flies and gnats hover persistently over Jorge's rotting leg.

Lorena, the Kid's wife, retrieves water from the well. She yanks hard on the cord again and again to bring up the pail from the bottom. She's pregnant. And skinny. The Kid is about to be a father of two. Jorge and his wife are giving the young family food and a place to live on land Jorge bought after winning a bit of money in the national lottery. The land's just enough to provide for them. Jorge's sons, nineteen-year-old Pepe and twenty-five-year-old Jorge, cultivate maize and beans in their *milpa*. Next to it stand two old structures with walls of mud and straw, and roofs patched together with a combination of laminate and plastic. The whole property, about the size of half a soccer field, is cut out of a sugarcane plantation that now seems the embodiment of neglect. Even in tiny El Salvador, remote corners exist. The buildings used to be small warehouses and shelters for the laborers, a place where they could eat their midday beans and tortillas out of the sun. The plantation has been abandoned.

The place looks like a moonscape. A bleak and lonely moonscape.

The Kid is washing with a bucket in front of a sink filled by the well water that Lorena is pumping. He has his hand cannon loaded and nearby. The hand cannon is made from two pieces of metal tubing and a nail. The lengths of tubing are soldered carefully together, and the contraption is loaded with a 12-caliber shotgun cartridge. To fire its single shot, you pull one piece of tubing out of its metal sleeve and slam it back hard, so that the nail pierces the shell and the pellets burst out. The Kid hasn't been without his weapon at his side since he's arrived in this latest circle of hell.

Near the property are the abandoned tracks of a line that used to transport coffee in western El Salvador's golden days. A little further on, at the outskirts of the village of El Saral, are just a scattering of adobe houses where poor campesinos and Barrio 18 members live. It's not far from Las Pozas, but its reputation is far worse. Few people want to live in El Saral since the Eighteens took over. It's one of the gang's more remote bastions. To the Kid, it's Comanche territory. That's why the hand cannon has become like an extra limb.

The Eighteens have been prowling around nearby to check out the new arrival. They're keeping their distance but, sometimes, at night, they fire a couple shots into the air to make their presence known. To tell the Kid, in bandit's language, that they're watching him. That neither he nor his family are welcome.

Jorge's younger son, Pepe, spends the afternoon giving Marbelly rides on his bicycle on a dirt path cutting through the old cane field. The mosquitoes are out in force, hovering and biting. But Marbelly loves these bumpy rides and, every afternoon, when Pepe comes home from working the fields, she asks him to take her.

This afternoon an Eighteen is hiding behind a mulato tree with a pistol in his hand, ready to ambush Pepe and Marbelly. Two other Eighteens, reinforcements, are hiding in the sugarcane.

Marbelly is drinking a Frutsi, a cheap soft drink sold in various artificial colors in plastic bottles. Marbelly's Frutsi is red. She's having fun. Neither she nor Pepe have any idea what's waiting for them behind the holy tree of the skinned, the Xipe Totec.

The Kid, who had been working with Pepe, keeps pouring water over his body to wash off the heat and the dust. Lorena keeps yanking on the well's cord. The Eighteen keeps waiting. Old man Jorge keeps rotting. And Marbelly is getting nearer to the ambush.

The Eighteen steps out from behind the tree.

"Stop," he yells to Pepe, not wanting to kill him without at least giving notice.

Pepe hurls Marbelly, along with the bicycle, to the opposite side of the path. He dives into the cane and starts running. The red Frutsi spills all over Marbelly's chest, soaking her shirt.

Pop. Pop. Pop.

The Eighteen fires three shots. The bullets smack the ground just yards from Marbelly, but they weren't aimed at her. The pail

254 THE HOLLYWOOD KID

full of water splashes down into the bottom of the well. Lorena runs toward the gunshots, toward her daughter. A shelf falls over as the Kid runs toward the gunshots, toward his daughter. He's carrying his hand cannon. Jorge doesn't move. He can't.

The Kid readies his weapon. Lorena doesn't carry anything but the child in her undernourished belly.

Marbelly screams. Her shirt is stained red, and she's laid out on the ground. The Kid looks at her and sprints past. He thinks Marbelly is covered in blood. Lorena runs toward her. The Kid doesn't stop. He's running after the Eighteens.

"Ah! No! Sons of bitches!" he yells. He thinks they've shot his daughter. He's become the Beast.

He fires his single shot. The Eighteens keep running. The Kid, barefoot and wearing nothing but his underclothes, keeps after them through the cane fields. He doesn't catch them, but he keeps going. He crosses the line into Barrio 18 territory. He keeps going. He's possessed. He wants to kill. He doesn't have any ammo left, just a load of hate and a useless tube in his hand. He runs until he can't run anymore.

He stops. Turns back.

If the Kid thought that the shack was his personal hell, he was wrong. There are other hells. Sugarcane grows in some of them.

The Kid and his family settled into this dangerous corner of the world in March of 2014, just a few days before the ambush. Life in El Refugio had become untenable. The basket of provisions had stopped coming altogether by November of 2013. The Kid had to go out and beg for money on the streets, flashing the warped MS tattooed on his hand in hopes it would scare people enough to give up a dollar. Sometimes it worked, sometimes it didn't. He ended up sixty dollars in debt: owing money to the woman who sold them the corn drink *atol*, to the man who sold them wood for their stove, to the corner store, to the tortilla woman.

Without food, without money, and with Chepe Furia and almost all the Hollywood Locos veterans behind bars, there was no reason for the Kid to stay in El Refugio. Detective Pineda wasn't even assigned to that station anymore. They'd transferred him to La Libertad, on El Salvador's central coast, to chase after gang members. The Kid couldn't handle the shack anymore. He and his family moved to old man Jorge's house at the beginning of March, to hide away in the midst of the corn and sugarcane fields. Who knows how the Kid and Jorge met, or why the man had such a soft spot for him that, even though they were close to Barrio 18 territory, he would take him in and put him in the same hut as his own kids. Old man Jorge said yes to something the whole world said no to.

Before leaving the shack for their new hideout, the Kid slipped out one morning with Lorena to show her the strange family that would host them for a few months. He showed her how to get there.

The prosecutors had delivered what to the Kid was the final affront. They offered to take him to a secure location—but without Lorena, without Marbelly, and without his unborn baby.

"In that case no. I don't give a shit if they kill me here. But I'm not going alone," Lorena remembers the Kid angrily telling the prosecutors.

Later, on another March morning, the Kid told Lorena that they were leaving, that they'd waited long enough in the shack, and that it was time to hit the road. He had a plan. He would leave in the morning to guard the path. And then she would come in the afternoon.

"If those sons of bitches come looking for me, tell them that I split. Act crazy and start crying. Say that I left you."

The Kid swiped a neighbor's bicycle and left.

Sergeant Pozo, the cop who had convinced the Kid, years ago, to talk to Detective Pineda, showed up around noon that day. He asked where the Kid was. Lorena, as deft as her man at maintaining silence, only spoke two words: "He left."

Pozo looked for him, checking under the beds. But there wasn't much space to hide in that shack. None, in fact. You can see under the rickety beds without having to bend down. The place was tiny. A tiny shack and a tiny little dried-up yard. Dead earth. Where the Kid managed to live for over four years without going crazy. He held up so they would pardon his multiple murders. He held up because they promised him security and a basket of provisions ... that damn basket.

Officer Pozo tried to find out more.

"How come? Where'd he go?"

Lorena offered a longer response this time. One word longer. "I don't know."

Lorena asked Pozo for some money so she could leave as well. She lifted Marbelly into her arms over her large pregnant belly and boarded a microbus toward La Hermosa church, right at the turn-off to El Saral. She got off the bus and walked down a narrow path, the way the Kid had shown her, toward old man Jorge's house. The Kid wasn't there when she arrived. In a gesture of thanks to Jorge for opening his home to them in that abject corner of the country, the Kid was out harvesting corn with Jorge's two sons.

The state's protected witness decided he needed to protect himself and his family. He trusted his hand cannon more than he trusted his country.

But Sergeant Pozo can be a bloodhound when he wants to be. Hours after Lorena arrived at old man Jorge's, Pozo showed up. He talked angrily to the Kid and then, promising to come back when they needed the Kid for any proceedings related to the Turín well, he left.

Old man Jorge was a campesino in the most traditional sense. Together with his two sons, he lived off the land he worked. If the land provided, they ate. If the land did not provide, they went hungry. But, a few years back, he had a stroke of luck. He played the lottery and won enough to buy a plot of unwanted land in the west. He says God told him to play the lottery. But then his luck, so dry for most of his life, dried up again. He fell into a hole and cracked his right tibia. His sons took him to the hospital in Chalchuapa, where they gave him a cast. But the old man couldn't handle the immobility or the itching. He ripped off the cast, popping a splinter of bone through his skin. The wound soon began to suppurate.

Old man Jorge took to his bed. His wife washed off the blood and pus with wet rags. But the infection was serious. Jorge blamed his plight on a curse that his nearest neighbors had cast on him. It's witchcraft, he would exclaim, festering away. The Kid wanted to help. He tried to undo the curse with his own spell. He trapped a live bat, put it in a bag, rubbed the bag against the bad leg, and then buried the bat in a secret spot among the sugarcane. The Kid had told Lorena that he had "the book from hell, the black book." Lorena didn't ask.

There can be few images as dark, depressing, and macabre as that of the Kid rubbing a live bat on the putrefying leg of old man Jorge on the edge of an abandoned sugarcane field in western El Salvador.

The infection, not surprisingly, followed its course.

Who knows why, but the old man loved the Kid. Lorena remembers that he even offered to let them build a house on the property. "There's land enough. You'd fit," he insisted, hoping the outlaw would settle down. He also offered to sell part of the harvest so the Kid could buy "a good gun" and, along with his two sons, kill the Eighteens of El Saral.

During their stay in that infernal landscape, we continued to interview the Kid and his family, but there was none of the calm of El Refugio days. We were interviewing an outlaw now. The Kid, grasping his hand cannon and with a machete tucked into his waistband, slipping down narrow paths between the cane and the corn, would meet us at predesignated points. Out-of-the-way, forgotten locations, random landmarks along the highway: the big ceiba tree, the mulato tree. And old man Jorge's sons were typically in tow. Even if they didn't sit in on the interviews, they hovered close by.

We rendezvoused one day on a narrow road that connected Atiquizaya to Las Pozas and San Lorenzo. At the designated meeting point there was a small bicycle workshop. Three kids, staring at our unfamiliar car, made a few phone calls. Moto-taxis rolled up and started making rounds. The drivers slowed as they passed to peer at us. The neighborhoods surrounding our meeting spot were all controlled by Barrio 18.

After a while the Kid, nervous and bathed in sweat, broke out of the brush. He had the hand cannon tucked into his pants as if it were a pistol, a machete in his hand, and was wearing a black ski mask similar to what he wore in court as Yogui. He glanced around for our car, ran over, jumped in the backseat, and hissed: "Step on it, go, go, go!"

We still had to drive through Atiquizaya. Not only was he nervous about his former clique that wanted him dead, he was also worrying there'd be a police checkpoint that would force us to stop. Carrying a hand cannon is against the law. Once we made it onto the highway toward Santa Ana, we stopped at a small hotel where couples pay seven dollars for four-hour sessions. The grim hotel, its walls painted a pallid pink, didn't even have a name.

"The enemy is going to hunt me down one day," the Kid said. "There's money on my head. I'm not part of the Mara anymore. I'm just someone who wanted to be different. What I can tell the world is this: maybe there's evil in the gangs, maybe there's even evil in the government ... All that I can tell the world is that nothing in this world belongs to us. It was all created by God ... I wish I could go back to when I was a kid and decide to not jump into the Mara ... I tell the youngsters: Don't do it. It's a pact with death."

He rambled on for a few moments, talking about God and the Beast. He took a sip of Coke, staring at the door of the stuffy little room. He spoke about death. A dusty fan rattled in the corner.

"What would you say to the people you killed?" we asked him.

"I didn't want to do what I did to them, but I was ordered to. I had to follow through. It was the pact of the Mara. I didn't want to do it. If they could be here now ... I'd ask forgiveness for what I did, and from their families, too. I made a lot of mistakes. I killed him, killed her, killed all of them ... And now I'm waiting for what's coming. There's someone behind all this that wants to see me suffer. The Beast, she's everywhere, fighting to bring me down."

"You were one of MS-13's most feared sicarios. Are you proud of that?"

"I don't have a thing to show for it. Not even the shoes on my feet. I'm not saying I'm great. I'm not saying I'm awful. I'm saying, I fucked up my life when I got involved in this."

"And now what?"

"Farm. Grow food to eat and wait until they find me. Because I know they're going to come someday. I live every moment knowing that the Beast is behind me, wanting to pull me down. She comes to me, bursting into flames in my dreams. The Beast is a black beast, a black horse that takes control, like in the Apocalypse, wiping peace off the earth. A black Beast that carries a pointed sword ... Back home, my daughter asks me: 'Do you love me?' How am I not going to love her, if she's my own blood? My wife, too. Sometimes, when she's sitting next to me, I tell her, 'Get out of here.' She feels bad and thinks I don't want her around, but that's not it. I just don't want the Beast to come for me and get someone else instead."

"And if that were to happen? If you lost your daughter or your wife?"

"I'd go back to what I was before. I'd start again. It would be like ... emptying a honeycomb of all its honey. Maybe I don't have a fuckload of soldiers, but it would be some heavy shit. If there's some idiot gangster who wants to try something like that, just let him come, I'll be waiting. I'll live in the mountains, in the woods. I'll be ready for him."

We talked for more than an hour. Miguel Ángel then told us where to drop him back off. It was in El Refugio, at a dirt path that led through a patch of weeds and dead trees. He put his ski mask on, took out his machete and his hand cannon, and slipped back into the shadows.

After the Eighteens' failed attempt, the Kid and old man Jorge's sons took turns between them, keeping guard over the property and working in the *milpa*. Two of them would go to work and the other two would be on lookout with the hand cannon. At night, they took two-hour shifts. When one of them needed to go to the next hamlet over, the other two would set themselves up at strategic posts along

the way. They lived like men
from long ago. Protecting their
lives and their food in the middle
of the wilderness.

The Eighteens kept on circling
the property. They stopped being
so cautious, stalking the cane
fields at night with flashlights
that lit up the families' mud huts.
The Kid and the brothers waited
for the Eighteens to make their
move.

A few weeks after the Frutsi
reddened Marbelly's chest, the
Kid decided to get out.

"They're going to kill the girl
or they're going to kill all three
of us," he said to Lorena. "It's all
going to hell."

The Kid with machete and hand cannon,
mid 2014, a few months before he was
murdered.

He said goodbye to his family in campesino style, showing little
emotion.

And he took off to where it all started. He headed toward Las
Pozas.

Old man Jorge died a few months later. Like so much in the
Kid's life, the old man rotted to death.

22
Truce

truce [noun]: 1. The cessation of hostilities
between two adversaries for a determined period.

The Kid's story has one consistent thread: everything always turns out badly. Everything always happens at the wrong time. His fate only heads in a single direction: from bad to worse.

By the time the Kid returned to Las Pozas in the middle of 2014, fleeing from old man Jorge's infernal cane fields, El Salvador had taken an unexpected turn. When the Kid decided to leave his shack the country was being rocked by something extraordinary, which would have lasting repercussions even after it was smothered. The gangs had set aside their mutual hatred and redirected their energies against two principal targets: the Salvadoran state, and traitors—traitors like the Kid who collaborated with the state.

In March of 2014, something had begun to break in El Salvador. Government efforts toward building a gang truce, which started in 2012 and got the world talking about this tiny and violent country, had begun cracking.

What in 2014 was officially crumbling (though there was never anything very official about the process) began on Saturday, March 10, 2012. That day, suddenly, the madness paused. The barbarity halted. That day, there were ten murders in all of El Salvador. Maybe the number doesn't sound like much to celebrate. Ten murders in a single day, in a country with only 6.6 million people, is a lot of murders. And yet, it was an important decrease. Four less than the previous month's tally. The following day, Sunday, March 11, a day of congressional and mayoral elections, only six families mourned their loved ones. In a country used to lamenting at least ten murders a day, six seemed like something close to peace.

Salvadoran peace is less war, not no war.

Authorities claimed that the relative tranquility was due to increased police activity around the election. But the explanation was inadequate. It seemed especially unlikely when, the next day, Monday, March 12, there were only two murders in all of the 13,000 square miles of national territory. Something didn't make sense: it was as if, one day to the next, Mexico City had suddenly become pollution-free and nobody could explain why.

The first hypotheses from journalists and researchers focusing on the gangs pointed to the jails. Something must have been happening in there. Something to do with the imprisoned but powerful leaders. All logic pointed to these hot, forgotten, pestilential holes where the state jammed tens of thousands of its men and women to pay for their crimes. Nobody imagined that the reduction in homicides had been orchestrated in the calm of an air-conditioned office by high government officials.

President Mauricio Funes was the country's first leftist president.

He came to power in 2009 after running as a candidate for the Farabundo Martí National Liberation Front (FMLN), an old coalition of former guerrilla fighters, and defeating Rodrigo Ávila, of the right-wing Arena party. Ávila had twice been the national director of the police under previous Arena administrations. The Funes campaign attacked Ávila on the terrain of national security. Why should El Salvador vote for a police chief who not only couldn't solve the gang problem, but had overseen a period in which the problem had gotten much worse? Why vote for a chief of police who had seen El Salvador become the most murderous country on the planet?

When Funes won the 2009 elections, he was practically seen as the country's messiah.

He had attracted the votes and the hopes of not only the left, but also of many in the center and even on the right. Young people saw Funes as different from the typical political dinosaurs. He appeared to be a serious candidate who could bring together the country's disparate interests. Even the business sector and, most importantly, the oligarchy stopped demonizing him as a bearded guerrilla commander. There was every reason to think he would be a conciliatory president.

Before entering politics, Funes was a respected journalist. In a media world used to complacency, he anchored multiple television news shows in which he asked hard questions of politicians and officials. In 2000, he traveled to Cuba and was one of the few Latin American journalists to interview Fidel Castro in Havana. On that occasion, he also interviewed two Salvadorans—former soldiers Ernesto Cruz León and Otto Rodríguez—who had been accused of terrorism and condemned to death in Cuba. Both men had links with the international terrorist and ex-CIA agent Luis

Posada Carriles, who in 1976 blew up Cubana de Aviación Flight 455, killing all seventy-three passengers and crew members. Funes the journalist forged a good relationship with Fidel Castro and the Cuban political elite, assuring him strong support from the Salvadoran left, especially among the ex-comandantes who revered Fidel as a sort of patriarch.

Funes was able to inspire confidence on both sides of the aisle. His election seemed to bode important changes in Salvadoran public policy. His slogan was: "This time it's different. Mauricio, President."

When Funes won, thousands of Salvadorans swarmed the Masferrer roundabout in San Salvador, close to the presidential residence, waiting for him to address them from the stage erected by the FMLN, roaring "Mauricio, Mauricio, Mauricio."

A community of ex-FMLN combatants in eastern Chalatenango, a region under guerrilla control during the war, threw an enormous party. The hoary *guerrilleros* wept and drank aguardiente. The crippled veterans and the war orphans celebrated throughout the night. After seventeen years of sacrifice, asymmetric war, and so many buried comrades, finally, they had won.

There were rapid changes. Almost all the ministries were put under the direction of onetime *comandantes*, men and women of the old guard. New chiefs of police were named, ex-guerrillas who had joined the force after the war, hoping to change it.

The gangs and their sympathizers supported the Funes campaign in their own way. In a beer hall, years later, a national Barrio 18 leader would explain to us that it wasn't a well-planned or democratic process. It was, however, inevitable. The hard-right Arena administrations had been increasingly confrontational with the gangs over the last eight years. The FMLN stood for a different strategy. They talked about investing in society, increasing opportunities for the youth, and curbing violence.

"The *guerrilleros* were poor, they fought for the poor. We're poor as well, and we're also fighting to change our lives," the gang member told us. Then he paused, looked intently at both of us, and tilted back his Golden beer.

A country longing for change, clamoring for salvation.

Funes appointed Manuel Melgar, who'd been a guerrilla *comandante* in the '80s, as minister of security and justice. Melgar had also been a member of the Revolutionary Party of Central American Workers (PRTC), one of the organizations that came together to form the FMLN, and which had carried out one of the most controversial acts of the war: the June 1985 killing of four US marines stationed in El Salvador. Thomas Handwork, Patrick Kwiatkoski, Bobbie Dickson, and Gregory Weber had been drinking beer on a day of leave at a Chili's restaurant in the Zona Rosa, in the posh San Benito area of the capital, when they were gunned down.

The United States never forgave the attack. Manuel Melgar, even after rising to the position of presidential advisor, was never granted a US visa.

But the hoped-for changes failed to materialize. The *comandante* didn't achieve significant advances in security. The number of homicides went up, more neighborhoods fell to the gangs, and the police corruption crisis worsened. With mounting US pressure to remove his security minister, Funes had no option but, in November 2011, to ask for his resignation.

President Funes then leaned on one of his confidants, General David Munguía Payés, who had helped him forge connections with the army during his campaign and was appointed minister of defense when Funes first came into office. When Melgar stepped down, Payés was asked to replace him.

Under the guidance of General Payés, the gangs agreed on a truce.

In those relatively bloodless days of March 2012, five months after General Payés took over the post, almost nobody, including many state intelligence officials from whom he concealed the truce strategy, knew what was going on. The chief of police claimed, predictably, that the drop in murders and the apparent torpor of the gangs was due to the increase in police operations. In other words, to more patrols, arrests, and large-scale raids. More of the same. The Arena strategy.

The government covered up the only non-violent effort they were making to curb gang violence, while continuing to hail the violent strategy that had never worked. Salvadoran politicians knew that the country wanted to see blood spilt in order to stop the blood from spilling. They still work on this assumption.

Some state intelligence officials, suspicious about the transfer of prisoners within the penitentiary system, contacted journalists at the online newspaper, *El Faro*. They gave them important information about these high-level transfers, in exchange for anonymity.

On March 14, 2012, along with three other writers at *El Faro*, we published the following story: "Government Negotiated with Gangs to Reduce Murder Rate." The article explained that on the night of March 8, thirty leaders of the Mara Salvatrucha 13 and two groups of Barrio 18 members were transferred from the maximum-security prison in Zacatecoluca (known as Zacatraz) to prisons with less stringent security protocols. Zacatraz is the only facility in the country that follows the US prison model. Two prisoners per cell, inmates separated from visitors by thick glass, uniforms, food on

trays, and so on—nothing like the filthy chaos that other prisoners are resigned to in, for example, Ciudad Barrios (for MS-13) or
Cojutepeque (for Barrio 18), where the state is unable to do anything beyond keeping the inmates inside. What goes on in those
prisons with the inmates, or with their visitors, mattered little to
those on the outside. They are basically carceral villages where the
inmates even construct their own shacks. Food is distributed in a
single bucket for each unit, where the recommended occupancy
per cell is exceeded by ten to twenty inmates. And yet, there are
advantages. These dungeons are rife with drugs, alcohol, and
"conjugal visits" that the state makes no effort to control. Some
of the transferred leaders, like El Diablito of Hollywood, or El
Croc of Hollywood, hadn't touched a woman in years. And their
new homes permitted both conjugal visits and cell phones. (There
were some phones in Zacatraz, but getting them in was hard and
expensive.) Here, the leaders could confer with inmates in other
prisons as well as street leaders. Moving the top dogs to these laxer
prisons allowed them to retake control of El Salvador's cliques.
The national *ranfla* of MS-13 has since been active and organized.
And that was all part of the state's plan: to give power back to the
leaders because, as General Payés would later say, it doesn't make
any sense to try to negotiate with someone who has no power.

This was the gist of what *El Faro* published on March 14, 2012,
and in several follow-up articles.

Politicians summoned the media, in an effort to explain themselves. General Payés convened a press conference. It was the first
time a top FMLN official had made a public statement about the
reduction in homicides. With a stern, impassive face, he declared
that the transfers were the result of new intelligence gleaned
from inside the prisons: bold police investigators had uncovered

that inmates were hatching an appalling plan to breach the walls of Zacatraz with antiaircraft missiles and break the leaders out. This sounded unlikely, given that Zacatraz's inmates are held in a sort of underground bunker. Payés looked stymied when a journalist asked the obvious question: Why, then, were the inmates being moved to lower security prisons? Wouldn't they be more secure inside another maximum-security facility? Payés ducked the question.

Communication between the prisons and the streets had never been better. The homicide rate remained low. In the barrios, the gang members were upholding their end of the bargain. Some clique leaders had received orders from the transferred prison bosses that they should stop the killing.

One June afternoon in 2012, El Ogre, from the Big Crazy clique in Soyapango (one of the haphazard cliques created by El Diablito of Hollywood in the 1990s) was drinking beer with his homeboy Chuky in a bar close to the University of El Salvador. The bar was called Mi Pequeño Jardín (My Small Garden), located in the Zacamil neighborhood, which is Barrio 18 territory controlled by the powerful Tinnys Locos Sureños. But El Ogre and El Chuky weren't bothered. Their leader had signed onto the truce. He'd told them they couldn't kill each other, that they needed to stop playing around, end the potlatch of reciprocal violence. They felt like they were on vacation. However, there was never any order to stop the extortions. They could still threaten, beat people up, and even rape. The only hard rule—Biblical—was *thou shalt not kill*.

Ogre and Chuky went to a brothel before starting to drink. They had sex with prostitutes who were under control of Barrio 18 in downtown San Salvador, close to Parque Libertad. This was the territory of one of the oldest and most powerful Barrio 18 tribes in the country: the Raza Parque Libertad. After the brothel, Ogre and Chuky bought a few grams of cocaine and went to Mi Pequeño Jardín for a drink.

"You have to make the most of it, see," Ogre told us. "When could we ever come here to drink? It's full of women. When could we go mess around with the whores under their control? Never. Who knows how long this is going to last, how long we're supposed to hold back from going after the homeboys. So we got to take advantage." He pulled a bag out of the sleeve of his black shirt and held it in his palm like a treasure. Coke is one of the drugs the Mara Salvatrucha 13 forbids its members to use.

El Chuky, meanwhile, like a secretive accomplice, nodded at everything El Ogre was saying, adding occasional grunts of approval. The bearish Ogre, followed by the squat Chuky, got up and headed to the bathroom.

General Payés, confronted with indisputable evidence from *El Faro*, finally admitted in September 2012, while sitting in his ministerial office, that the truce was a plan hatched by him and approved by President Funes.

Each barrio went public with the truce in its own way. In some places, such as in the crowded neighborhood of Ilopango, they organized meetings in schools where members of the Mara Salvatrucha 13 and Barrio 18 hugged each other and begged the community—looking on in shock—for forgiveness.

In Ciudad Barrios, the MS-13 prison where La Ranfla—the prison-based gang organizing committee—was based, the drama group Teatro del Azoro (consisting of four Salvadorans and one Spanish actress) staged the play *Los más solos* (The Loneliest Ones). It was an odd performance. The inmates went out to the yard to see a play about desperate inmates. El Diablito of Hollywood himself received the troupe, taking the actresses on a tour through the prison dungeons along with Carlos Tiberio Valladares, El Snyder, one of the other MS-13 big shots. Both El Snyder and El Diablito were deported from the United States in the 1990s.

Gang leaders on both sides gave a joint press conference from Mariona prison, where they'd been transferred.

As if things weren't strange enough, General Payés tapped Raúl Mijango to handle the truce negotiations. Payés himself never met with any of the gang members, leaving Mijango to take care of the weekly meetings. Mijango had been a *comandante* of the Revolutionary People's Army, another of the guerrilla groups that was later folded into the FMLN. He was one of their most skilled military strategists. After the war ended, he worked in various leftist organizations and was an FMLN member until the year 2000, when he left the party for ideological reasons. He kept a low profile until he reappeared in 2012, surprising the entire country with his new role as the lead mediator between the Mara Salvatrucha, the Barrio 18, and the state.

An army general and an ex-guerrilla, working together to make peace between the gangs.

Another of General Payés's strategies was to ask for help from a respected priest: the bishop to the armed forces, Monseñor Fabio Colindres, assigned to both the military and police forces. Paolo Luers, a German who arrived in El Salvador in 1981 to join the armed struggle of the FMLN, contributed to the truce negotiations as a communications specialist. After the war, Luers opened the bohemian bar, La Ventana—a meeting place for intellectuals and artists—and was an analyst and commentator on various television shows until 2012.

Mijango, Colindres, and Luers were the three principal

negotiators in a truce process that was regularly denied at the official level.

President Funes himself repeatedly denied that his administration had anything to do with the truce. He would only admit to endorsing the pacification efforts led by the Catholic Church and various NGOs. Funes maintained his hard stance even though General Payés had already admitted the fact to *El Faro*.

Meanwhile, the murder rate remained low, and, in the midst of this tense period of peace—an armed peace—Salvadoran society held its breath. In some sectors people were hoping that the social conflict the gangs had unleashed would dissolve. And there were reasons to believe this might happen. The general secretary of the Organization of American States (OAS), the Chilean José Miguel Insulza, along with El Salvador's papal nuncio, attended a meeting with gang leaders in prison.

In 2010, El Salvador had a murder rate of 64.7 for every 100,000 inhabitants. In 2011, the year before the truce, the rate climbed to 70.1. In 2012, the first year of the truce, the rate dropped to 41.2. In 2013, the rate was 39.4, the third lowest of the century. Even with the truce, of course, the country still maintained a level of homicides—higher than Mexico's—that the UN classifies as an "epidemic." In El Salvador, not only gang members are killed, but people who have nothing to do with gangs. And not all gangsters obeyed the new rules of restraint. Killing was how they communicated. Killing was a question of honor. Some were being asked to spare members of an opposing gang who had killed their family members, or members who, like the Kid, in exchange for immunity, were collaborating with the state to put them in prison for decades.

It was a strange, precarious opening in El Salvador. Dozens of international journalists traveled the country with tour guides. Not long before, gang members would have killed them for even setting foot in their territory.

And then El Salvador rammed home its tragic lesson: a population raised under the threat of a crackdown will gravitate toward the logic of a crackdown. The popularity ratings of the truce were terrible. People repudiated the strategy, even as it was drastically lowering the murder rate.

Everything was falling apart in 2014, when the Kid decided to return to Las Pozas. The Constitutional Chamber had dealt a fundamental blow to the truce when it declared that it was unconstitutional for a soldier to occupy a ministerial position. In mid-2013 the father of the truce, General Payés, became the armed forces minister. The Ministry of Security and Justice was handed over to Ricardo Perdomo, previously head of the State Intelligence Agency. Perdomo banned former guerrilla Raúl Mijango from entering the prisons, cut off communication with gang leaders, severed the gang leaders' access to the media, raised the number of police operations in neighborhoods controlled by gangs, and persecuted the mediators of the truce. In short, he set out to demolish the truce. The Funes government and the FMLN, concerned about the 2014 presidential elections, became increasingly afraid to fight for the strategy that had yielded such remarkable results in lowering the murder rate.

Prison perks were slashed. Visits were restricted. Lower-ranking gang members castigated their leaders for letting themselves be duped. The government did not understand that you can't play with beasts without getting clawed. In March 2014, almost two years after the truce began, Salvador Sánchez Cerén (a former guerrilla commander and Funes's vice president) won the election.

The FMLN retained their seat at the table. The truce, however, was sidelined and, in January 2015, the new president ordered its outright cancellation.

"We can't go back to the strategy of trying to understand and negotiate with the gangs, because that's illegal now," Sánchez Cerén explained in a press conference. "They've placed themselves outside the law, they've become violators of the law, and so our obligation is to pursue them, punish them, and ensure that justice determines an appropriate outcome."

In March, the president ordered thirty of the gang leaders that had been transferred to lower-security jails to be returned to Zacatraz. The government, faced with mass rejection of its peace policy, prioritized raising its popularity over lowering the homicide rate. That March was one of the most violent months of the century so far: 500 murders. The year 2014 would close out with a rate of 61.1 homicides for every 100,000 inhabitants. And 2015 would descend into total mayhem: 103.6 homicides for every 100,000 inhabitants. A higher death rate than in countries at war.

To put it succinctly, the Salvadoran government had betrayed the most murderous gang in the world.

Some gang leaders had foreseen the fiasco and already chosen the successors who would take their place in the streets, anticipating that conditions in Zacatraz would be even more severe when they returned.

The gangs began plotting their revenge in the form of a new war: the gangs against the state. For the first time, it was not the main objective of MS-13 members to annihilate members of Barrio 18. The two groups agreed on some ground rules, mostly to do with respecting each other's territory, and set their sights on attacking those who had defrauded them.

On June 19, 2014, police officer Jaime Molina was busy in the vegetable garden in his backyard in Los Magueyes, in the city of Ahuachapán. A group of gang members surrounded him, threatened him, and started beating him. Jaime tried in vain to defend himself. The intruders cut up his body with machetes. By the end of that year, thirty-two officers had died in similar raids. Another eighty-eight were killed in 2015, and sixty-six in 2016. Dozens of soldiers and prison guards were also targetted. Some were chopped to pieces while still alive. Videos of the murders were disseminated.

Little by little the police started responding like gangsters. In his 2016 article, "Just like the National Guard," Roberto Valencia, a reporter for *El Faro*, likened the police force created after the peace accords to the state-sanctioned torture apparatus that had wreaked havoc during the civil war. Valencia showed that between January 2015 and August 2016, in the twenty months after President Sánchez Cerén declared the truce to be over, the police killed 693 alleged gang members. The statistics show that six suspected gang members were killed for every policeman who just came away with an injury in these "mutual skirmishes." For every policeman who was killed, fifty-three gang members died in the shootouts.

By that time, few in El Salvador avoided using the word 'war' to describe what was going on. What began as a truce in search of peace turned into a war crueler than the one government officials had been trying to end. The gangs were bent on revenge against people in uniform, and against traitors like the Kid.

In 2017, ex-president Funes fled to Nicaragua to avoid prosecution for illicit enrichment. In a raid on one of his homes, the prosecutor's office found a bizarre jumble of luxury items: a baby stroller valued at several thousand dollars (similar to those used by British royalty), collectible weapons, high-end cars, copper-plated boots, a bronze bust of himself, expensive cigars bearing etchings of his face, a lavish amount of clothes and shoes including a Ferragamo pair worth more than $6,000, and dozens of other frivolities that suggested a very different life from that expected of the "people's president."

In 2017, the prosecutor's office found him guilty of illicit enrichment to the tune of nearly half a million dollars. The following year he was accused of mounting a network to steal over $350 million dollars from the public treasury. He remains an outlaw expatriate in Nicaragua, often tweeting his self-justification.

Our current era of powerful mafias and ill-advised public policies against gangs did not begin with Mauricio Funes's backsliding. In fairness, he had implemented novel stratagems that yielded positive results. His problem was that he was scared of the polls.

In April 2003, President Francisco Flores (of the far-right Arena party) held a press conference in the Dina neighborhood of San Salvador, which was then controlled by Barrio 18. Unbeknownst to the president, a commemorative mural was displayed behind him in homage to a murdered gang member, Uncle Barba, a famous drug dealer considered one of the founders of the Barrio 18 in El Salvador. Completely oblivious of the significance, the cameras rolled while the security guards paced around in their black uniforms. Flores was here to launch his first Iron Fist Plan—the first antigang plan of its kind in the history of El Salvador, and which aimed to crush the gang problem. Dressed in a brown jacket and jeans, the president spoke tough words as the elite of the Salvadoran police dragged supposed gang members out of their houses and exhibited them like circus animals. He boasted of the harshness of his laws, of how implacable his government would be toward gang crime.

But the strategy bombed. The locals who were carted away were released just a few months later, due to lack of evidence. Many young men were detained merely for sporting tattoos and baggy pants. The state had tried to arrest what it didn't understand.

The Iron Fist, although a disaster in terms of improving public safety, was nonetheless massively popular.

It also proved a success for the Mara Salvatrucha and the Barrio 18. As with the deportations of the early 1990s, when they conquered the Salvadoran prison system, this public policy allowed them to colonize new territory. Young men harassed by the police for merely dressing like gang members were encouraged to join a gang, since they had little to lose by doing so. The damage caused by President Flores's national safety plan is still felt throughout El Salvador. (Flores had his karma to reckon with. After months on the lam, he turned himself in in 2014, accused of misappropriating several million in earthquake relief funds from Taiwan. He died of a stroke in 2016 while awaiting trial.)

And yet most people were so happy with his unprecedentedly repressive measures that, following Flores's term, they backed another Arena candidate in 2004, Antonio Saca. He was well loved in El Salvador for having been the Channel 4 sportscaster during the 1998 World Cup in France. Saca was also a millionaire radio magnate.

Sorely lacking in creativity, ignoring the dismal results of his predecessor, and failing to visit a single gang-controlled neighborhood, Saca launched his own plan, the Super Iron Fist. The Super Iron Fist was identical to the Iron Fist, only supersized. That's to say, there were more raids, more captures, more operations, and he sent, though always only briefly, more gang members to prison.

The increase of gang members in the prison system, however, caused severe problems, the worst of which erupted in August 2004, the first year of Saca's term. The common criminals of the largest prison in the country, officially named La Esperanza (the Hope), but better known as Mariona, determined to kill more than 400 members of the Barrio 18. The Eighteens, armed with grenades, launched a countermassacre. Of the thirty-two dead, only eight were gang members. The following week, one headline in a local paper read, "A Place in Hell Known as Mariona."

The Saca administration hardly acknowledged the massacre or its cause. They transferred the gang members, as had been previously done with the MS-13, to a facility designated exclusively for them. And that was that. The isolating transfer contributed enormously to the buildup of gang power hubs, which used the prisons as their headquarters.

"The party is over for these thugs," was Saca's motto during his presidency. And people bought it.

All these measures would soon be regretted. By the end of Saca's presidency, El Salvador had become the most murderous country on earth. But at least we can still rely on karma. In October 2016, the party was over for Saca. It was during his son's wedding, held at one of the most expensive and exclusive convention centers in El Salvador, Hacienda de Los Miranda. In full view of the elegant guests, the prosecutor's office accused him of stealing public funds and laundering money, and police escorted him from the table of honor to a patrol car.

As of 2018, Saca, after pleading guilty to money laundering and corruption charges, remains in that place in hell he had ignored for so long: Mariona prison.

◄◄

For the Kid, the outcome of all this was tragedy. An Iron Fist policy, plus a Super Iron Fist policy, plus a truce, plus the betrayal of that truce, turned him into a prime target, a traitor, a friend of the treacherous government. There was no one on his side anymore.

23
Hell

Hell [noun]: 1. In various mythologies and religions, a place
inhabited by the spirits of the dead.
2. A place or situation that causes great suffering or discomfort.

May 2014. The Kid has returned to Las Pozas. He's back in the
exurb of San Lorenzo where he'd spent parts of his childhood,
where he first came to know the Mara Salvatrucha 13. Seventeen
years ago, Chepe Furia rolled up in his pickup, looking for the
Cockroach's bar, armed to the teeth and radiating the potent, enigmatic gang lore from his days in Los Angeles.

This is where the Kid and the Beast first met.

Now, after years of looking for him, that Beast has found him
once again. The Beast knows the Kid lives in Las Pozas, and that
it's time to hunt.

It's evening here in Las Pozas. A member of the Hollywood
Locos, Lethal, stops under the shade of a ceiba tree at the barrio's
entrance, the same tree where Chepe Furia once plied the lost

boys with Cuatro Ases. Lethal notices the Kid at the edge of the soccer field. He jumps off his motorcycle and cuts across the field. The Kid, nervously looking over his shoulder ever since he came to town, has already spotted him. Lethal's wearing a motorcycle helmet, but his slanted eyes are unmistakable. Lethal was just a pup when the Kid was on the clique's highest rung. The Kid runs past the goalpost. The wooded hills have always been a place of refuge for him. He scrambles up the slope. Lethal fires, but the Kid boasts some fancy footwork. He slides to the ground, bounces back up, and keeps on running. He's been a soldier for more than a year, a gangster for more than ten, a traitor for almost five—he knows how to dodge a bullet, especially if the hitman has terrible aim.

The Kid counts the shots—six, seven, eight. He spots a tree with a fat trunk and runs toward it—nine, ten, eleven, twelve, thirteen. He doesn't lose count. The tree is so close. Fourteen, fifteen. It's rare for a magazine to hold more than fifteen bullets, which is why the Kid chooses this moment to turn and challenge him. From behind the tree he taunts him to come closer. Unable to complete the mission that would have made him famous among the Hollywood Locos, Lethal runs toward his motorcycle and speeds away.

The Kid returns to his house, which sits in front of the soccer field on one of the neighborhood's five, dusty, dead-end streets. He knows the Beast. He knows she won't bother him again today.

After only a month, the Kid and Lorena had left the cane field where bullets constantly chased them. But the bullets followed them straight to Las Pozas. Besides the bullets, they were also fleeing poverty, and poverty, like the air, is everywhere, impossible to escape.

At home, Rosa Tobar, the Kid's mother, is also rotting to death. Five months after the Kid's father, Jorge García, hung himself,

Rosa Tobar took a man home. This man was old and had been a member of the now defunct National Guard, the military police force that terrorized Salvadorans from 1912 to 1992. The man also slept with one of Rosa's daughters, the Kid's half-sister, but this didn't put her off. The ex-guardsman stayed a few days, between December 2013 and January 2014, having sex with the widow of the broken-armed *miquero* who'd hung himself from a beam on his back patio like a piñata. And then he vanished. A few days later, the elderly Rosa Tobar began to give off a foul odor from her crotch. Then came the rancid gas and diarrhea.

Her kids can only afford to treat her with medicine bought at a corner store. Her son and neighbors say she's lost her mind. Sometimes she confuses the Kid with her late husband. She calls him Jorge García, and the Kid scolds her. Other days, she refuses to let anyone in. If a neighbor comes by she'll open a window and try to scare them off.

"The Beast, you sons of bitches, the Beast," screams Rosa Tobar at the children who knock on her door, hoping to catch a glimpse of her before running away, laughing. She curses them, making the *garra salvatrucha* claw sign with her hand.

"Yeah, the Beast is going after my old woman," the Kid says calmly, as if he were talking about something natural and inevitable. Rosa Tobar will die two years later. She will die, according to his diagnosis, of the same ailment as old Jorge: generalized decay.

Bullets and rotting flesh—tenacious ghosts—continuously haunt the Kid.

In the house live not only the Kid and his family, but also his sister Sandra and her family. Sandra was the young girl who was repeatedly raped by the foreman while her dad got drunk on Cuatro Ases. She doesn't talk much. Actually, she doesn't talk at all. At least not with strangers. She lowers her eyes, hunches her shoulders forward and goes to some solitary inward place. Sandra is with a forty-five-year-old man known as Ñingle.

Ñingle served a fourteen-year sentence in various prisons. He was released a couple of years ago, then arrested again when a plea-bargain witness accused him of small-time drug peddling. He spent another year in prison before being acquitted. After that he went back to Sandra and their children—only to find his brother-in-law living with them, a man with a death sentence hanging over his head, a state collaborator, just like the guy who'd landed him in prison. Ñingle doesn't like it. The Kid doesn't, either.

"The Kid was the guy who handed me over the first time," says Ñingle to anyone who will listen. "He's why I did fourteen years."

If you ask Ñingle about the Kid, he won't miss a beat before telling you his side of the story. He says he was a marijuana distributer. He admits this frankly: "I trafficked marijuana." He'd climbed the ladder and no longer carried pounds of it across the river from Guatemala, but pushed through Guatemala all the way to the department of Petén, on the border with Mexico. If the Mexican state of Sonora is the golden gate of drugs and arms trafficking into the United States, Petén is the golden gate into Mexico. All the big Guatemalan drug traffickers have owned land in Petén on the banks of La Pasión River, which runs north to the jungles of Tabasco state in Mexico.

In the 1990s, Ñingle moved hundreds of pounds of marijuana packed in plastic barrels. The former prisoner, who lived under the rule of La Raza in the penitentiary system, says he'd picked up around 700 pounds of marijuana and, along with the Kid who was still a teenager, buried them close to his house in Las Pozas. He also buried cash. "A shitload of cash," says Ñingle. And weapons, too, at least one .357 gun and an M-16 rifle. One day in 1999, when the Kid was around fifteen and a newly minted member of the MS-13, some police officers came by the house and arrested Ñingle. He was surprised when, at the trial, they only accused him of peddling 100 pounds. Nothing more. Ñingle is sure it was the Kid who turned him in. The Kid confessed as much, one drunken night.

The Kid, Lorena, and Marbelly live in the more dilapidated part of the house, a kind of garage with a partition made of sheet metal, sticks, concrete blocks, and dried earth. Lorena is three months away from giving birth to their second daughter.

Ñingle regards the Kid as an intruder and, worse, as the traitor who made him spend fourteen years in a hole. And his sister, Sandra, barely impinges on the Kid's thoughts. Her gaze seems permanently lost and her two kids hide under her skirt, fearful of this new stranger. For Rosa Tobar, meanwhile, it's hard to focus on anything. The pain in her innards, from which the Kid spilled out thirty years ago, prevents her from seeing the world around her.

One day Ñingle explodes. He yells at the Kid without daring to name the reason. When he first went to prison, he'd left behind a newly jumped teenager. Now that he's out he finds a murderer before him, one feared throughout the state. Ñingle shouts that ever since the Kid arrived, the house has filled up with pot smokers and vagrants. He insults him. In turn, the Kid responds the only way he knows how.

"Miguel Ángel grabbed hold of his machete and said: 'Come on then, you son of a bitch, come on out! But don't give me any of your shit 'cause I'll cut your head off,'" Lorena would tell us two years later, her words undercut by a nervous titter. "Ñingle wouldn't come out. He locked himself in the toilet, he was so scared."

The Kid, sick of his brother-in-law's temper, hacks with his machete into an almond tree behind the house, next to the latrine where Ñingle is cowering.

"Come out then, you son of a bitch, come out," snarls the Kid, keeping his hatred from boiling over by hacking the small almond tree to the ground. This is the last time Ñingle will challenge the Kid. He won't risk that machete slicing into his neck.

It's in this hellhole that Jennifer Liset, the Kid's second daughter, is raised. Before she's officially named, her father calls her Little Burrito. She is light-skinned and has her father's eyes, except they're innocent and pure. Lorena uses some old rags and a couple of hats to cover the baby. She barely has any milk. The baby works to suckle every last nutrient from her mother's thin body. When there's nothing left to squeeze out, she wails.

The Kid and his family are all malnourished. "Everyone's hungry," shrugs Héctor, his father-in-law, whose *milpa* barely produces enough corn and beans to feed his own dependents.

The Kid has no job. He misses the skimpy food basket he'd been receiving in El Refugio. He fled from what he thought was life at the bottom of a ditch, but he's since discovered new lows. First, in old Jorge's cursed sugarcane farm. Now, in the only place that's left in the world, his own home. The prosecutor's office hardly ever comes by. He's now only useful for a case no one's interested in— that of the bodies in the Turín well.

He's needy and alone in a country that, after pitifully trying to hide its face, has shown what it truly is: nothing but war, repression, and hatred. All he can do is make use of his past life, of that sloppy MS tattoo on his hand. The mark that made him a gang member on the Day of the Cross, May 3, when he became a son of the Beast.

When their hunger becomes unbearable, the Kid goes out with his machete. He risks his life to reach the crossroad that leads to San Lorenzo, and he asks for money from taxi drivers. It's not exactly extortion, not exactly robbery. It's the gray area between demanding and begging for money. With what he gets he'll buy a bit of corn, bean, pasta, perhaps a little more. Day by day, his family is dying of hunger.

Sometimes, when he can't milk the moto-taxis, he'll follow his father-in-law to the *milpa*. He'll labor for free, hoping to be paid in corn, but his hands have forgotten, or perhaps never learned, the secrets of the earth. The machete has less ugly functions than those given to it by the Kid. In this land of campesinos, all he understands of the *campo* is how to turn it into a mass grave.

When he and Héctor rest under the shade of a tree, sheltered from the pounding sun, they talk, though they don't understand each other. Héctor speaks of *milpas*, beans, compost, and rain. He says it's bad to plant beans under a new moon because they won't grow. He talks about the pests that feed on beans, and the type of pesticide best to fight them off. But the Kid doesn't understand that language anymore. Death has deformed him. He tries to confide in his father-in-law, telling him about visions and prophecies, about beginnings that never begin and endings that never end. Hector doesn't understand. That stuff doesn't grow, it doesn't bear fruit or feed hungry families.

So the sicario and the campesino go on working the land in silence.

"He couldn't. He tried but he couldn't. When he plucked the beans, he'd stuff little bunches of them under his arms but they'd always fall. He let the weeds grow tall. He couldn't even drive the stakes in. I'd tell him how, I'd show him—do it carefully, don't let

them get scuffed, don't let them peel," Hector would tell us, years
later, shortly after lowering the Kid's body into his grave.

Héctor is scared of the Kid. In fact, when fourteen-year-old
Lorena went off with him, the police advised Héctor to press
charges for statutory rape. Héctor refused. He had other kids to
think about, and knew the Kid would find him and kill him if he
took legal action.

In this hellhole, unlike the sugarcane field, at least the Kid is not
ogled like a circus freak. He's not some suspect intruder. Here in
Las Pozas he is who he is, Miguel Ángel Tobar, the Hollywood Kid.
Those looking for him know who they're looking for. Dozens of
young MS-13 hitmen want to earn their marks by delivering the
Kid over to the Beast. They dream of the moment when, after murdering the traitor, they start getting call after call from the prisons,
faraway voices cheering their accomplishment.

The last to try was Lethal. The Beast almost got him. The Kid
saved himself with the tricks he'd learned as a soldier, but the Beast
stayed close behind. She had smelled blood, and nothing was going
to stop her until she tasted it.

Since then, there's been a stream of cars staking out the Kid's
house. Their occupants don't do anything. They don't yell, they
don't threaten, they don't shoot. They simply make their presence
known, reminding the prey that the hunt continues. Sooner or
later they will make their move. But the Kid has always been a step
ahead. He never leaves the house without a machete in his hand.
The visitors drive off then. They're afraid, too. This prey isn't just
any prey. As the Kid himself once said, "He has nails and teeth, and
they're very sharp, the better to fuck everyone up with."

To the Kid, his assailants are not anonymous figures. They're
Cocheche, Ades, Las Pescadas, El Burro, Gin, and another handful

of boys and men who knew him well when he was still considered one of the clique's foremost heroes. The great killer of *chavalas*, the perfect sicario, the grasper of enemy hearts. Today they want to kill him, but they're also afraid to get close. They're hunting an animal braver than they are.

The Kid's enemies know where he is. The Eighteens of El Saral know. The police officers accused of handing Rambito over to Chepe Furia know (and fear that the Kid will reconsider, putting them back in the dock.) The entire Hollywood Locos Salvatrucha knows where he is. The Beast, too, knows.

This is why the Kid sometimes suffers from paranoia. He's alone. The whole world against him, his machete, and his hand cannon.

Sometimes the paranoia reaches a fever pitch, and the Kid goes out in the middle of the night with his grenade in hand to lurk among the cherry trees in front of his house, waiting for one of his killers so he can blow him up. Recently, he drew another picture of the Beast.

One of his neighbors, one of the few who comes to see him and give him some marijuana now and again, thinks he needs help: "He only talks about killing and dying, he's obsessed."

Once, while watching a soccer game in the local field, the Kid thought he noticed the gaze of a gang member in the eyes of the players. He chased the whole team out of Las Pozas with his machete.

Other times he'd change course on his way back from picking up small quantities of pot in Guatemala. When he heard or saw owls or roadrunners, birds of bad omen according to western campesino lore, he'd turn around. Believing the birds were warning him of nearby enemies, he'd go hide, and bury his pot. Even the nature around him hummed of death.

Months went by. In June 2014, impossible though it seems, matters take a turn for the worse. Hell is closing in, the Beast crouches just around the corner.

The Kid crosses back from Guatemala with a few ounces of pot in his pocket. He's bringing it for others, in exchange for a hit or two. Some rural policemen detain him, finding his stash and weapon. He begs them to let him go, telling them he's a protected witness, rattling off the names of the police officers he knew: Detective Pineda, he says, Sergeant Pozo. Nothing doing. The cops take him to the outpost of Ahuachapán.

Salvadoran outposts are like miniature jails. Sometimes the police squeeze up to 300 detainees in spaces designed, at most, for fifty. Legally, a person can only be detained for up to seventy-two hours in one of these cells before being freed or transferred to a prison. But this law, like so many others, is simply ignored: there are men and women who serve their entire sentences in these reeking cages. They are never let out for exercise. They receive no visitors.

These unlucky people, just like in the prisons, are divided into MS-13 members, the two factions of the Barrio 18, and "civilians."

"Are you a civilian? You're not mixed up in anything?" one of the officers asks the Kid. He repeats that he's a plea-bargain witness, who musn't be placed in a cell with the MS-13 or the Eighteens. The officer, whose query had been sarcastic, opens the cage housing the MS-13s and pushes him in.

These gang members are young and don't recognize him right away. After all, the Kid abandoned the clique almost five years ago. He lies. He says he'd been part of the Centrales Locos Salvatrucha in the capital, years ago. Says he retired in 2000.

The Kid knows how to handle even the worst situations, largely because the worst situations have been his entire life. He's a convincing liar when he needs to be. So many years in the Mara Salvatrucha 13 taught him how to toy with the minds of murderers.

"I've been deprogrammed, but I'm always on the lookout for the *bichas* so they won't break my ass, and if one lets himself get smoked out, then I'll smoke him out," the Kid tells his fellow inmates.

The police officer, when he realizes the Kid has gotten off the hook so far, walks up to the bars and says: "Nah man, this here's the Kid, the one who turned witness in El Refugio, the one who trapped the leader of the Hollywoods."

A cage. The Kid. The Beast.

The gang members, like rabid animals, encircle him. They're barefoot and shirtless. But the Kid has a plan B. He's got no plan B for anything else in life, but always a plan B for confronting death. Always. While the police doctor performed his routine examination, the Kid filched a blade lying on his desk, a small scalpel.

"Shuddup you son of a bitch. You have no more right to talk. One word and we'll smash your face in," spits the leader of the cage.

The Kid doesn't stop talking. He starts cursing.

The MS surround him. The Kid whips out the tiny scalpel. He screams. He rants. He threatens. Before long, the young gangsters are hollering for their lives.

"Knife, knife, knife!" they scream.

The police intervene before the scene turns into a bloodbath and pull the Kid out of the cell. They kick him over to a metal post in front of the MS-13 cell and tie him up. Now the inmates have the upper hand again, taunting him:

"Oh yeah, you son of a fucking bitch, so you're the Kid, the guy who castrated Chepe Furia!"

Miguel Ángel directs his response to the leader of the cell, with

whom he'd done a hit job years ago, though the youth didn't recognize him at first.

"Yep, so what're you going to do about it? You're the Silence,
bicho, you son of a bitch. Who wouldn't recognize you? Just tell me
where, when, with what."

The policemen don't want to take any more risks. They call their
bosses on the phone. A commissioner returns the call, tells them
he's a protected witness and orders them to give the Kid a lift to
Las Pozas. They let him go and sentence him to community work,
though he won't live long enough to do it.

The Kid makes it back home, without his marijuana but also
without a scratch, just a bruise from one of the police officer's boots.

Since the Kid became a protected witness in El Refugio, since he
became a traitor to the Mara Salvatrucha 13 in 2009, the Beast has
never gotten so close. The Beast had him alone, cornered, but the
Hollywood Kid, once again, slipped her grasp.

The Kid is more paranoid than ever. He doesn't sleep and trusts
no one.

Cars continue to idle in front of his house.

The Kid chose Las Pozas in part because of its reputation, because
it's known for its rough, ruthless people. He thought maybe that
would keep the Hollywood Locos at bay. Two pot-dealing brothers
live on one street corner, and they have an M-16, which earns them
the same sort of respect the owner of a Mercedes-Benz might enjoy
in a middle-class neighborhood. Near the amate tree at the neighborhood's entrance lives El Siri, who once belonged to a gang from
the warring 1980s called 11 Puntos—toughs who made a living
stealing cattle, knowing they'd be summarily shot if they were ever
caught by the army or the guerrilla. There's also an ex-hitman who
spent eleven years in prison, and now cultivates yucca plants and

trades in marijuana wholesale. And a gaggle of young boys who smoke the marijuana and assault whomever they can. They're lost boys, like the Kid was when Chepe Furia arrived on the scene; kids waiting for someone to give them a purpose in life.

But Las Pozas is also home to Pai Pai, Las Pescadas, El Emo, and Gin—all of them MS-13 collaborators. The Kid smokes with them and tries to read their minds. He knows they want to walk him, just as he walked so many others. He keeps them close, but doesn't trust them. Those kids will be adulated by all the western cliques if they kill Miguel Ángel, or just deliver him alive. They dream of one day being able to offer him up to the Beast, to finally receive her approval.

"When I smoke with El Emo, I look into his eyes; when I take a hit I control that son of a bitch with my gaze. I want him to see I'm in control," the Kid insists.

He's trying to convince himself that he has a sound strategy, that he's not helpless as dust in the wind, that he's not trapped in a hell with no way out.

Las Pozas is a dead end. Beyond, you're in another country. With another story, other crews, and other beasts. For the Kid, this is a dead end. He doesn't know it yet, but it's his final stopping place, before the bullets bite him for the first and last time. But this was also a beginning. This is where he met Chepe Furia. This is where he met the gang that branded his life forever.

Here, in hell on earth, the Beast will soon end her son's life.

24
Death

death [noun]: 1. Cessation or end of life.

2. Destruction, annihilation, ruin.

Friday, November 21, 2014. The Kid has been biking over dusty streets since early in the morning. He left Las Pozas with his machete, but without his hand cannon. He felt sure of himself that morning. He rode his bicycle down Portillo Street to the municipality of San Lorenzo. As everyone here knows, unlike Atiquizaya, Ahuachapán, or Chalchuapa, San Lorenzo is a peaceful place. There hasn't been a single homicide here this year.

It's a tiny blotch of a place. A good little town.

The Kid is on a mission: to give his second daughter a surname. To legally recognize her and proclaim before the state of El Salvador: I, Miguel Ángel Tobar, am the father of Jennifer Liset Tobar, born three months ago.

In his bag, the Kid, now thirty years old, has his and Lorena's ID cards. Lorena recently turned eighteen.

The Kid walks into the town hall, three blocks away from the police post in front of the small central plaza and the Catholic church. They tell him he needs to come back in the afternoon, because his daughter's birth certificate, necessary to legally recognize her, hasn't shown up in their system. They'll be able to locate the document by that afternoon, they say, and then he'll be able to officially recognize her as his daughter, Jennifer Liset.

Instead of going all the way home, the Kid goes part of the way back up the road and kills the time somewhere between San Lorenzo and Las Pozas. At around two in the afternoon, he cycles through the region of El Portillo, heading back to the town hall in San Lorenzo. Many people come to visit this town, following the main road that runs parallel to the San Lorenzo River. The fresh water flowing in the middle of this hostile heat allows cashew and the regional flower, loroco, to flourish. The river is beautiful, and the area around San Lorenzo is peaceful. That combination is necessary for tourism to flourish in this country. It's not enough for a place to be pretty. There are plenty of lovely mountains that only serve as giant cemeteries. The river attracts swimmers; local women sell food and rent outhouses where the swimmers can refresh and relieve themselves. One of the women who charges for the use of her bathroom is Esperanza. Esperanza knows the Kid. They're around the same age. She's known him since before he betrayed the Mara Salvatrucha 13.

Cockroach, the barman of Las Pozas, says that back in 2009 Esperanza's husband used to drink in his bar. He'd drink and kiss and touch a young girl called Wendy, who would let herself be kissed and touched in exchange for sips of Cuatro Ases. Wendy was a regular in the bar. She was already an alcoholic by age sixteen. Sometimes, with a deadly hangover, she'd beg and beg Cockroach to give her a quarter liter of Cuatro Ases, just to make it through the hangover. When asked about this, Cockroach proudly replies: "I gave it to her so she'd stop hurting." Cockroach also relates the way the drunks of Las Pozas would fuck Wendy and then keep on feeding her liquor. More and more liquor, more and more drunks penetrating her. Day in, day out. One night, full of angry suspicion, Esperanza came to look for her husband at the bar. It was late, and the doors were locked. Esperanza yelled abuse and threats. Cockroach, her husband, and Wendy listened to her raving, but didn't open the door.

Days later, Cockroach recalls, Esperanza came by and complained to him: "My husband was here with that little slut, wasn't he?"

"Sure, he was here, but why would I've told you that, so you could come and cause problems in my bar?" He advised Esperanza to keep her husband on a tighter leash at home, and not air out their problems at his bar. He had enough to handle with the Eighteens of El Saral coming by to drink and then the MS yelling, threatening him, and going out to patrol the streets armed with machetes and guns.

Esperanza swore she'd kill Wendy, the barman remembers, and then she left.

Wendy, in her teenage ignorance, and surrounded by men for whom the concept of rape is pretty hazy, was also going out with a member of the Barrio 18. After spending several crazed weeks at the bar, Wendy wound up murdered by machete, at the hands of an MS-13. She was Lorena's cousin, and the Kid was witness to that carnage.

As with so many similar cases in this country, the murder was never solved. Wendy might have been killed on Esperanza's orders, as the Kid tried to claim, or simply because she said too much while sleeping with someone from Barrio 18.

Ever since the Kid returned to Las Pozas in 2014, Esperanza called the police every time she saw him pass by the river in El Portillo. And she boasted of calling the police on the Kid to as many residents of San Lorenzo as would listen.

Biking back to the town hall, the Kid takes dirt paths to avoid the main street. He bumps into Esperanza and demands she give him the two dollars he needs to pay for the birth certificate that, by now, past two in the afternoon, must be ready. Esperanza forks them over reluctantly. She'll later tell this part of the story over and over.

The Kid enters the town hall. He approaches the main counter. They tell him to wait a few minutes, that everything is ready for him to legally name his baby daughter. He spreads out on a bench, clasps his hands behind his head, and relaxes. A city employee whom he recognizes comes in. They shoot the breeze for a few minutes.

The Kid seemed relaxed, the same employee would later say.

The mood changes, however, when a boy from the outskirts of San Lorenzo gets off a rickshaw in front of the town hall, dropped off by two men who speed away toward El Portillo. The young man swaggers in, flicking his head and eyes all around. The Kid tenses. He prepares to get up. They exchange a few aggressive words. "Huh," says the Kid, "what the fuck, bitch?" "Oh yeah? What's up, Kid?" The young man heads back outside. The city employee tells the Kid: "I think you better leave. I think there's gonna be a shootout." The Kid rushes to the desk, signs some papers, and takes Jennifer Liset Tobar's birth certificate. All the employees leave the room. The Kid races away, pedaling back up the path toward El Portillo.

A street sweeper, Chele Campolón, is at work. The Kid greets him in a hurry. "Hey, hey," he says, speeding away on his bike. A moto-taxi growls down the street. Shots ring out. A woman cries out hysterically: "They're killing each other, they're killing each other!" Curiosity getting the best of him, Chele Campolón runs toward the gunshots. Two men riding a moto-taxi speed past him. Chele Campolón sees a bicycle on the ground.

A body lies sprawled on its back.

On a November day, during the month of the dead, under the shade of a mango tree and next to a budding mulato—God's tree, the tree that dies in order to give life, the Xipe Totec—lies the body of Miguel Ángel Tobar, the Hollywood Kid.

His eyes are open. His head is tilted back. If he were alive, he'd be staring at a budding mulato tree.

A few weeks before his murder, Miguel Ángel is pictured with Lorena, holding Jennifer Liset, in the backyard of the Las Pozas house. Miguel Ángel has Marbelly in his arms.

Part IV

Alive

25

In Search of the Kid

January 9, 2018. We arrive at the cemetery of Atiquizaya at three in the afternoon. It seems like not one more body could fit in this graveyard. If many more come, they'll have to bury them in the ravine, close to the cluster of houses where some local kids are popping their heads up to peer at us.

The last time we were here was more than three years ago, the day they buried the Kid. That day, the members of what was once his clique, the Hollywood Locos Salvatrucha, wrecked his funeral. They didn't let people finish crying, they didn't let the evangelists finish singing, nor did they allow his relatives time to bury the national flower with dignity and care. They didn't let the traitor go in peace.

Since that day, no one has come to visit the blanket of dirt that covers the Kid. Not one family member. Once, a cemetery employee came to offer Héctor, the Kid's father-in-law, a cement cross that someone had left behind. The campesino wisely preferred to decline the gift. "I didn't want to risk having to dig another grave just for putting up a cross."

Before coming to the cemetery, we stopped by the town hall. We identified ourselves as journalists and said we were on our way to visit the Kid's grave. The town hall thought it best to send two security guards along with us.

The manager of the cemetery greeted us. He's a tough-looking guy, around fifty years old. His right forearm is deformed by an enormous scar: an amorphous scorpion tattoo that he acquired after the war in honor of his battalion. He gave himself the tattoo one drunken night, using car battery fluid and a sewing needle. The scorpion is the symbol of the Atlacatl Battalion, the most ferocious wing of the military during the Salvadoran war, financed and trained by the CIA and notorious for massacres like El Mozote, where up to 1,200 civilians were slaughtered in 1981. Carlos, the killer turned undertaker, doesn't hide his past. He wears it with pride. He still refers to Colonel Domingo Monterrosa, the leader of this death squad, as "*mi coronel* Monterrosa." Carlos's ringtone is the Arena marching song, whose lyrics include: "El Salvador will be the tomb where all the reds end up."

Carlos is the uncle of a jailed Hollywood Locos Salvatrucha member, and his sister is the wife of El Stranger, now serving time for the murder of Rambito. El Stranger has retired from the gang. As his homeboys would say, he's a penny beggar now. He's a traitor, just like the Kid, whom he'd tried to kill for years. El Stranger, so Carlos says, is now dying of brain cancer in the stinking prison of Sonsonate, here in western El Salvador.

El Salvador is a cruel parody of itself. Carlos, who killed in the civil war, now lives by burying the dead of a new war fought within his own family. Different war, different kinds of tattoos.

The veteran of the cruelest battalion stopped doing cocaine—which he'd used as a form of escape after the war—twenty-one years ago. He stopped drinking—which he'd done to drown his memories—twenty years ago. He's an evangelical now. He says he was rescued by God. This is the story of so many, the syncretism of a whole country inside one man.

The cemetery is plastered in gang insignia: a solitary black claw drawn on the wall behind us; an "MS" with horns and the initials of the clique, HLS; the words "see, hear, and keep quiet" scrawled on another wall; other gang signs and letters marking the tombstones. Carlos says that when Eighteens die in the area, they're not buried here but in the cemetery of El Refugio, which is their turf. In El Salvador, even the dead belong to a gang. Even the dead belong to a clique.

"That was a special case. The Kid made history here," Carlos says, remembering the Kid's burial. "It was historic."

"Yeah, for me it was historic when they killed him. It was sad because they didn't even get him out of the bag. Only his face was visible when they put him in the ground, and he looked like a Chinaman. It was a black bag. Things were tense that day in the cemetery, and I thought: Maybe there's gonna be a big shootout here ... Well, that's all."

That's all. More death.

"Where is the Kid's grave?"

"Right here," he says, pointing to a mound of dirt.

The mound is crowned with a blue cross and a wreath of red flowers. Plastic flowers are nailed onto the cross. Behind it grows a small izote bush.

"This one?" we ask in disbelief.

"Yeah. This one. Thing is," Carlos goes on, "we just don't have enough space. There's nothing left of the Kid underground. So we didn't even have to dig anything up, we just dug right down and buried another body."

"You're saying there's another body on top of the Kid?"

"Right." Carlos lifts the wreath of red flowers. Carved into the cross is a name: "Mercedes de J."

The red flowers are not for the Kid. The blue cross isn't for him either. That izote bush is not the same plant his family hastily stuck in the earth in front of the menacing eyes of the gangsters. That one, Carlos tells us, "dried up and died." This grave, in fact, isn't even the Kid's grave. This grave is someone else's. For other mourners to come and grieve.

The Hollywood Kid, Miguel Ángel Tobar, once known as the Clown, the protected witness of the Salvadoran state, was swallowed whole by the Salvadoran west. He's now nothing but dirt and roots. He has forever escaped this rotten corner of the world.

"He was serious business. He denounced some seventy maras," Carlos says.

Carlos isn't alone in his exaggeration. He isn't the only one building a legend out of the life of a murderer, a witness, the son of a *miquero*, a man who's so similar to so many other men in this country. A town hall janitor says that when they killed him, the moto-taxi of the hitmen looked like a hearse, and a nurse ran toward the town of San Lorenzo, screaming, "They're killing each other! They're killing each other!" Others say the Kid walked bare-chested down the dusty streets of the west with a giant machete in his hand, and, as he passed, the residents would close their windows and lock their doors, crying, "Here comes the Kid! Here comes the Kid!" Others, who didn't witness his death, describe how he fought off his assassins, wounding them with the blade of his machete.

The Kid goes on killing, fighting, resisting death. The struggle between the Kid and The Beast continues. The battle intensifies. It goes on and on.

Miguel Ángel Tobar has no peace, not even in death.